D1526137

Dress and Gender

Dress is one of the most significant markers of gender identity, yet it has rarely been explored in depth. This volume opens up fascinating aspects of the relationship between gender and dress by covering a great variety of ethnographic areas reaching from Asia, Europe, and Africa to North and South America. The time span is equally wide-ranging and offers present-day material as well as studies based on historical data.

Ruth Barnes is an art historian who has done field research on textiles of Lembata, in Eastern Indonesia. The results are published in her book *The Ikat Textiles of Lamalera: A Study of an Eastern Indonesian Weaving Tradition*, and in several articles. She also has worked with ethnographic collections at the Pitt Rivers Museum, Oxford. Currently she is preparing a catalogue of the Newberry collection of Indian block-printed textiles at the Ashmolean Museum, Oxford University.

Joanne B. Eicher is a professor in the Department of Design, Housing, and Apparel at the University of Minnesota. Her current fieldwork focuses on the significance of dress and textiles among the Kalabari of Nigeria. She has authored *Nigerian Handcrafted Textiles* and *African Dress: A Select and Annotated Bibliography*, and coauthored *Dress, Adornment, and the Social Order* and *The Visible Self: Perspectives on Dress.*

Cross-Cultural Perspectives on Women

General Editors: Shirley Ardener and Jackie Waldren,
for The Centre for Cross-Cultural Research on Women, University of Oxford

Vol. 1: Persons and Powers of Women in Diverse Cultures
Edited by Shirley Ardener

Vol. 2: Dress and Gender: Making and Meaning
Edited by Ruth Barnes and Joanne B. Eicher

Vol. 3: The Anthropology of Breast-Feeding: Natural Law or Social Construct
Edited by Vanessa Maher

Vol. 4: Defining Females
Edited by Shirley Ardener

Vol. 5: Women and Space
Edited by Shirley Ardener

Vol. 6: Servants and Gentlewomen to the Golden Land: The Emigration of Single Women to South Africa, 1820–1939
Cecillie Swaisland

Vol. 7: Migrant Women
Edited by Gina Buijs

Vol 8: Gender: Symbols and Social Practices
Edited by Vigdis Broch-Due, Ingrid Rudie and Tone Bleie

Vol. 9: Bilingual Women: Anthropological Approaches to Second Language Use
Edited by Pauline Burton, Ketaki Dyson and Shirley Ardener

Vol. 10: Gender, Drink and Drugs
Edited by Maryon MacDonald

Vol. 11: Women and Missions, Past and Present
Edited by Fiona Bowie, Deborah Kirkwood and Shirley Ardener

Vol. 12: Women in Muslim Communities: Religious Belief and Social Realities
Edited by Camillia Fawzi El-Solh and Judy Mabro

Vol. 13: Women and Property, Women as Property
Edited by Renée Hirschon

CROSS-CULTURAL PERSPECTIVES ON WOMEN | VOL. 2

Dress and Gender

Making and Meaning in Cultural Contexts

Edited by

Ruth Barnes and Joanne B. Eicher

BERG

Providence / Oxford

BRESCIA COLLEGE
LIBRARY
62310

Published in 1992, paperback edition, 1993 by

Berg Pubishers, Inc.

Editorial offices:
221 Waterman Street, Providence, RI 02906, U.S.A.
150 Cowley Road, Oxford OX4 1JJ, UK

© Ruth Barnes and Joanne B. Eicher, 1992

All rights reserved.
No part of this publication may be reproduced
in any form or by any means without the permission
of Berg Publishers.

British Library Cataloguing in Publication Data

Dress and gender: Making and meaning in cultural contexts. – (Cross-cultural perspective on women)
I. Barnes, Ruth II. Eicher, Joanne B. III. Series 391.009

ISBN 0 85496 720 6 (cloth)   0 85496 865 2 (paper)

Library of Congress Cataloging-in-Publication Data

Dress and gender : Making and meaning in cultural contexts / edited by Ruth Barnes and Joanne B. Eicher.
p. cm.
Includes bibliographical references and index.
ISBN 0–85496–720–6
1. Costume—Sex differences—Cross-cultural studies. 2. Costume—Social aspects—Cross-cultural studies. I. Barnes, Ruth, 1947–. II. Eicher, Joanne Bubolz.

GT525.D74 1991   91–15885
391—dc20   CIP

Printed in the United States by E. B. Edwards Brothers, Lillington, NC.

Contents

Preface

Ruth Barnes and Joanne B. Eicher

The seed for this volume was planted in the spring and summer of 1988, when Joanne Eicher was on sabbatical leave at the Centre for Cross-Cultural Research on Women (CCCRW), Queen Elizabeth House, Oxford. We each had worked with research topics of dress and cloth, and while aware of the importance of both in a social and historical context, we shared a concern about problems of definition arising out of the existing literature on the topic. When Shirley Ardener asked us to convene a workshop on dress, we decided to take an interdisciplinary and cross-cultural approach in relating dress to gender. We solicited contributions from anthropologists, art historians, and scholars trained in textiles and clothing. Our original intent was to develop a dialogue of colleagues from the United Kingdom, continental Europe, and North America, but this was extended to include participants from Australia and Asia as well; the fieldwork used as a base for analyzing the topic included Asia, Africa, Europe, the Middle East, as well as North and South America.

The workshop titled "Dress and Gender: Making and Meaning" was held in April 1989 in Oxford, under the auspices of the CCCRW. Presenters whose papers were available for inclusion in this volume are: Rebecca Bailey, Suzanne Baizerman, Ruth Barnes, Helen Callaway, Catherine Cerny, Louise Cort, Penny Dransart, Joanne Eicher and Mary Ellen Roach-Higgins (joint paper), Danielle Geirnaert, Leedom Lefferts, Julia Leslie, Susan Michelman, Cherri Pancake, Lidia Sciama, and Malcolm Young. Although O. P. Joshi from India could not attend, his paper was read. Tonye V. Erekosima, who also was not able to attend, has coauthored a paper with Michelman for this book. Presenters whose papers were not available for publication were Catherine Daly, Jenny Littlewood, and Julie Marcus. As invited discussants, Shirley Ardner, Joy Hendry, and Howard Morphy added constructive comments.

The essays published in this volume are all based on material presented during the workshop. The intellectual stimulation and vitality of discussion presented impetus for revisions of the manuscripts. We are most grateful to all participants for the effort and concentrated attention they gave to their contributions as well as the timely manner in which they met publication deadlines.

We want to acknowledge help from many sources for the completion of this book. Funding for travel for Joanne Eicher came from the Office of International Education and the College of Human Ecology, International Programs, University of Minnesota. Substantial financial help for word processing came from the Department of Design, Housing and Apparel, University of Minnesota. By name, we wish to thank Bonnie Maas Morrison, Buckman Professor and Head of Design, Housing and Apparel; Charleen Klarquist, word processing specialist, without whose help this volume could not have been finished; as well as Mary Heltsley, Dean; and Shirley Baugher, Associate Dean, College of Human Ecology. Unnamed are those who supplied travel funds for our participants to attend the workshop and those who helped in the tedious processing of manuscripts to be sent for editing. Whether support came from the participants themselves or others, we appreciate that the workshop took place. We would also like to thank Annette Weiner and Jane Schneider for convening the Wenner-Gren conference on Cloth and the Organization of Human Experience in 1983 at Troutbeck, in Amenia, New York, that brought us together for the first time.

RUTH BARNES
Department of Eastern Art
Ashmolean Museum
Oxford

JOANNE B. EICHER
Department of Design,
Housing, and Apparel
University of Minnesota
St. Paul

Introduction

Ruth Barnes and Joanne B. Eicher

Throughout the history of the human race, people have wanted to change the appearance of their bodies. Archaeological evidence and contemporary practices around the world have shown that humans add clothing, paint, or jewelry, and even alter the shape of their body parts. Hardly a society exists where some form of alteration or addition is not considered essential as an emblem of the person as a social being. Textiles or skins as dress may be fundamentally protective, but they also have social meaning. Decorative ornaments that are added to the body (such as earrings, bracelets, and finger rings) or markings imposed (such as tattoo, cicatrice, or paint) show a person's position within the society. A cultural identity is thus expressed, and visual communication is established before verbal interaction even transmits whether such a verbal exchange is possible or desirable.

Dress as a cultural phenomenon has several essential attributes. First, a person's identity is defined geographically and historically, and the individual is linked to a specific community. Dress serves as a sign that the individual belongs to a certain group, but simultaneously differentiates the same individual from all others: it includes and excludes. This property of inclusion and exclusion is also carried over into the meaning of dress within the group. Dress is an indication of the general social position of the person in the society. The prestige accorded one's social position may vary within a lifetime, as when related to age, or when closely connected with the political or spiritual power a person achieves. Social position bestowed at birth may be affected by class, caste, or lineage of descent, depending upon the society into which one is born. As an emblem of power, one's position may be communicated by a crown, staff, or robe. Dress is also a symbol of economic position. Textiles and jewelry, for example, can acquire great value as expressions of personal or communal well-being.

But attributes of identity as related to the social positions held by an individual are all affected by the gender identification of the dressed person. Gender distinctions are a crucial part of the construction of dress, whether they are made on biological or social grounds. All contributions in this volume address this topic, as dress affects the appearance of humans as social beings.

Dress and Cultural Identity

According to the stories of origin told by the people of the Andes and discussed here by Dransart, the ancestors entered this world "fully clothed, wearing the dress which identified the sex and the ethnic origin of the wearer." The places where they came into being were identified and venerated as points of origin, thus connecting the specific dress of an ethnic group to its place of origin and legitimizing it. Their dress identifies them as members of a certain group and simultaneously distinguishes gender. That the place of creation is closely linked to the ancestors intensifies the connection between dress and ethnic origins, as the ancestors are celebrated in the form of appropriately dressed mummies. This theme, the social significance of ethnically identified dress, is implicit in most of the chapters in this volume. We may see it explicitly expressed in Michelman's and Erekosima's description of the development of Kalabari dress throughout the physical and social advancement of a person's life. Specific forms are characteristic for either masculine or feminine. What is striking in particular about the Kalabari evidence is that external and definitely non-indigenous material is appropriated and assimilated into a form that is specifically and unmistakably local.

Important in almost all instances is that the identity expressed in dress is maintained. Cultural self-definition is a prominent part of Callaway's analysis of British social dress in the colonial empire, and is equally essential to Leslie's account of the prescriptive behavior that is deemed appropriate to a faithful Hindu wife. An additional element enters these considerations, though, and is taken up by Joshi in his description of contemporary Indian women's dress. Social identity expressed in dress becomes not only an answer to the question of *who* one is, but *how* one is, and concerns the definition of the self in relation to a moral and religious value system.

Personal quality, as related to moral or religious allegiance, is considered in several chapters. The Jewish skull cap that Baizerman discusses is a sign of a man's degree of religious orthodoxy, and can even be considered an expression of his political position in present-day Israel. As Lefferts shows, the Theravada Buddhist monk indicates through the shape and color of his robe his position in a cosmological scheme, one in which he renounces the "world of desire," yet he wears a cloth that with its patches is modelled on the rice fields of that same world. In an analysis of a seventeenth-century Japanese narrative, Cort follows the disintegration of a woman's life – and her final salvation – through illustrations of her dress. She also points out that feminine literacy, a quality much valued in seventeenth-century Japan, could aptly be expressed through the patterns of a robe. The allusion to personal quality and its relationship to gender identity is present in a peculiar way in the quilted garments Cerny discusses: quilted clothes are personal and individualistic, and they evoke the history and the values of American frontier societies. The patchwork quilt is an immediate feminine point of reference, and with it is implied the real or imaginary gift of creative power in the face of adversity.

Cultural identity expressed in a particular form of dress is found throughout this volume. As noted, though, dress is also linked to gender, and further distinctions are made depending on definitions of gender. The result may give a revealing image of the qualities associated with "feminine" or "masculine." What is crucial here is that the message communicated is understood by both wearer and viewer.

The Construction of Dress: Making and Meaning

How do we define dress? This particular problem is addressed by Eicher and Roach-Higgins in the first essay. Their survey of the literature on the topic reveals ambiguity, even in recent publications. Although it is important that the terminology of dress include the wide range of materials and actions that constitute appearance, dress is not only visual; it may also include touch, smell, and sound. It has an impact on the viewer, but also on the wearer. The sensual effect of certain textures on the skin may be experienced as either positive or negative. Certain textile designs may delight or displease the person wearing them, as is apparent from Cerny's report on the comments of quilters, and from Young's quotations of police women's reactions to their dress uniforms.

The analysis of dress needs to place the complete *objet d'art* into the context of a total cognitive structure. A definition must allow room for all types of body supplements and modifications. The effect of the narrow, restrictive term "costume," for example, is demonstrated in

Barnes's discussion of the writings of scholars who used the Royal Anthropological Society's *Notes and Queries* as a guide for their investigations. In this case, which deals with several societies from the Naga Hills of northeast India, the result reveals astonishing discrepancies between the ethnographic report and the tangible, visible evidence.

To understand the role of dress in a given society, an analysis of the creative act of making dress is essential. Usually the production of objects that are to be worn is itself gender-specific; this is particularly in evidence when we discuss the weaving of textiles or the working of metals to make jewelry. Metalworking seems to be usually in the hands of men and is therefore one of the few gender-specific technological activities. Weaving, by contrast, is not as clearly affiliated with one gender. In small-scale societies, however, it is commonly found that the production of specific textiles is divided according to gender. Even in the one case described here where gender boundaries have been relatively flexible, in Pancake's essay on Guatemalan weavers, the making of specific ethnic textiles is undertaken by women. The article shows that gender boundaries are blurred when weaving is done for the production of an export trade.

The gender-specific production of textiles may be directly related to the meaning of cloth in a society. Weaving has a particularly strong metaphoric interpretation in the Southeast Asian context. This is evident in all three papers dealing with the region (Barnes, Geirnaert, and Lefferts). The entire process, including the preparation of the thread, may be likened to the creation of life. The completed product, the cloth, can reflect culturally important images in its design or pattern by representing mythological beings, the ancestors of the community, or the rice fields that give sustenance.

Although technologically distinct from loom weaving, the interlacing of betel baskets described by Geirnaert nevertheless uses similar motifs. As a very personal container, the basket is closely linked to its owner (and the gender of the owner) and becomes a receptacle for his or her spiritual essence or soul. Here the production of textiles (and, incidentally, of the betel bags) is closely associated with women, and their reproductive capability is metaphorically linked to the making of cloth. The concept of textiles as being made from "threads of life" is strongly expressed and clearly affiliated with the feminine gender. Barnes argues that this is balanced, on the other hand, by the masculine activity of headhunting. For the Naga, two types of dress were of particular importance: one was a body cloth – usually a large cloak – woven by women once a man had performed certain elaborate feasts of merit; the other the headhunter's dress, a complex costume construction assembled by the man, where the textile takes a very minor role. Among the Naga, then, two versions of dress are constructed by women and men, respectively. Both forms of dress are worn to display personal achievement and, by implication, individual power and social position.

The making of textiles to express merit is equally explicit in Lefferts' discussion. The monk's robe is an outward sign of his achievement of merit. However, while a Naga weaver takes much time over producing a "cloth of merit," the monk's robe when still woven in the home, was produced in as short a time as possible, to emphasize that it represented a separation from the "world of desire" which is bound by time and space. The amount of time spent on making the object is of great importance, and is closely related to the value attached to it. Specific qualities are associated with the production. Fertility and well-being have been mentioned in the Southeast Asian context, but it is equally important in the dressing and elaboration of ancestral representations in the Inka tradition. The elaborate dress construction that follows the "coming out" celebration for a Kalabari woman after the birth of a child is another instance.

A peculiarly Mediterranean theme is developed by Sciama, who links the making of a particular textile to feminine virtue. The virtue of a woman is closely connected to her sexuality, and is determined according to her sexual behaviour. Connecting the making of a particular textile with a moral attitude is not a typical association. However, this association is also implicitly present in the production of quilted apparel (Cerny), and, to some degree, in the making of the *kippa sruga* (Baizerman), an object that is crocheted by a woman for a male for whom she feels affection. Far from being a value-free activity, the construction of the dress article may hint at the essence of its meaning.

Form and Function

The relationship between the form and purpose of dress remains to be considered. Even when garments are used for a specific and apparently mundane purpose, we may find that the form they take is not always purely dictated by rationally appropriate requirements. Bailey discusses the historical development of maternity clothing, for example, and shows that medical opinions, supposedly with a scientific base, in fact clearly follow changing social attitudes toward pregnancy.

Setting the pregnant woman apart and treating her as potentially vulnerable in her state is indeed common to many human societies. What is unusual, though, is the development of a specific dress code for her, as developed in the Western world since the end of the nineteenth century.

Gender-specific dress is of course closely linked to sexuality. In Bailey's case, however, pregnant women are seen to be removed from their feminine sexuality and placed into a dress category that emphasizes a form that is different from what is "fashionable," hence considered sexually attractive at a particular time. A similar process of de-sexing the female is evident in Young's article. As he describes, women in the British police force become the objects of crude jokes and comments, all focusing on their lack of, or uninhibited abundance of, sexuality. Prescribing the wearing of certain dress articles to enhance the feminine sexual appearance is essential to Leslie's paper. Her account even includes references to the presentation of the Hindu woman in space, as the preparation of the room is part of the dressing. A similarly total performance is also present in Michelman's and Erekosima's account, especially as they describe the development of feminine dress over time: acquiring dress items is linked to sexual maturation and culminates in the *iriabo* ensemble that represents a Kalabari woman's identity as a procreative female and the celebration of motherhood. In the Mediterranean context, as described by Sciama, the wearing of lace trimmings on a particular part of the body can change the meaning of lace from a sign of positive, virtuous sexuality to a symbol of negatively perceived licentiousness. Wearing lace, as well as making it, is again linked to the moral concept of virtue.

Even commonly worn or carried articles of dress may reflect a profound meaning. The ever present betel bags of West Sumba (Geirnaert) reveal, in their design and quality, the status, age, and gender of the owner. One motif in particular, the *mamuli*, represents female genitalia, and is the pervasive symbol of feminine fecundity and thus is only represented on the betel bags of women of childbearing age. The Thai division into gender-specific textiles reflects, in the designs appropriate to each, the attitude to the position of men and women. The feminine, in this case, is firmly part of the world of desire, while men are given the opportunity to change over to the distinctly different world of the monk. The masculine textile is set apart by its design from the representative patterns of the feminine cloth.

In her description of Japanese robes, Cort notes that there is no gender-specific shape, but that the patterning on the cloth makes the distinction: elaboration for particular ceremonial or temporal occasions, and varying degrees of refinement to express differences of class. Baizerman shows that the cap worn by the Jewish Israeli (made by a female, worn by a male) is a clear indication of the degree of his religiosity or worldliness, even of his social or political attitudes. In these examples it is not so much the structural form that varies, but the designs that enhance the object.

Form as a totality of dress, on the other hand, appears in the headhunter's ensemble as well as in the dress of merit (Barnes), in the ethnically specific and gender-differentiated dress of the Inka empire (Dransart), and it is overwhelmingly present in the uniforms prescribed for British policewomen (Young). The dress preparations described by Leslie as desirable for the orthodox Hindu woman also involve the entire body, and they should change according to her menstrual cycle and to her husband's presence or absence. In the totality of dress, the touchstone is not the woman herself, but her relationship to her husband. Dress here expresses loyalty to the point of devotion: proper dress becomes a sign of submission.

The requirement for submission, implying the effect of power, is looked at from the reverse position by Callaway and Young. Both develop the theme of dress in relation to manipulation of power and authority. Callaway interprets the insistence on dress formality by British colonialists as a visible sign of certain moral and social attitudes closely connected to concerns of personal and national dignity. Although this dress may have communicated a sense of self-discipline and assumed social superiority, its ultimate function was to uphold the balance of power. Within this structure of dress display, men and women take on quite distinct positions which reinforce the inequality of gender roles.

Young also approaches this inequality in his investigation of the attempts on the part of the British police force to accommodate female colleagues. This "invasion" of females into a strongly masculine group leads to the attempt, through uniform requirements and prescriptions, to androgynize those females and subject them to informal ridicule. Dress here has become a vehicle for political authority, subjecting the individual to its power. In the extreme situation of uniform rules, it has reversed its property of being an extension of the self by negating the gender identity of the wearer.

As we review these articles, a point made by Howard Morphy as discussant remains clear: dress is both an indicator and a producer of gender.

1

Definition and Classification of Dress

Implications for Analysis of Gender Roles

Joanne B. Eicher and Mary Ellen Roach-Higgins

Dress is a powerful means of communication and makes statements about the gender role of a newborn child soon after birth.[1] Although newborn childrens' first dress may be gender-neutral, their sex soon prompts kin or other caretakers to provide them with dress considered gender-appropriate within their particular society.[2] Further, specific types of dress, or assemblages of types and their properties, communicate gender differentiations that have consequences for the behavior of females and males throughout their lives.[3] This essay includes a review of scholarly works related to dress and gender roles and an assessment of the problems we have encountered in dealing with terminology and classification systems used in these works.[4] We summarize our response to the problems by presenting a sociocultural definition of dress and a classification system for types of dress that are compatible with this definition. We also discuss the relevance of the system in analyses of relationships between dress and gender roles.

Although in this paper we emphasize the use of the classification system to clarify and unify the content of anthropological and sociological study of dress and gender, the system is applicable to all work on the sociocultural aspects of dress. A major advantage of the system is that it brings together a number of related concepts, travelling under various names, within different theoretical and research contexts, under the rubrics "body modifications" and "body supplements."

Early Anthropological Perspectives on Dress and Gender Roles

Statements that anticipated a social anthropology of dress and gender[5] date to the second half of the nineteenth century, when various new sciences of human behavior were taking shape in both the United Kingdom and the United States. Such statements occur in Spencer's *The Principles of Sociology* (1879)[6]; Darwin's *Origin of Species* (1859), *The Descent of Man, and Selection in Relation to Sex* (1871), and *The Expression of Emotions in Man and Animals* (1872)[7]; Tylor's *Primitive Culture* (1871)[8]; Morgan's *Ancient Society* (1877)[9]; and Westermarck's *History of Human Marriage* (1891).[10] In these works, the authors explained variations in forms of dress according to principles embodied in theories of social evolution, and sometimes attributed differences in the dress of females and males to differences in the sexes' respective levels of social evolution, with males being at a higher level. In making such attributions, these nineteenth-century scholars were no doubt influenced by what they saw around them, that is, the relatively plain dress of men that contrasted sharply with the elaborate fashions of women. They were also influenced by the sometimes exotic (to Western eyes) material from which they were extracting data to support their theories. This material included extant accounts of experience in non-Western settings by people of diverse interests: travellers, explorers, traders, colonial officials, and missionaries; as well as historical and literary works, especially those by classical Greek and Roman writers.

By the twentieth century, social anthropologists were increasingly disenchanted with theories of social evolution. They questioned the value of the evolutionists' speculations regarding the origins of types of human behavior, as well as their attempts to determine universal, fixed stages of social development to explain variations in human behavior that differentiated groups of people. They also questioned whether sound social theory could be based on the potpourri of secondary sources used by the evolutionists to support their theoretical propositions.

Among the questioners was Crawley, the first anthropologist to give extensive and serious attention to dress and to relate it to a wide range of human behavior. In his almost book-length entry entitled "Dress" in the *Encyclopedia of Religion and Ethics* (1912:40–72), Crawley partially followed the pattern set by the social evolutionists. He discussed origins of dress; interspersed throughout his work references to dress at the evolutionary levels of savagery, barbarism, and civilization; and supported his generalizations about dress with numerous examples from a variety of secondary written sources. His move away from the evolutionary stance is apparent in his reluctance to claim that anything more than speculations can be made about origins of dress. It is also apparent in his refusal to apply the evolutionists' concept of survivals in his interpretations of dress.[11] The most noteworthy features of Crawley's work, however, are its comprehensiveness, his many keen observations on dress that remain as applicable today as in his own time, and his stance on "sexual" dress – what we would call gendered dress. His position, pivotal to his whole work, is that of the many possible social distinctions that can be communicated by dress, the most important one is sexual, in current terms based on learned gender roles.

As the twentieth century progressed, the oncoming generation of social anthropologists stressed personal, on-site fieldwork as a means of obtaining accurate, scientific data regarding the form and meaning of material and nonmaterial inventions of cultural groups. Among these innovators were ethnographers such as Bronislaw Malinowski and A. R. Radcliffe-Brown and their students (identified with the methodology of the United Kingdom), and Franz Boas and his students in the United States.[12] Lynch, in comparing the work of British and American ethnographers of this period, noted that the Americans tended to place stronger emphasis on collection and analysis of a wide array of material objects. This difference is of some importance for the study of dress because it encouraged orderly and detailed study of the sociocultural significance of material products used as dress. She cautions, however, that one cannot take this as a hard and fast rule, since a lively exchange of ideas between ethnographers from the two countries led some individuals to choose research methods and theoretical orientations contrary to such a distinction (Lynch 1989).

Ethnography, Dress, and Gender

Since the early years of the twentieth century, anthropologists have produced an impressive body of literature. However, none has offered as comprehensive a view of the anthropology of dress and gender as Crawley. This does not mean that British and American anthropologists have completely ignored dress and gender since that time. Especially after 1960, distinguishing characteristics of dress of females and males that intrigued Crawley also caught the attention of anthropologists intent on analyzing cultural similarities and differences between various societies. However, their analyses have tended to be treatments of limited aspects of dress published in monographs, occasional journal articles, and book excerpts, or information included incidentally in the general coverage of the material culture of a group of people.

Among relatively short works are those by Benedict (1931), Bunzel (1931), Bohannan (1956), Messing (1960), Murphy (1964), Roach and

Eicher (1965), Mead (1969), Schwarz (1979), Cordwell (1979), and Hamilton and Hamilton (1989). In entries in the *Encyclopedia of Social Science* entitled "Dress" and "Ornament," Benedict and Bunzel, respectively, followed a nineteenth-century tradition set by Westermarck and others for considering dress as clothing and ornament. As they shied away from global generalizations about clothing and ornament and warned against trying to find universal sequences in their forms, they reflected the general move away from theories of social evolution toward the more cautious approach of twentieth-century ethnographers.

Bohannan (1956) limited his observations to body modifications among the Tiv of Nigeria, emphasizing the practice of scarification. He noted that designs of scarification, a requisite for beauty among both females and males, varied by sex and in some cases had erotic meanings. Messing (1960) discussed only the Ethiopian *shamma*, a generic wrapped garment worn by both sexes, and gave examples of how differences in volume, color, texture, surface design, and manipulations of the wrapped shape communicated a variety of meanings, including the sex of the wearer. Murphy (1964) concentrated on the wrapped facial veil of adult Tuareg males. According to his interpretation, the veil announced the public roles of males, which were not available to females. He further observed that a male's manipulation of the veil facilitated his enactment of somewhat conflicting roles within a complex kinship system.

Roach and Eicher (1965) provided a broad perspective appropriate to the study of the anthropology of dress in brief essays that served as overviews to a series of readings; however, they made only brief mention of the relationship of dress to gender, or "sex roles," as they were called at that time. Mead gave some attention to details of dress of the male and female Maori of New Zealand. However, his main emphasis was on technical aspects of their traditional body coverings (enclosures). Schwarz made a plea for anthropologists to pay greater attention to dress and expanded some of his ideas by discussing the relation of the dress of females and males to the social structuring of life among the Guambianos of Colombia. Cordwell concentrated on cosmetics and other modifications of the body but did not analyze distinctions between the dress of females and males. Hamilton and Hamilton (1989) focused on the dress of adult females of the Karen hill tribe of Thailand.

Several book-length monographs have dealt with limited aspects of the dress of females and males. Strathern and Strathern, in *Self-Decoration on Mount Hagen* (1971), emphasized the body modification of males; as did Faris (1972) in his analysis of Nuba body painting, particularly of males. Rugh (1986) focused on the folk dress of females in a number of Egyptian villages. In a study confined to one Palestinian village, Weir (1989) determined that, contrary to a popularly held view that traditional garb is highly standardized, the garments of these Palestinian women varied widely in surface design and other properties. O'Hanlon (1989) scrutinized both body modifications and body supplements, primarily of the males, in the New Guinea village of Wahgi.

As this sample of publications indicates, increasing attention is being paid to gender and dress by British and American anthropologists. What is lacking is a method for summarizing how dress is both a repository of meanings regarding gender roles and a vehicle for perpetuating or rendering changes in gender roles. Our view is that the intertwined problems of terminology and conceptualization inhibit not only the clear evaluation of the contribution of past and current research, but the formulation of sound theoretical perspectives on which to base research. In the next sections we address these problems.

Problems with Classification and Terminology

Some publications intended as guides for fieldwork offer classificatory systems and terms for describing dress. Probably the best known of these are the Royal Anthropological Institute's *Notes and Queries in Anthropology* (1951) and Murdock's *Outline of Cultural Materials* (1961). In each of these, authors subdivided dress into the familiar categories of clothing and ornament. A more recent book on methods edited by Ellen (1984), *Ethnographic Research: A Guide to General Conduct*, offers no classification system, but refers the fieldworker back to both *Notes and Queries* and Murdock's *Outline* as general starting points for generating initial checklists of terms to try out in on-site study. Thus this volume also helps perpetuate the clothing and adornment dichotomy. Other authors who have attacked the problem of classification and terminology are Doob (1961), Roach and Eicher (1973), Conn (1974), Roach and Musa (1980), and Anawalt (1981). Conn continued the clothing and adornment categories. Doob declined to use these categories and opted to use in their stead "changes in appearance," which he further subdivided into changes of the body and changes on the body. Anawalt, emphasizing only the construction of garments, divided them into five somewhat overlapping categories: draped, slip-on, open-sewn, closed-sewn, and limb-encasing.[13] Roach and Eicher classified types of dress as reconstructing, enclosing, and attached. Roach and Musa considered body modifications, enclosures, and attachments. Our assessment of the works surveyed leads us to the conclusion that systems for defining and classifying types of dress are frequently incomplete, and that the terminology used is ambiguous and inconsistent.

As we address the problems of classifying types of dress, we recognize that the dressed person is a *gestalt* that includes body, all direct modifications of the body itself, and all three-dimensional supplements added to it. Further, we acknowledge that only through mental manipulation can we separate body modifications and supplements from the body itself – and from each other – and extract that which we call dress. Despite these limitations, we choose to focus on the concrete reality of dress that has describable properties, such as color, shape, texture, surface design, or odor. We also take the position that the direct modifications of the body as well as the supplements added to it must be considered types of dress because they are equally effective means of human communication, and because similar meanings can be conveyed by some property, or combination of properties, of either modifications or supplements. For example, the design and color of a facial scar (a body modification) can be as accurate a means of conveying high social status as a supplemental robe of a particular shape and color. However, rarely do the stated or implied classifications of dress found in the literature take into account all possible categories of body modifications and supplements or their properties. Classification of dress as draped or tailored, for instance, presents a very limited view of dress. It concentrates attention only on variations in body enclosures that surround the body in cloth or other pliable materials, such as animal skins or plastic sheetings. Left out is a whole range of body modifications, from skin coloring to perfumes and hairdress. Likewise, those who opt for the use of the word clothing as a single category to encompass all types of dress run a similar risk, for the term clothing also restricts dress to the assemblage of items that happen to cover the body in some way.[14] The omission of body modifications from the study of dress can be a serious loss, for it may lead to false conclusions regarding the social significance of dress. For example, modifications in hairdress may communicate information that has more influence on how human beings see and understand themselves and others than supplements such as robes, foot coverings, or jewelry.

The use of the term "appearance" as a category that subsumes various types of dress also has its limitations. In some ways appearance is more than dress and in other ways less. It is more than dress because it takes into account body features, movements, and positions, as well as the visible body modifications and supplements of dress. It is less than dress because it leaves out what may be some of the most intimately apprehended properties of dress, that is, touch, odor, taste, and sound.

Accompanying the problems of classification are vexing questions about the use of terminology. In designating types of dress, writers frequently use ethnocentric, value-charged terms such as mutilation, deformation, decoration, ornament, and adornment. When they use these terms, they are usually applying their own personally and culturally derived standards to distinguish the good from the bad, the right from the wrong, and the ugly from the beautiful, and thus inevitably reveal more about themselves than about what they are describing. They are also forgetting that dress considered beautiful in one society may be ugly in another, and that dress considered right in one social situation may be wrong in another.

When classifiers label a type of dress or some aspect of it as ornament, adornment, or decoration, they are clearly making a value judgment regarding its merits as an aesthetically pleasing creation. Similarly, their calling a type of dress a mutilation or deformation indicates they have judged it to be nonacceptable. What they omit is whose standard they are applying – and this is a critical omission, for the classifiers' application of these evaluative labels is no guarantee that the wearers, or other viewers, concur with their judgments.[15] Terms thus far discussed as value-laden (mutilation, deformation, ornament, and adornment) are also ambiguous terms. They are ambiguous because they reveal relatively little about type of dress, but a great deal about functions. Like the term "cosmetic surgery," they involve and emphasize the dual functions of dress: as a means of communication between human beings and as an alterant of body processes.[16]

Viewers who label types of dress as mutilations or deformations are registering conscious or unconscious disapproval of certain kinds of body modification, perhaps scarification, tooth filing, or head binding. Their negative reactions are based on what these types of dress communicate to them. Facial scars, for example, may communicate interference with body processes in a way that seems to threaten health and survival. They may also communicate ugliness within the value system of the viewer's own culture group, because their observable properties lie outside the cultural range of body modifications that can be accorded a degree of attractiveness. In other words, their usage is so sharply different, culturally speaking, that they simply are not eligible for consideration as marks of attractiveness or beauty by the viewer who comes from outside the culture. A displayer of scars within one culture and a person with a face lift in another may each undergo risk in order to achieve social approval. Thus scars and face lifts are more alike than different; a search for beauty and a general disregard for risks to health or body functioning is indicated by each.

An additional term that is popular in current literature, but difficult to interpret, is "physical appearance." Some writers use the term to indicate qualities of the natural body, others to identify characteristics of the body and any direct body modifications (as in skin color or hair shape and texture). Still others use the term to summarize a totality consisting of body and garments, jewelry, and other supplements, as well as any direct body modifications. Such fluctuation in usage introduces ambiguity in concept and limits the usefulness of the term physical appearance in discussions of dress, or, for that matter, in discussions of body characteristics.

Defining Dress

In our discussion so far we have been intentionally supporting use of the word "dress" as a comprehensive term to identify both direct body changes and items added to the body, and have presented reasons for rejecting a number of overlapping, competing terms found in the literature related to dress. We have also stressed an important sociocultural aspect of dress: that it is imbued with meaning understood by wearer and viewer. Having taken this sociocultural stance, we define dress as an assemblage of body modifications and/or supplements displayed by a person in communicating with other human beings. Defined in this general way, the word dress is gender-neutral. This general usage does not rule out that, in specific contexts or with specific inflections, the word may be used to convey socially constructed, gendered meanings. When specifically preceded by the article "a" or converted to the plural form, the word dress, according to current usage, designates feminine garments. Similarly, when used in the verb form to designate dressing the male genitals to the right or left in the custom tailoring of men's trousers, it takes on a masculine meaning. A further virtue of the term dress is that its use avoids the potential value bias introduced by words like ornament or decoration, and the lack of clarity or completeness inherent in terms like physical appearance and clothing. The classification system we present in the next section follows from the general definition of dress we have presented.

A Classification System for Types of Dress

Three previous works moved terminology and classification systems away from the built-in contradictions of the long-used clothing-versus-ornament schema. Doob (1961) took a step toward isolating what we call dress by considering changes in the appearance of humans as changes of the body and changes on the body. What he left out were the properties of dress that evoke other than the visual sensory responses, that is, odor, taste, sound, and touch. Roach and Eicher (1973) and Roach and Musa (1980) presented systems that went beyond the visibly observable aspects of dress to include these other categories. The classification system that follows in Table 1 is based on ideas set forth in these earlier works.

The range in types of dress, as shown in the classification system, allows us to provide a method for accurately identifying and describing types of dress that relate to gender roles and other social roles.[17] It also allows us to appreciate the potential variety in dress. In the classification system, we focus on the first part of our definition of dress: an assemblage of body modifications and supplements. Listed in the left-hand column are the major categories of dress – modifications and supplements – and their subcategories. As the subcategories show, parts of the body that can be modified include hair, skin, nails, muscular-skeletal system, teeth, and breath. Body parts can be described in regard to specific properties of color, volume and proportion, shape and structure, surface design, texture, odor, sound, and taste. Supplements to the body – such as body enclosures, attachments to the body, attachments to body enclosures, and hand-held accessories – can be cross-classified with the same properties used to describe body modifications.

By manipulating properties of body modifications and supplements, people communicate their personal characteristics, including the important distinctions of gender. Even when forms of dress and their properties are largely shared or similar for both sexes, gender distinctions can be clearly communicated by a minimum of manipulations of dress. For example, if the hair of males is expected to be cut short and that of females is expected to grow long in a particular society, the shape and volume of hair immediately communicate to observers the gender of the individual under scrutiny.

Relevance of the Classification System in Analysis of Dress and Gender Roles

The definition of dress and the classification system we present unites two major human acts (modifying the body and supplementing the body) that invite sensory responses to and interpretations of the resulting outward similarities and differences of human beings. The preponderance of visually recorded properties in our classification system indicates that we can expect the visual stimuli of dress to outweigh the impact of other sensory stimuli, such as sound, touch, odor, and taste, in establishing gender identity. An additional reason why the visually observable properties may have more impact is that they do not require close proximity to be noticed by others. On the basis of this heavy weighting of visual impact and what we know about theories of communication, we can expect dress to precede verbal communication in establishing an individual's gendered identity as well as expectations for other types of behavior (social roles) based on this identity.[18] The importance of dress in the structuring of behavior, as Polhemus (1989) points out, is that some of the information that is transmitted from person to person by dress is not easily translatable into words. Moreover, to give a detailed verbal report of all the information an individual's dress communicates (including gender) would be both time-consuming and socially clumsy.

At birth, when a child lacks verbal skills as well as the physical power and motor skills required to manipulate dress, adult caretakers (kin or surrogate kin who come to the aid of the child) act as purveyors of culture by providing gender-symbolic dress that encourages others to attribute masculine or feminine gender and to act on the basis of these attributions when interacting with the child. Because establishing gendered forms of dress for males and females provides a visually economical way to reinforce the fact that wearers have the sex organs that are the primary physical distinctions between the sexes, dress serves the macrobiological as well as the macrosocial system. Distinguishing sex by dress can encourage not only sexual overtures in socially approved ways, but also mating, which, in turn, as it leads to birth of children, guarantees the continuity of both the species and society. On a more micro level, members of the kin group who are likely to establish gendered dress for the newborn are also those who are most likely to have a stake in the mating that assures the continuity of the kin group. Only the name of an individual (where distinguished by gender) can compete with dress as an effective social means for communicating the sex of an infant (or a person of any age) to others who then know what gender expectations to apply in making their responses to the dressed individual.

Each society, or subgroup of a society, has its own rules regarding which body modifications or supplements should declare gender roles; to our knowledge, all make their declarations. A ribbon, but a

Table 1.1 Classification System for Types of Dress and Their Properties*

Types of Dress**	Properties							
	Color	Volume & Proportion	Shape & Structure	Surface Design	Texture	Odor	Taste	Sound
Body Modifications								
Transformations of a. Hair b. Skin c. Nails d. Muscular/ skeletal system e. Teeth f. Breath								
Body Supplements								
Enclosures a. Wrapped b. Suspended c. Pre-shaped d. Combinations of ab,ac,bc,abc								
Attachments to Body a. Inserted b. Clipped c. Adhered								
Attachments to Body Enclosures a. Inserted b. Clipped c. Adhered								
Hand-Held Objects a. By self b. By other								

© Mary Ellen Roach-Higgins and Joanne B. Eicher

tiny attachment tied to a wisp of a baby's hair, can announce a gendered identity as feminine. Similarly, within a specific cultural group a short haircut can be a body modification that invests a baby with a masculine identity. The examples given indicate that either a specific supplement or a specific body modification may be a significant symbol that elicits gender expectations and an anticipation that through time children will learn to direct their own acts of dress according to gender expectations. Age, therefore, is closely allied to gender in social expectations for type of dress. Furthermore, language is a strong ally in reinforcing social rules for dress of "a boy," "a girl," "a man," "a woman." As they grow older and develop increasing physical and social independence, children learn by trial and error to manipulate their own dress according to rules for age and gender. They usually acquire these rules via direct advice from adults or older siblings, or by following role models of the same sex, such as admired friends or publicly acclaimed individuals. For the most part, societies are lenient with young learners. Even when rules for gender-distinct dress are strict, children are likely to have more leeway in dress than adults. Thus a young boy may wear only a shirt when both shirt and preshaped trousers are *de rigueur* for a man, or a young girl may wear trousers when a skirt is proper for a woman.

Acquiring knowledge about gender-appropriate dress for various social situations extends to learning rights and responsibilities to act "as one looks." Accordingly, gendered dress encourages each individual to internalize as gendered roles a complex set of social expectations for behavior. These roles, when linked with roles of others, represent part of social structure. Since each person's rendering of any

---

* This system also appears in Mary Ellen Roach-Higgins and Joanne B. Eicher, "Dress and Identity," *Clothing and Textile Research Journal*, Vol. II, 1992. This system is based on previous work as follows: Mary Ellen Roach and Joanne B. Eicher, *The Visible Self: Perspectives on Dress*, Englewood Cliffs, NJ, 1973; Mary Ellen Roach and Kathleen Ehle Musa (now Campbell), *New Perspectives on the History of Western Dress*, New York, Nutriguides, Inc., 1980. We wish to acknowledge suggestions from various students and colleagues. Bruce Olds, University of Wisconsin-Madison journalism student, suggested the hand-held category. Gigi Bechir, University of Minnesota sociology student, suggested that breath can be modified. A discussion with colleagues at a Design, Housing, and Apparel seminar at the University of Minnesota convinced us to use "types" rather than "forms of dress."

** Both body modifications and body supplements can be further classified according to (a) general body locus, e.g., head, neck, trunk, arms, and legs, or (b) more specific locus, e.g., lips, nose, eye-lids or lashes, ears, hands, ankles, feet, breasts, genitals.

social role is unique, this social structuring is constantly recreated (in its details) at the same time that its general configuration may appear to remain constant.

Prescriptions for dress according to gender and age may become increasingly complex as individuals progress through various life stages and participate in multiple societal systems, such as the religious, economic, and political. In each of these systems, differences in forms of dress for females and males can define, support, and reinforce the relative power and influence of the sexes. When specific differences in color, structure, surface design, volume, or texture distinguish dress of males and females, differences in social rank and power can be made obvious. Thus the differential in power and rank of males and females that determines who shall sit on the left and who shall sit on the right of the aisle in church can be made palpably visible by even slight differences in dress.

In the late twentieth century, in areas where technology is highly developed and the economic system is supported by a largely white-collar society, the male white-collar worker's biological presence has been diminished by the shape and volume of his business suit that masks his body contours. By comparison, shape and volume (in proportion to body size) of females' business dress reveals body contours more than the dress of males. This example of females' dress contrasts with dress in some less technologically advanced areas of the world where adult females, often to comply with religious codes, shroud their bodies in veils. It also raises questions regarding the relation of dress and the integration of females into positions of power equal to those of males within the respective economic systems. In some societies an interesting similarity exists between the body veil as a concealing gender-specific wrap for a female, and the Western business suit of a male as a somewhat rigid, preshaped body veil. However, the former is sanctioned by the religious system; the latter by the economic system.

As we have discussed ways in which gendered dress may be incorporated into religious and economic systems, we have touched on the relationship of dress to gender and power. We now turn specifically to this relationship within institutionalized political systems. The most important political information that the dress of people within a political system can convey is the right of the wearer to make decisions on behalf of people within a particular governmental unit. And the most important aspect of this dress, particularly for police and military personnel, is that it commands instant recognition of the right of the wearer not only to make decisions but to use force to maintain social order or wage war. A uniform based on a gendered-enclosing, preshaped, trousered outfit for males is at present a global standard for police and military dress. When females have entered this traditional realm of males, they have generally accommodated to wearing a preshaped uniform while maintaining feminine distinctions in modifications of hair or facial skin color. The uniforms, because they cover bodies, downplay the sexual characteristics of the wearer, as do requirements for identical color, texture, and general shape and structure. Another example of political dress is the voluminous enclosing robe of a judge. Although the robe can be unisex, shoes, modifications of hair, and any cosmetics that complete the judge's dress are usually not.

Some types of political dress are neither body-hiding enclosures nor uniforms. Instead, they are small attached, inserted, hand-held, suspended, or rigid preshaped objects. They include badges, buttons, ribbons, rings, medallions, crowns, and staffs. Often these smaller objects take on rich political meanings because of their "rarity." Four stars on a general's epaulets, an array of ribbons on a veteran's military uniform, a mayor's ribbon-suspended medallion, a pope's tiara, and an emperor's jewelled crown all communicate meanings relative to specific rank and temporal power of the wearer. They are available to women only if a society allows women to take the political positions these objects announce. In some cases, a queen's crown may only proclaim her husband's power, not her own.

Conclusions

In this paper we have developed a perspective for use in analysis of dress and gender roles. This perspective includes a definition of dress and a classification system for types of dress. We have also explored how the definition and system can free our discussions of dress and gender from some of the old assumptions, such as the necessity to classify all dress as either clothing or ornament. A few scholars have utilized perspectives closely allied to ours in analyzing the cultural significance of dress. As example, we refer to studies by Kroeber (1919), Kroeber and Richardson (1940), and Robinson (1976). Their work involved developing methods for measuring properties of dress and searching for ways to link historical fluctuations in properties of dress to fluctuations in other cultural phenomena. Kroeber and Richardson measured aspects of dress that can be readily interpreted as volume and proportion, and also as shape and structure, as these properties were exhibited in a historical sequence of women's fashionable and largely preshaped garments. Several decades later Robinson showed that measurement techniques similar to those used by Kroeber and Richardson could also be applied in studying a type of body modification, that is, trimmed beards. These studies suggest that scholars can classify and make judgments about a variety of types of dress and their properties without resorting to biased, ambiguous terms or getting bogged down with the vast global accumulation of nomenclature for specific units of dress.

With our topic, dress, accurately identified, we can proceed to formulations of questions concerning what choices from a seemingly open-ended universe of body modifications and supplements – and their properties – individuals and social groups make. Within a given cultural group, we can explore whether dress tends to have a narrow range of types to identify gender roles and direct behavior of males and females in gender-specific ways versus an elaborately detailed system of distinctions with alternate choices. We can consider whether body supplements, versus body modifications, prevail in establishing gender distinctions or whether some balance is maintained. We can also compare the influence of variables such as age, sex, and technology, and types of kinship, religious, economic, and political systems on gender distinctions, as well as the points of variability in dress that support these distinctions.

Another topic relevant to the United States since the late 1960s is the types of dress that can support equality in economic roles of men and women. In a kind of natural experiment, women working in white-collar jobs began to choose tailored business suits with a jacket similar to a man's suit jacket, worn with either trousers or skirt. Such dress was adopted by women maintaining ideologies from relatively conservative feminist to radical feminist. Somehow this ensemble stood, in the ideology of the time, as a claim for equal opportunity for women and men, particularly in the economic arena. As time went by, masculine properties in colors, texture, garment shape, and even the suit itself, gave way to more feminine-distinct features in dress, such as bright colors and surface designs in fabric. As a result, radical feminists felt betrayed (Lind and Roach-Higgins 1985; Strega 1985). However, what had occurred was easily predicted by anyone who gave serious thought to Bohannan's study of the Tiv reported in 1956. The suit as a political statement had yielded to fashion, just as among the Tiv men and women the old fashion in design and texture of scarification gave way to the new. Those who felt betrayed failed to accept or recognize that fashion (often mistakenly considered characteristic only of societies with complex technology) is a pervasive social phenomenon that may prevail over ideology, taking over a once politically potent symbol and drawing it into the fold of fashion. This takeover in no way rules out that dress functions as a powerful though often underestimated system of visual communication that expresses gender role, which is usually intertwined with age, kinship, occupational, and other social roles throughout a person's life. From womb to tomb, the body is a dressed body, and caretakers typically introduce the young to gender-differentiated dress and often dress the dead in gendered garb. Thus each human being enters and exits life in dress appropriate for the sociocultural system into which he or she is born and from which he or she departs.

Notes

1. We distinguish between the terms "sex" and "gender," but early writers whose work we discuss did not use the term "gender." Only since the 1960s have social scientists made a concerted effort to assign the term "sex" to biological distinctions between females and males and the term "gender" to variations in social roles learned by females and males. We also point out that, as adjectives, female and male emphasize biological differences between the sexes, while feminine and masculine indicate differences in social roles, hence gender.
2. We can expect dress of the newborn to vary from one social group to another, and to change through time in each group. Examples of gender-neutral dress supplied at birth include hospital-provided diaper, long-sleeved undershirt, and knitted cap in the United States in the 1990s; a coating of oil and a touch of ochre around the fontanelle among the Nuba in the late 1960s (Faris 1972); a paste of ground camwood applied to the head among the Tiv of the 1950s (Bohannon 1956).
3. Of the two general functions of dress, communication is of primary concern for social anthropologists. The other general function, altering body processes, is, for the most part, a matter of concern for biophysicists, members of the health professions, or moralists.
4. We limit our examples to works published in the United Kingdom and North America.
5. The dates given are the earliest we determined for publication of material in book form. Some of Spencer's chapters appeared earlier as articles published simultaneously in journals in the United States, United Kingdom, and additional European countries.

6. From among the early writers, Spencer, in *The Principles of Sociology*, presented one of the more extensive treatments of dress, devoting three chapters to the topic. Since Spencer's point of view was determinedly evolutionist, he searched for types of dress that distinguished primitive people from nineteenth-century western Europeans, whom he considered to be representatives of higher levels of social evolution. Further, his observations on dress foreshadowed those of later social scientists, particularly Goffman, as he emphasized that various types of dress serve as guides to interpersonal conduct within the daily and special "ceremonies" of life. Goffman acknowledged this debt in an article "Symbols of Class Status" (1951) and in his book *Relations in Public* (1971). Spencer also emphasized the effects of dress on social patterns of authority and deference in human encounters, giving numerous examples of how different types of men's dress make clear, or reinforce, these patterns. At first, his failure to pay much attention to women's dress seems ironic; however, this omission may carry a message. Perhaps he simply did not perceive women as exerting much control in encounters among those people he regarded as primitive – or, for that matter, among people who had developed what the nineteenth-century evolutionists considered the civilized state epitomized by western European nations, with elaborate political organizations designed for exercising social control.
7. In *The Descent of Man, and Selection in Relation to Sex*, Darwin attributed developments in dress by both sexes to a general inborn similarity in the mind of "man." At the same time, he perceived innate differences in attention paid to dress by men and women, attributing to females a "greater delight" in activities of dress than men (Darwin, C. n.d.: 884, 901). In *The Expression of Emotions in Man and Animals* he carried his ideas further, proposing that females have greater sensitivity to others' views of dress than do men. This explanation, although based on a belief in innate differences, led him a step away from a strictly evolutionary stance regarding sex differences in dress. (Darwin, C. 1955: 325–46). In fact, this concept expressed a rudimentary social-psychological viewpoint, greatly resembling that of contemporary symbolic interactionists, who posit that people's self-evaluations of their presentations of the outwardly observable self are learned through their social interactions with other people.
8. Tylor was perfunctory in his treatment of dress of both males and females in *Primitive Culture*. He did mention dress as he set forth his doctrine of survivals, but mainly cited a few historical changes in form that, by analogy, exemplified how cultural survivals from earlier stages of social evolution may persist in the "more important matters of life." Despite his downplaying of the social significance of dress, and observable survivals in it, subsequent generations of writers on dress – from various disciplines – apparently thought otherwise and regularly included virtually obligatory sections on such survivals in their work. These writers include: G. Darwin (1872), Veblen (1899), Webb (1907), Hurlock (1929), and Flugel (1930).

9. Morgan, in his work *Ancient Society*, devoted a chapter to the "organization of society on [the] basis of sex," but offered no comment on how dress may be related to such social organization, or the interpersonal conduct it implies. Instead, he followed his special interest in kinship designations almost exclusively in the discussion of this topic. We take note of him, however, because of the meticulous detail with which he delineated what he perceived as material and non-material progress made in each of the six stages of social evolution that culminated in the attainment of the seventh stage: civilization. These six preliminary stages included three levels of savagery and three levels of barbarism. From his mental mapping, we can extract how he saw the dress of human beings fitting into a great evolutionary scheme. Briefly, he saw humans entering the first social level of savagery naked, the first level of barbarism in skin garments, and arriving at civilization in woven garments.
10. In his *History of Human Marriage*, Westermarck, like Spencer, gave considerable attention to what we are calling dress. Unlike Spencer, however, he restricted his discussion to primarily one topic: "primitive" people's use of self-decoration as a way of enhancing "sexual attractiveness." In his discussion, he used, and perhaps helped set, a pattern that anthropologists generally still follow: the practice of separating dress into the two overlapping categories of ornament and clothing.
11. Hodgen pointed out that Crawley was one of several anthropologists who spoke out in opposition to the use of the doctrine of survivals, questioning the assumption that savagery survived among contemporary people, especially peasants, as bits of "fossilized thinking" (Hodgen 1977: 146, 164).
12. We recognize the negative connotations frequently implied in the use of the term "social evolutionist." In 1952 Radcliffe-Brown noted a tendency for the term "evolutionary anthropologist" to be used as a kind of abuse. When Morgan was so disparaged, Radcliffe-Brown defended Morgan's view as one of progress and not as evolutionist, commenting that such anti-evolutionists as Franz Boas believed, like Morgan, in progress (Radcliffe-Brown 1963: 203).
13. Anawalt (1981) credits Barnett (1942) and Boucher (1966) as sources for her categories. Barnett proposed that all material objects have three properties: principle, form, and function (a garment wrapped around the body exemplifies the principle of being draped, the garment's shape is its form, and its function is covering the torso). Boucher provided the names of the five categories that Anawalt modified.
14. Other terms that leave out many or all body modifications are apparel, garb, attire, and costume. We are especially aware that non-Westerners are sensitive to having their dress called costume by Westerners, for they feel the term sets them apart as quaint, freakish, immoral, or deprived, when they are simply following their own customs in dress.
15. We do not rule out that careful describers of dress can avoid their own

bias when recording other people's evaluations of types of dress. However, the literature does not indicate this is universally done. Moreover, as the next section explains, whence the knowledge or whence the valuing is of little consequence, since these terms are only remotely related to the task of describing type of dress.

16. Dress may be a direct alterant of body processes in the case of some body modifications, such as tooth filing or cutting body tissues to introduce lip plugs. It can also be an alterant as it serves (as a cloak may) as a micro environment and an interface between body and the macroenvironment.
17. The classification system itself is applicable in any study of dress, not just to the study of dress and gender.
18. Gregory P. Stone, in an article titled "Appearance and the Self" (1962), points out that appearance in face-to-face interaction precedes discourse, and he uses the word "program" to categorize the dress that an individual wearer presents to another for "review," stating that when program and review coincide, the self of the wearer is validated. His ideas are of relevance here, as he would point out that one's gender, as presented by one's program of dress, establishes a basis for consequent verbal interaction with others who review the wearer's dress.

References

Anawalt, P., *Indian Clothing Before Cortés*, Norman: University of Oklahoma Press, 1981.

Barnett, H.G., "Invention and Cultural Change," *American Anthropologist*, Vol. 44, 1942, pp. 14–30.

Benedict, R., "Dress," *Encyclopedia of Social Science*, New York: Macmillan Co., Vol. 5, 1931, pp. 235–37.

Bohannan, P., "Beauty and Scarification Amongst the Tiv," *Man*, Vol. 56, 1956, pp. 117–21.

Boucher, F., *20,000 Years of Fashion: The History of Costume and Personal Adornment*, New York: Abrams, 1966.

Bunzel, R., "Ornament," *Encyclopaedia of Social Science*, New York: Macmillan Co., Vol. 5, 1931, pp. 496–97.

Conn, R., *Robes of White Shell and Sunrise*, Denver: Denver Art Museum, 1974.

Cordwell, J., "The Very Human Arts of Transformation," in J. Cordwell and R.A. Schwarz (eds.), *The Fabrics of Culture*, The Hague: Mouton Press, 1979.

Crawley, E., "Dress," *Encyclopaedia of Religion*, New York: Charles Scribner's Sons, Vol. 5, 1912, pp. 40–72 (reprinted in Crawley, E., *Dress, Drinks, and Drums*, London: Methuen and Co., 1931, pp. 1–175).

Darwin, C., *The Expression of Emotions in Man and Animals*, New York: Greenwood Press, 1955 (1872).

———, *The Origin of Species* and *The Descent of Man, and Selection in Relation to Sex*, New York: The Modern Library, n.d. (1859 and 1871, respectively).

Darwin, G., "Development in Dress," *MacMillan's Magazine*, 1872, pp. 410–16.

Doob, L.W., *Communication in Africa, a Search for Boundaries*, New Haven: Yale University Press, 1961.

Ellen, R.F., ed., *Ethnographic Research: A Guide to General Conduct*, London: Academic Press, 1984.

Faris, J., *Nuba Personal Art*, London: Gerald Duckworth, Inc., 1972.

Flugel, J.C., *The Psychology of Clothes*, London: The Hogarth Press, 1930.

Goffman, E., "Symbols of Class Status," *British Journal of Sociology*, Vol. 2, 1951, pp. 294–304.

———, *Relations in Public, Microstudies of the Public Order*, New York: Harper and Row, 1971.

Hamilton, J.A. and J.W., "Dress as a Reflection and Sustainer of Social Reality: A Cross-Cultural Perspective," *Clothing and Textiles Research Journal*, Vol. 7, 1989, pp. 16–22.

Hodgen, M.T., *The Doctrine of Survivals*, Folcroft Library Editions, Manchester: St. Ann's Press, 1977 (1936).

Hurlock, E., *The Psychology of Dress*, New York: Ronald Press, 1929.

Kroeber, A.L., "On the Principle of Order in Civilization as Exemplified by Changes in Fashion," *American Anthropologist*, Vol. 21, July 1919, pp. 235–63.

———, and J. Richardson, "Three Centuries of Women's Dress Fashions: A Quantitative Analysis," *Anthropological Records*, Vol. 5, No. 2, 1940, pp. 111–53.

Lind, C., and M.E. Roach-Higgins, "Fashion, Collective Adoption, and the Social-Political Symbolism of Dress," in M.R. Solomon (ed.), *The Psychology of Fashion*, Lexington, Massachusetts: Heath and Co, 1985, pp. 183–92.

Lynch, A., "Survey of Significance and Attention Afforded Dress and Gender in Formative American and English Anthropological Field Studies," manuscript, University of Minnesota, 1989.

Mead, S.M., *Traditional Maori Clothing*, Wellington: A.H. and A.W. Reed, 1969.

Messing, S.D., "The Non-Verbal Language of the Ethiopian Toga," *Anthropos*, Vol. 55, No. 3/4, 1960, pp. 558–60.

Morgan, L.H., *Ancient Society*, Tucson: University of Arizona Press, 1985 (1877).

Murdock, G.P., *et al. Outline of Cultural Materials*, 4th ed., New Haven: Human Relations Area Files, 1961.

Murphy, R., "Social Distance and the Veil," *American Anthropologist*, Vol. 66, No. 6, Part 1, December 1964, pp. 1257–74.

O'Hanlon, M., *Reading the Skin: Adornment, Display and Society among the Wahgi*, London: British Museums Publication, 1989.

Polhemus, T., "Style Groups: The New Ethnicities," seminar paper, Oxford University, 1989.

Radcliffe-Brown, A.R., *Structure and Function in Primitive Society*, New York: Free Press, 1963.

Roach, M.E., and J.B. Eicher, *Dress, Adornment and the Social Order*, New York: John Wiley and Sons, 1965.

———, *The Visible Self: Perspectives on Dress*, Englewood Cliffs, New Jersey: Prentice–Hall, 1973.

———, and K.E. Musa (now Campbell), *New Perspectives on the History of Western Dress*, New York: Nutriguides Inc., 1980.

Robinson, D., "Fashions in Shaving and Trimming of the Beard; The Men of the Illustrated London News, 1842–1872," *American Journal of Sociology*, Vol. 8, March 1976, pp. 1133–39.

Rugh, A.B., *Reveal and Conceal: Dress in Contemporary Egypt*, Syracuse: Syracuse University Press, 1986.

Royal Anthropological Institute, *Notes and Queries in Anthropology*, 6th ed., London: Routledge and Kegan Paul, 1951 (1874).

Schwarz, R.A., "Uncovering the Secret Vice: Toward an Anthropology of Clothing and Adornment," in J. Cordwell and R. A. Schwarz (eds.), *The Fabrics of Culture*, The Hague: Mouton Press, 1979.

Spencer, H., *The Principles of Sociology*, Vol. II–1, New York: D. Appleton and Company, 1879.

Stone, G.P., "Appearance and the Self," in A. M. Rose (ed.), *Human Behavior and the Social Processes: An Interactionist Approach*, New York: Houghton Mifflin Co., pp. 89–118.

Strathern, A. and M., *Self-Decoration on Mount Hagen*, London: Gerald Duckworth and Co. Ltd., 1971.

Strega, L., "The Big Sell-Out: Lesbian Femininity," *Lesbian Ethics*, Vol. 1, No. 3, Fall 1985.

Tylor, E.B., *Primitive Culture*, New York: Harper and Brothers, 1958 (1871).

Veblen, T., *The Theory of the Leisure Class*, New American Library Edition, New York: Mentor Book, 1958 (1899).

Webb, W.W., *The Heritage of Dress: Being Notes on the History and Evolution of Clothes*, London: E. Grant Richards, 1907.

Weir, S., *Palestinian Costumes*, London: British Museums Publication, 1989.

Westermarck, E., *The History of Human Marriage*, Vol. 1, New York: The Allerton Book Company, 1922 (1891).

2

Women as Headhunters

The Making and Meaning of Textiles in a Southeast Asian Context

Ruth Barnes

The Pitt Rivers Museum in Oxford holds what is certainly the greatest and best-documented collection of artifacts from the villages of the Naga Hills, a mountainous region of northeast India, bordering on Burma.[1] Two collectors, in particular, provided the bulk of the material: J. H. Hutton and J. P. Mills, both at one time British colonial officers in the Naga Hills. Their presence in the area corresponds roughly to the years between the two world wars. Although stationed in the Naga Hills primarily to fulfill their duties to the colonial service, both men took great interest in the habits and customs of the people they were to administer. They considered it part of their professional duty to learn as much as possible about local habits, social institutions, and languages, and to publish what they learned in scholarly publications. To Hutton and Mills the service to the colony and the pursuit of anthropological investigations were mutually complementary and, in general, not in conflict. An emotional attachment and respect for the people of the Naga Hills added to their commitment. Between them they published five monographs on different Naga groups that are still the primary sources for the area, as well as numerous articles (Hutton 1921a, 1921b; Mills, 1922, 1926, 1937).[2] Their books are detailed and densely packed with information, yet all follow a peculiar pattern.

For their monographs, both were influenced and guided by the methods of investigation proposed in *Notes and Queries*, the Royal Anthropological Institute's handbook and guide to ethnographic fieldwork questions, which led to a standardized structure of their books. Whichever volume one opens, the chapter sequence is identical: (1) General (or Introductory), (2) Domestic Life, (3) Laws and Customs, (4) Religion, (5) Folklore (or Folktales), (6) Language. Incidentally, the ethnographic information that is put into each chapter also follows an identical sequence. The Introductory, for example, contains: Origin and Migrations, Clans, Appearance, Dress, Ornaments, Weapons, Character.

The purpose, of course, is to achieve an objective form of presentation, as free as possible from the personal leanings or interests of the ethnographer. The aim is to be scientific. The result is peculiar to a particular period in the history of anthropology, and it succeeds in creating an abstract structure that does not take its lead from Naga life. Although full of ethnographic facts and details, the account makes no attempt at reflecting a structure – physical or conceptual – of a Naga society.[3]

The Pitt Rivers Museum Collection

How do the academic writings of Mills and Hutton compare to their ethnographic collections? At the time, a study of material culture was still an essential aspect of anthropological research. To some degree, the research into material culture was connected to the profession's theoretical interest in questions of evolution and diffusion, but, as we shall see, the detailed documentation of the collection can only be interpreted in a sociological sense, within the context of social meaning.

Both Mills and Hutton shared their interest in material culture with Henry Balfour, the first curator of the Pitt Rivers Museum. He urged them to send any tools, costumes, musical instruments, and other artifacts, with documentation where possible, to the museum in Oxford, where it was to become part of the great teaching collection. Between 1914 and 1938 Hutton donated 2,018 specimens, and Mills gave 2,079 objects between 1920 and 1938. In addition, both bequeathed their photographs.

The documentation they attached typically notes the village of manufacture or acquisition, and usually includes the indigenous terms for the objects. Occasionally, the information includes the personal name of the last owner, or of the man or woman who made the objects. These individuals can sometimes be matched up with archival photographs or sketches. In addition, Hutton and Mills kept up a constant correspondence with Balfour about the usage, meaning, and local distribution of the objects they collected. Thus, while the monographs that were written about the Naga Hills were academic with a tendency towards abstraction, attempting a generalized picture of these societies, the Pitt Rivers collection gives very specific and particular evidence.

The collection also makes it visually obvious that a great deal of diversity existed in the Naga Hills, with ethnic identity frequently shifting or overlapping. Hutton, in an article written more than thirty years after living in the Naga Hills, noted that "the differences in language, custom, dress, appearance and psychology, seemed so marked that the inherent unity of the Naga tribes tended to be obscured by their differences. . . . All this meant that one could not see the forest for the trees" (Hutton 1965:16). Keeping this in mind, I nevertheless want to consider particular aspects of the collection without always making ethnic distinctions. A detachment from the immediate, specific context may be deplorable in many instances, but it can also occasionally provide a broader vision. Although many differences in social and material culture exist among the peoples of the Naga Hills, certain underlying principles common to the area can be emphasized.

What insight, if any, can we gain from the detail of the Pitt Rivers collection? First of all, the nature of the collection already says something about what was important in material terms to the various Naga societies. Although all aspects of material culture are represented – including not only the completed objects, but also the tools necessary to produce them – there is no doubt that it was costume, in the widest sense, and all forms of body ornament that were predominantly available. Of the more than 4,000 items in the Hutton-Mills collection, more than 20 percent are large textiles that were worn as clothing. In addition, smaller textiles, such as loincloths or belts, must be added to the loom-woven part of the collection. Furthermore, if one adds other articles of dress and ornament, such as leggings, bracelets, necklaces, and headdresses, a conservative guess brings the total close to two-thirds of the number of objects. For the museum researcher, the initial impression is one of overwhelming detail. Yet in the monographs, both Hutton and Mills had dealt with the topic of "dress" in a few pages in their introductions.

Interpretation of the Collection

The categories for particular textiles are described with great precision. Cloths and dress are first of all gender-specific.[4] That in itself is, of course, not surprising, but seems to be a commonplace feature of human societies. Far more refined categories confront us, often specifically associated with particular lineages and individual status reached within the community. It is status that I will consider here, rather than the association with specific lineages, although many cloths are affiliated with both simultaneously.[5]

Of particular value in this respect is Mills's collection from the Ao Naga, both because his documentation is especially detailed and because certain general aspects of Naga dress are precisely described by his Ao informants. The characteristics that emerge are as follows. Apart from the gender distinction already mentioned, there is a differentiation by age. Elaboration of dress only develops as men and women mature. Of paramount importance in that respect are so-called feasts of merit, a series of ceremonial feasting married men and their wives engage in. They involve the slaughter of animals, culminating in the sacrifice of the ritually and symbolically important *mithan*, and the generous feeding of the entire community and of allied lineages from outside the village. To commemorate the series of feasts, stone monuments or, in some areas, forked posts are set up (Plate 2.1). Each feast increases the status and "merit" of the person(s) involved (Hutton 1921a:230–33; 1921b:227–29; Mills 1922:136–44; 1926:257–62; 1937:181–95). A new stage is always associated with a particular type of textile, which may, furthermore, be distinctive to a particular lineage.

However, the acquisition of the right to a specific cloth, as associated with the feasts of merits, has to be seen separately from, and to some degree in contrast to, the other specific dress elaboration of Naga societies.[6] The latter is closely affiliated with headhunting. All Naga groups were formerly intensely involved in ritual warfare, culminating

Plate 2.1 Forked post. (Hutton, J.H. The Sema Naga: opposite p. 37)

ideally in the capture of an enemy's head. From a certain age onward (once an adolescent boy had entered the men's house, called *morung*) physically active men went on headhunting raids, and the successful headhunter gained the right to elaborate dress. Before returning to the cloths associated with the feasts of merit, the general characteristics of this form of dress should be described.

The headhunter's dress is a composition of various parts, of which the woven textile is a minor aspect, sometimes even no more than a loincloth. Essential is the headdress. This can be varied, but basically there exist two types among different ethnic groups; one is a skullcap of bear skin, with tall feather ornaments added, and the other is a helmet with prominent horns (Plates 2.2 and 2.3). Tusks, teeth, earrings, smaller feather ornaments, human hair, and brass discs may all be added to create a composite structure that is to some degree an expression of the individual man's imagination. The headhunter wears a necklace with a pendant, armlets and anklets, bracelets and an ornament

Plate 2.2 Ao warrior. (Pitt Rivers Museum Collection, J.P. Mills photographs)

Plate 2.3 Konyak warrior. (Fürer-Haimendorf, C., *The Naked Naga*: Ill. 25)

across the front or back (called "enemy's teeth"), as well as a small basket at the back, to hold *panji*, spike traps used when retreating after a war raid. The basket may have the attachment of a "tail" with long fringes of hair (Plate 2.2). Components of the total ensemble are put together by the man himself, and most parts are made either by him, or by other males.[7] Even to the loincloth he wears, which – as is all weaving – is done by a woman, he will add shell ornaments, sometimes encrusting it so thickly that the textile is visually insignificant.

If we compare this costume, worn by the headhunter at the ceremonies following a raid, to the large cloths associated with the completion of certain feasts of merit, the following differences are obvious. The headhunter's dress is made up primarily from parts that come from outside the village: skins, feathers (from wild birds), claws, tusks, and wild animals' teeth; the form that is created plays on the image of the "forest dweller," especially by including the long tail. Of course this is appropriate for the occasion, as the headhunting party leaves the order and security of the village and goes into the wild, uncontrolled forest and into the danger of enemy territory, seeking to find a victim. Before the raiding party can return into the community, word has to be sent ahead so that preparations for the appropriate welcome can be made. The return to the village after a successful raid is an essential part of the headhunting, and it culminates in the display of the trophy, either on a skull tree or in the men's house (Plate 2.4). At this point of entry, the warrior's costume is put on and is displayed in dances that may last for days.

The cloths that one gains through feasts of merit, on the other hand, are single large textiles, worn often as mantles over the shoulder. Shells, beads, or hair tassels may be added, but the costume of status is primarily made up of the textile (Plate 2.5). While the headhunter's dress emphasizes the wildness of the forest in its composite parts, the cloths of a feast of merit underline, by contrast, order and precise structure. The former is assembled by men, the latter is always made by women. This brings up a further and significant distinction.

Both types of dress are closely connected to ideas of status and merit in Naga society. Both headhunting and feasts of merit (the latter associated with the ceremonial sacrifice of animals and the setting up of stone monuments) are a way of gaining social status. Hutton noted that both aspects of village life, headhunting and feasts of merit, are central to understanding certain values of Naga communities (Hutton 1928:399–400). Both activities are considered to increase personal and communal fertility, as is reported in all accounts from Naga societies.

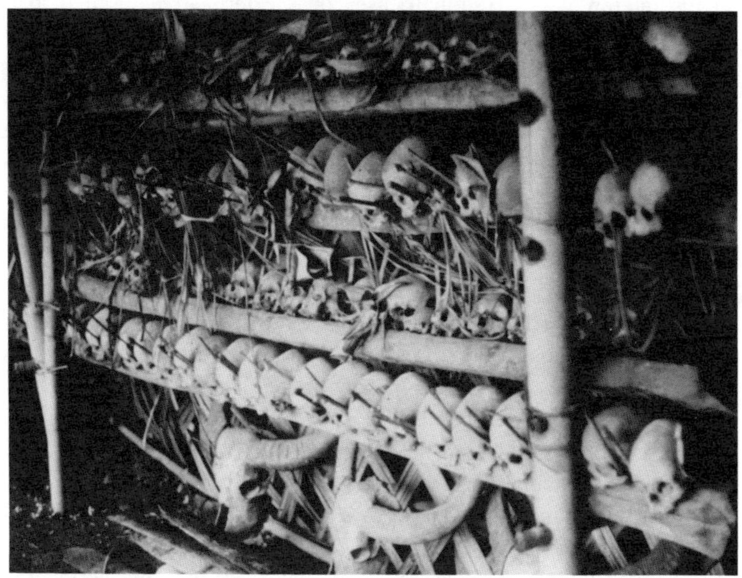

Plate 2.4 Skulls displayed. (C. Fürer-Haimendorf, unpublished)

Plate 2.5 Cloth of merit. (Pitt Rivers Museum Collection: 1928.69.715)

In his interpretation, Hutton focuses on the term *aren*, used in particular by the Ao Naga (Mills 1926:112, 257). Both he and Mills describe *aren* as spiritual strength and personal prosperity. Hutton goes so far as to interpret headhunting as the transfer, via the head, of *aren* from one person to another. This interpretive analysis actually is not supported by the ethnographic record. As both Mills and Hutton report, no Naga doubts that headhunting brings prosperity to the warrior and the community, but it is unclear what happens between cause and effect.[8]

What is certain, however, is the opinion that the warriors undergo great danger: literally, of course, they could lose their own heads. This kind of death is considered to be a particularly unpropitious one (Mills 1926:286). To be a headhunter means that one goes out into the forest, which in this case is wild and dangerous and ritually distinct from the village, but brings back fertility for the well-being of oneself and the community. Participation in a successful raid is an essential prerequisite for a young man who wants to marry (Hutton 1921a:165). Headhunting is entirely a male activity: women are present once the head is integrated into the village, but to the act itself they are peripheral.

Feasts of merit are similarly concerned with the visual display of fertility, now seen as physical, material prosperity. By having the means to entertain the entire community, one can show that one has *aren*. Material wealth is seen metaphysically and implies personal fertility. By initiating the display of wealth, further wealth will be gained by the individual and the community. The emphasis here is on order and balance within the community. Although the feasts are held by men, only married men can perform them, and their wives have a crucial role in the preparations and carrying out of the event. Both male and female are needed to perform the ceremony, and most significantly, both a husband and his wife, as well as their children, gain the right to wear certain cloths after the feasts have been held. Although the appropriate cloth is won through the man's initiative to hold the feast, the textile itself need not be gender-specific, as Mills reports for the Ao *aosü*. The cloth is the essential marker of achievement in the household, a sign of spiritual blessing. The textile of distinction, however, is made by women. Not only are women involved in the actual feast, the preparation, and the serving of food and drink, but by weaving the cloth they produce one of the essential emblems of the acquired merit.

To return briefly to the comparison between the warrior's dress and the cloak of the feast of merit, it has been noted that the headhunter's dress includes the use of material that comes from animals of the forest, and to some degree even alludes to animal characteristics, such as the tail worn by several Naga groups (such as the Lhota and Ao). The implication is that the headhunter, wearing his dress after the raid, emphasizes that the action of his success has been outside the village community. Moreover, the costume is made up of numerous elements from different materials. By contrast, the dress one gains as a result of a merit feast consists primarily of a large textile, worn as a wrap-around cloak or skirt. The woven cloth has a structured form, first in the regularity of warp and weft, and second in its clear geometric patterns that emphasize the horizontal and vertical lines already inherent in the weave. The cloth is never cut and tailored.

Yet the two forms of dress should not be seen as symbolically opposite, just as it would be incorrect to imply a simplistic opposition between village and forest. The village community represents social order in this life, but the forest does not necessarily stand for lack of order. Instead, certain animals of the wild can bring special powers to humans and are spoken of with great respect. Such animals are, in particular, the tiger, leopard, elephant, and bear. Hunting them successfully results in restrictions and prohibitions (Mills 1937:100). There is a widespread belief that certain people have a close affinity with specific tigers or leopards, and that the life of the human and the animal are connected (Hutton 1921a:243–44; 1921b:200; Mills 1922:164; 1926:247; 1937:228). This connection gives special powers to the human and frequently results in him or her becoming an accomplished healer or magician. The hornbill bird, whose feathers or entire skulls are so often prominently incorporated in the warrior's headdress, can be a messenger from the spirit world of ancestors and divinity, and frequently appears in myths and tales (Hutton 1921a:391–93; Mills 1926:14). The forest that supplies so many attributes to the headhunter's dress, therefore, can be seen as an aspect of the spiritual world, and in that respect is different from the village, but not symbolically opposite.

The costume thus put together is worn to celebrate the successful transferral of fertility from the outside into the community. The transmission of prosperity in this case is horizontal. By contrast, the fertility gained in feasts of merit spreads vertically through the line of descent: a man's descendants continue to participate in his merit, although they also have to renew the feasts not to lose the right to certain textiles.[9] Women partake of the prestige gained through merit feasts, but they are separated from the status of headhunting. However,

I will argue in my concluding interpretation that they, too, engage in an activity that may be seen as analogous to the male pursuit of headhunting: as the producers of textiles they manipulate and transform material (raw cotton) into a shape that can become a person's foremost sign of physical and spiritual well-being and wealth. Unfortunately, the Naga ethnographies give scant and rather fragmented evidence for this hypothesis.[10] For that reason, I want to bring in comparative material from other parts of Southeast Asia, in particular Indonesia.

Headhunting and Textiles: A Southeast Asian Perspective

Maritime Southeast Asia in general has traditionally had a preoccupation with headhunting. The interpretation proposed above, which connects the custom to a concept of fertility and its manipulation, seems to hold generally true.[11] The capture of a head and its integration into the own community was formerly considered as important by the Iban of Borneo as by the Atoni of Timor or the Lamaholot of East Flores. In her survey of Indonesian textiles, Mattiebelle Gittinger says: "Textiles, headhunting, and fertility traditionally formed a symbolic triad in Indonesia" (1979:31). In which way are the three juxtaposed, and how is the relationship to be interpreted?

I have earlier considered the relationship between headhunting and fertility. The connection between the latter and textiles is common knowledge to scholars of Indonesia, but in this context it might be helpful to bring up a few generally perceived characteristics. First of all, textiles are *always* made by women in Indonesia, just as is the case in the Naga Hills. All aspects of cloth manufacture are exclusively carried out by women, from the cleaning and spinning of the cotton to the dyeing, weaving, and patterning of the cloth. Textiles, therefore, are considered to be "feminine" goods, and as such are essential to a complex of gift exchanges at various stages of life.

It is a commonplace that women are associated with fertility, as they bear children. In the Southeast Asian context, this theme finds particular elaboration. Women are physically capable of taking a being (the child to be born) through a rite of passage, birth. Their particular ritual role, therefore, is frequently associated with transitions of state in a person's life. Textile manufacture, far from being simply the making of a useful object, is seen as just that: a transformation from the raw material – the cotton that grows in the field, the dye plants that may have to be gathered in the woods – into the cloth that in its structure (the intertwining of warp and weft) and in its design can express fundamental concepts of the community.[12]

The making of textiles can be divided into two aspects: the making of the prerequisite vehicle (the thread), and the making of the cloth (its patterning and weaving). Both parts of the production can be interpreted metaphorically. The thread preparation, for example, is linked to the "thread of life" motif we all are familiar with in our own tradition. In the Indonesian context, Danielle Geirnaert has given an appropriate and meaningful interpretation of this motif (Geirnaert 1990). She has described how women of Laboya, in West Sumba, symbolically "glue" the two parts of a person's soul together while physically winding the cotton thread into a ball. She has also discussed spinning as "a strong metaphor for conception and new life" (1987:119).

The completed cloths, if ceremonially important, are often consciously linked with certain aspects of fertility. Among the Lamaholot of East Flores, Solor, and Lembata, the warp threads of certain textiles exchanged at marriage may not be cut, as they represent the continuous line of descent that is hoped to be initiated by the bride (Barnes 1989a:16–17). The same textile, in its patterns, may refer to a long line of descent, and hence by implication to continuing fertility. The most obvious image here is one showing ancestors linked by hands, feet, or a continuous spinal column, creating a picture that relates the present to the past. The cloth's iconography, therefore, relates to the past, the time of ancestors, while its structure, with the uncut warp, symbolizes the future.

Conclusions

We have seen so far that fertility can be related both to headhunting and to textiles. Is there also a link between the two? I would argue that the making of textiles, done exclusively by women, is comparable to the headhunting carried out by men. The missionary Howell noted in 1912, when writing about the Iban: "As students of Dayak life know well, the Sea-Dayak bachelor in order to win the affections of a maiden must needs get a head first; similarly the Sea-Dayak maiden to win the affection of a bachelor must needs to be accomplished in the arts of weaving and dyeing" (1912:63). No Iban woman was considered mature enough to marry and bear children until she had made a *pua*, a ceremonial cloth that was, among other ritual purposes, also the essential container for receiving a captured head. No man, on the other hand, could marry until he had participated in a successful headraid.

Howell also mentions that a certain part of yarn preparation, the laying out of the warp, is called "the warpath of the women" (1912:64). Both activities involve transition from one stage to another. The headhunter enters into danger outside his community to bring back something that will increase his own and the village's fertility, in the widest sense. The woman making a textile transforms an originally unstructured fiber into a cloth, often the prerequisite to certain ceremonial functions that are essential to the village's well-being. The most precious and sacred cloth is frequently red, for which the dye is not grown in the village or on cultivated fields, but has to be gathered in the forest. Its redness is considered to be dangerous to manipulate, as it is associated with blood, warfare, and headhunting. Among certain groups of the Lamaholot, only old women may make this type of cloth, as it would interfere with the fertility of a woman of childbearing age and endanger her mental stability (Barnes 1989b:54). The same restriction is given by J. P. Mills for the Ao Naga, with a similar explanation (Mills 1926:93). An age-related prohibition is also recorded for the Lhota Naga (Mills 1922:37).

To conclude, Plate 2.6 sums up better than any words what has been

Plate 2.6 Woman from Timor, eastern Indonesia, wearing the headdress and ornaments of a headhunter. (Koninklijk Instituut voor de Tropen, Amsterdam)

discussed here. The photograph shows a young woman from Timor who has just completed her period of seclusion after giving birth. To reintegrate her ceremonially into the community, she is dressed in the costume of the headhunter, here wearing a large man's cloth and the headdress and neck pendants of a successful headhunter. The "head" she has brought is, of course, the newborn child.

Notes

1. I began research on the Pitt Rivers Museum collection in 1986, after completing my doctoral dissertation (Barnes 1984; 1989a). My own field research was in eastern Indonesia on the island of Lembata, where I lived in Kédang from 1969 to 1971, and returned to the island in 1979 and 1982, for three and six months respectively. These shorter visits were spent in the village of Lamalera, where I focused on a study of *ikat* design and weaving.
2. Hutton later held the Chair of Anthropology at Cambridge University, and Mills became a Reader in Anthropology at London University.
3. By contrast, Christoph Fürer-Haimendorf, who carried out fieldwork for one year among the Konyak Naga (1936–1937), allows himself to be guided by his environment, and his account follows the year and its agricultural and ceremonial cycle as he experienced it (Fürer-Haimendorf 1939).
4. As the interpretation is based on the museum collection as it appears now, the present tense is used throughout the paper. I am aware that the material discussed is part of a historical past.
5. A woman's cloth from the Ao Naga, for example, is annotated with the following information: Chantongia Village; Skirt, black with thin red lines, of a woman of the *Chamirr* clan, whose father has *not* but whose grandfather and ancestors have done *mithan* sacrifices; Collected 20.1.1921.
6. Other village-wide ceremonies, especially involving dancing, may also require dressing up and ornamenting the body, but these occasions do not imply the same specifications for everyone.
7. Specialists may make wood carvings and brass ornaments.
8. Mills gives the following information for the Rengma: "In the case of most Naga tribes it is only by inference that we learn that the underlying idea of head-hunting is to increase the fertility of the killer's village by adding to its store soul-force obtained in this way from another village. The Rengma, on the other hand, says bluntly and openly that enemies' heads cause the crop to flourish and men and animals to increase" (Mills 1937:161). However, Mills's implication that a transference of soul-force

is referred to by the Rengma does not necessarily follow. For an analysis of various Southeast Asian ethnographic accounts of headhunting, and for the development of the "soul-force" concept, see Needham (1976).

9. See Pitt Rivers Museum 1923.85.294, an Ao cloth from Chantongia village collected by Hutton. The accession card reads: "Cloth worn by a man who like his father and grandfather has done the necessary ceremonies. Obtained from Takatoba who could not hope to qualify for wearing it as his father had."
10. Both Mills and Hutton emphasized that they believed Naga women to have high status, but they did not look at Naga life from the female perspective and they were not especially alert to the symbolic position of gender.
11. This interpretation refers to cultural areas where communal identity was (and often still is) primarily village-based, rather than to societies involved with the early historical state formations affected by Indian models, such as much of Java, Bali, and certain parts of Sumatra.
12. See the essays published in M. Gittinger, ed., as well as the article by Hoskins (Gittinger 1989; Hoskins 1989). Although both publications appeared after this paper was prepared, in general these detailed accounts support the interpretation offered here.

References

Barnes, R., *The Ikat Textiles of Lamalera, Lembata Within the Context of Eastern Indonesian Fabric Traditions*, D. Phil. diss., Oxford University, 1984.

———, *The Ikat Textiles of Lamalera: A Study of an Eastern Indonesian Weaving Tradition*, Leiden: E.J. Brill, 1989a.

———, "The Bridewealth Cloth of Lamalera, Lembata," in M. Gittinger (ed.), *To Speak With Cloth: Studies in Indonesian Textiles*, Los Angeles: University of California Museum of Cultural History, 1989b.

Fürer-Haimendorf, C., *The Naked Naga*, London: Methuen, 1939.

Geirnaert, D., "Hunt Wild Pig and Grow Rice," in R. de Ridder and J.A.J. Karremans (eds.), *The Leiden Tradition in Structural Anthropology. Essays in Honour of P.E. de Josselin de Jong*, Leiden: E.J. Brill, 1987.

———, "Kijora: A Thing for Lost Souls," in Pieter ter Keurs and Dirk Smidt (eds.), *The Language of Things: Studies in Ethnocommunication*, Leiden: E.J. Brill, 1990.

Gittinger, M., *Splendid Symbols. Textiles and Tradition in Indonesia*, Washington, D.C.: The Textile Museum, 1979.

———, (ed.), *To Speak With Cloth: Studies in Indonesian Textiles*, Los Angeles: University of California Museum of Cultural History, 1989.

Hoskins, J., "Why Do Ladies Sing the Blues? Indigo Dyeing, Cloth Production, and Gender Symbolism in Kodi," in A. Weiner and J. Schneider (eds.), *Cloth and Human Experience*, Washington, D.C.: Smithsonian Press, 1989.

Howell, W., "The Sea-Dayak Method of Making and Dyeing Thread From Their Home Grown Cotton," *Sarawak Museum Journal*, Vol. 1, No. 2, 1912, pp. 61–64.

Hutton, J.H., *The Angami Nagas*, London: Macmillan, 1921a.

———, *The Sema Nagas*, London: Macmillan, 1921b.

———, "The Significance of Head-Hunting in Assam," *JRAI*, Vol. 58, 1928, pp. 399–408.

———, "The Mixed Culture of the Naga Tribes," *JRAI*, Vol. 95, 1965, pp. 16–43.

Mills, J.P., *The Lhota Nagas*, London: Macmillan, 1922.

———, *The Ao Nagas*, London: Macmillan, 1926.

———, *The Rengma Nagas*, London: Macmillan, 1937.

Needham, R., "Skulls and Causality," *Man*, Vol. 11, No. 1, 1976, pp. 71–88.

3

Cut and Sewn

The Textiles of Social Organization in Thailand

H. Leedom Lefferts, Jr.

The Buddha organized and established his religion as a Middle Way between the extreme asceticism of early Hinduism and the life of relative ease of the layperson. This Middle Way evolved from the Buddha's own experiences in attaining enlightenment, which revealed that neither total deprivation nor unthinking self-absorption would lead a seeker to an understanding of the causes of suffering. This paper discusses textile composition and focuses on the *uncut* or *cut-and-stitched* composition of clothing to describe and illuminate the nature of different kinds of beings – laypeople and monks – in the cosmological system of Thai Theravada Buddhism. The importance of the decision to make cloth either unstitched or cut-and-stitched stems from the cultural environment in which the Buddha developed his theories. The requirements of the Middle Way observed by the Buddha for establishing the dress of those who followed him are necessary in understanding the meanings implicit in their dress of patched-together cloth.

The cosmological system of Theravada Buddhism, the variant of Buddhism practiced by many of the peoples of Sri Lanka and mainland Southeast Asia, posits an ascending series of thirty-one realms organized into three worlds (Reynolds and Reynolds 1982:16). The eleven realms of the lowest world, the *kamabhumi,* translated as "the world of desire," are comprised of hells, ghosts, animals, humans, and six different kinds of angels. The middle world, the *rupabhumi*, "the world with only a remnant of material qualities" (literally, "the world of form"), is made up of the lower sixteen levels of *jhanic* attainment. The third and highest world, the *arupabhumi*, "the world without material qualities," or "formlessness," is comprised of the highest four levels of *jhanic* attainment, including Nibbana. While people live in the world of desire, it may be posited that some humans and monks are moving toward participation in higher realms, the worlds of form and formlessness. This paper considers how the dress of the beings in question relates to their positions in this cosmological scheme.[1]

However, these textiles are ambiguous. The dress of laypeople and monks does not communicate such a clear separation as has been suggested in past formulations. This paper asserts that these newly discovered ambiguities lead to productive readings. The ambiguities themselves may highlight significant facets of the relationships among genders, persons, and beings in Thai society. An analysis of these relationships will contribute to the literature that demonstrates the importance of dress as a fundamental symbolic category in establishing, as well as reflecting, gender. In addition, this paper will show that, at least for Thai Theravada Buddhist culture, the unstitched or cut-and-stitched nature of dress may symbolize the status of the wearer in the Buddhist cosmological system and therefore may communicate the amount of power and merit accorded that person.

The Textiles of Early Buddhism

As a result of the discovery of the Middle Way, the followers or adepts of the Buddhist philosophy – both monks and novices – did not adopt the scanty garments or the ashes worn by many Hindu ascetics. When going to receive alms in a village, the Buddha prescribed that "a Bhikkhu should put on his waistcloth so as to cover himself all round from above the navel to below the knees, tie his belt round his waist, fold his upper robes and put them on, fasten the block [a belt] on, wash [his hands], take his alms-bowl, and then slowly and carefully proceed to the village. He is to go amidst the houses properly clad, with [his limbs] under control, with downcast eye, with [his robes] not tucked up, not laughing, or speaking loudly, not swaying his body or his arms about, not with his arms akimbo, or his robe pulled over his head, and without walking on his heels" (Rhys Davids and Oldenberg 1965–1969, *Kullavagga VIII,* 4:3). (All citations from the *Kullavagga* and the *Mahavagga* are taken from the 1965–1969 translation, and correspond to chapters and verses, unless a specific page number is given.) At the same time, however, the Buddha prescribed that the dress of the adepts should signify their separation from the world. In traditional Hinduism, clothing consisted of unstitched lengths of cloth: a shawl and lower body cloth for men, and a single garment for women.[2] To solve the problem of separating adepts from society while ensuring that these adepts respected the conventions of their benefactors and did not offend them by unseemly behavior or dress, the Buddha prescribed an important solution: the garments of adepts should be of rags sewn into the proper size and shape, or, alternatively, whole cloth was to be cut and then resewn into a garment. That the clothes were of rags or cut cloth would symbolize the nature of the adepts' separation from the allegiances of this world. That they were then sewn into prescribed shapes for robes would signify that the adepts were still part of this world and recognized the conventions of this world.

This dress and its derivation are explained in the *Vinaya*, the major work that gives the Buddha's solutions to various problems. The issue of robes seems not to have arisen until the organization of adepts, the Sangha, was sufficiently large to attract many laypeople who wished to gain merit by giving substantial gifts. Initially, the robes of the Buddha and the Sangha were called *pamsukula* robes and were "made of rags taken from a dust heap or a cemetery" (Rhys Davids and Oldenberg 1965–1969, *Mahavagga VIII*, 1:34). Picking rags and sewing them together appears to have been one of the duties of the adepts.

This situation existed for twenty years after the Buddha's enlightenment, according to a commentary by Buddhaghosa about the first presentation of robes to the Buddha by laypeople (See Rhys Davids and Oldenberg 1965–1969, *Mahavagga VIII*, p. 193, footnote 1).[3] At that time, King Paggota sent a "suit of *Siveyakka* cloth" to be presented to the Buddha. It is described as "the best, and the most excellent, and the first, and the most precious, and the noblest of many cloths and of many suits of cloth, and of many hundred suits of cloth, and of many thousand suits of cloth, and of many hundred thousand suits of cloth" (Rhys Davids and Oldenberg 1965–1969, *Mahavagga VIII*, 1:34–35). It was presented by the Royal Doctor to the Buddha. This was the first lay cloth accepted by the Buddha; from that time he permitted members of the Sangha to wear robes presented by laypeople, and robe-giving became a significant aspect of making merit. The text continues with the Buddha's acceptance of a woolen garment from Benares (Rhys Davids and Oldenberg 1965–1969, *Mahavagga VIII*, 2) and then of robes made of many different materials, such as linen, cotton, silk, wool, coarse cloth, and hemp, and robes made of a mixture of these (Rhys Davids and Oldenberg 1965–1969, *Mahavagga VIII*, 3).[4]

Accepting robes made from certain types of newly processed yarn did not prevent members of the Sangha from receiving *pamsukula* robes. Members of the Sangha could receive both robes made of whole cloth and robes of rags picked from cemeteries. However, it is certain that the newly made robes evidenced a tension between the Bhikkhu's motivation toward asceticism and the layperson's wish to make as much merit as possible.

The ongoing issue of robes was used by the Buddha to illustrate the nature of the society he was establishing among members of the Sangha. He prescribed that Bhikkhus should share with one another both the robes they gathered themselves and those they received from donors. He also stated that one Bhikkhu in each group should be selected to receive, store, and distribute robes.

The nature of the robes was also of concern. First, we have already seen that prescriptions governed the kinds of yarn from which a robe could be made. Second, the Buddha also prescribed the proper method for dyeing cloth received by the Sangha, stating that it should be of a uniform "yellowish colour like ivory" (Rhys Davids and Oldenberg 1965–1969, *Mahavagga VIII,* 11:1).[5]

Third, and most important for this discussion, the Buddha responded to complaints from laypeople that some robes were *akkhinnaka*, that is, made of untorn or uncut cloth. The Buddha said, "You ought not, O Bhikkhus, to possess akkhinnaka robes. He who does, commits a dukkata offence" (Rhys Davids and Oldenberg 1965–1969, *Mahavagga VIII,* 11:1).

The Buddha then specified a uniform design of cut-and-sewn pieces for the robes to be accepted and worn by members of the Sangha. To accomplish this, he took as his reference the humanly manufactured world around him. "[As] he set forth on his journey towards Dakkhinagiri, [he] beheld how the Magadha rice fields were divided into short pieces, and in rows, and by outside boundaries [or ridges], and by cross boundaries." He asked his prime disciple and brother, "'Could you, Ananda, provide robes of a like kind for the Bhikkhus?'" Ananda replied affirmatively and "provided robes of a like kind for many Bhikkhus." The Buddha, on seeing the construction of the robes, said, "'I enjoin upon you, O Bhikkhus, the use of an under robe of torn pieces, and of an upper robe of torn pieces, and of a waist cloth of torn pieces'" (Rhys Davids and Oldenberg 1965–1969, *Mahavagga VIII,* 12:1–2).

Traditional Thai Textiles

Today the robes of Theravada Buddhist monks in Sri Lanka and Southeast Asia maintain the pattern enjoined by the Buddha. Few, if any, robes are constructed of rags. Most that I have seen in Thailand and

Burma are available for purchase ready-made in markets, where they are bought by the laity and presented to the monks. Nonetheless, all of them are cut and sewn using a specified, standardized design – the staggered patchwork motif of rice fields with bunds.[6]

This paper proposes that understanding that monks' robes have a referent in the material world complicates what has otherwise been seen as an smooth upward progression in the production of textiles and the maintenance of social organization, from women through men to monks. It is still possible to interpret Thai Theravada Buddhist cosmological theory and social organization using traditional Thai textiles, but the "text" has now become more complicated, and links have appeared that were not evident before. Most of these connections result from the evidence presented in this paper that monks' robes have a referent in the material world.

This new reading stems from an earlier paper (Lefferts 1983) in which I divided the garments of women, men, and monks into three discrete categories. In that paper I disregarded what now appears essential – the difference between the whole-cloth skirts of laypeople and the cut-and-stitched dress of members of the Sangha. The importance of the uncut length of cloth is especially true for men's skirts, which are made of one piece. Women's skirts may have up to three pieces.[7] In order to understand this new conceptualization, I include a brief recapitulation of my earlier conclusions.

In my previous paper I depicted women's skirts (*phaa sin*) as evidencing the close association of women with the world of desire. This association could be fully derived not only from the designs in women's skirts, but also from the extraordinary amount of time women spend in the production of this textile. If a great amount of time is spent producing something of this world, it seems likely that there exists a strong attachment between the producer and the thing and this world. Reinforcing this notion are the designs on *phaa sin* – which have referents in the natural world or the constructed world of myth – such as pythons, watermelons, rice grains, chickens, casuarina trees, and mythical *naak* (in Sanskrit, *naga* means "serpents").

These *laay* (the Thai word for "designs") appear only on women's skirts and other textiles associated with women, such as pillow covers, flags, and blankets. For the body of the *phaa sin*, the designs are applied to the textile using the complicated resist-weft dye process known in Indonesia as *ikat* and in Thailand as *mat mii*. The separately produced upper and lower borders (subsequently stitched to the main textile) may be elaborated using supplementary weft techniques, which also require an extraordinary amount of labor. For pillow covers, flags, and blankets, supplementary weft techniques produce the design. Most of these supplementary weft textiles are items of exchange between the women who made them and the families of their husbands or the Sangha (Gittinger, personal communication, 1989). Note that the two major textiles associated with women, *phaa sin* and pillow covers, are sewn from more than one textile piece. The significance of this will be discussed later.

The motif of the *phaa sarong*, the men's skirt made of a single piece of cloth, is strikingly different from that of the *phaa sin*. It consists of a geometric grid of large rectangles separated by one or more white lines.[8] While the sarong may be made of the finest silk, especially since it is usually woven by a woman to be presented to an important man in her life, such as her husband, father, brother, or son, the pattern of the plain-weave cloth (as it is created solely through choice of warp and weft thread colors) requires no complicated dyeing or weaving. Thus, this garment takes less time to prepare than a woman's *sin*.

Two other textiles may be grouped provisionally with the sarong. The *phaa chongkraben*, a piece of unseamed whole cloth at least three meters in length worn as a skirt by men, has no motif, although it does have white bands near each of its weft ends. The *phaa ko maa*, a checked cloth, also unseamed and usually used as a shawl, may be pressed into service in a number of utilitarian ways. Because of the lack of a pattern (*laay*), a close association of men's textiles with the world of form, rather than the world of desire, may be posited. However, the colors of these textiles readily distinguish them from the "yellowish ivory color" of a Buddhist monk's robes.

Finally, under the previous formulation, monks' robes were seen as symbolic of their wearers' renunciation of this world. Both the uniform color and the lack of apparent (and stated) design (*laay*) of the robes established monks as different from laypeople. Information I have obtained about production of monks' robes prior to the machine production of textiles and modern marketing indicates that women wove these robes in one twenty-four hour period immediately prior to their donation as gifts to monks.[9] This ritual occasion accentuated the limits of time and involvement people were supposed to spend on something for a being who had renounced this world.

Thai Village Society

The above formulation of three distinct categories of textiles – the *phaa sin* with design, the *phaa sarong* with modulated colors, and the monks' robes removed from the others by apparent lack of design and color – articulates with other facets of Thai rural culture: social organization, the organization of space in Thai communities, and the linguistic categories of laity and monks. Of special importance are social organization and language.

In rural Thai society the inheritance of rice land as well as houses and house land occurs preferentially through the female line, from mother to daughter. Moreover, the initial residence pattern for a couple after marriage is matrilocal. Putting these two preferences together, we can see that most rural households form, over time, a continuity of women (Lefferts 1974).

In an interesting expansion of Lévi-Straussian exchange theory, men are exchanged between these households of women. Simply put, upon marriage men move from the houses of the mothers who bore and raised them to the houses of the daughters of other mothers.

However, the exchange of men is more complicated (Lefferts 1977). Ideally men become monks at some time in their lives, although most remain monks for just one "Rains Retreat," from July through October. These men often say that they enter the Sangha in order to increase the merit of their parents, especially that of their mothers (Tambiah 1970). Regardless of whether one becomes a monk for only a short period or for life,[10] monks are set apart in *wat* (monasteries), which remain integral to villages and are supported by villagers. Monks are treated with respect and speak and are spoken to in words reserved for elders or for their own category. They sit at levels higher than the laity, eat before laity, and are prohibited by injunctions set by the Buddha from touching or being touched by a woman.

One of the most obvious characteristics of monks – in addition to the dress, the shaved head and eyebrows, and the modest demeanor – is the linguistic category into which they are placed. Along with amulets, images of the Buddha, other sacred objects, and the Royal Family,[11] monks are classified as *ong*. This distinguishes them from laity (other than royalty), who are classified as *khon*. This distinction between *ong* and *khon,* with the other attributes given above, led me to think that monks are perceived as different kinds of *beings* from laity. Moreover, this trichotomy between women, men, and monks that was, in turn, built into a dichotomy between laity and the Sangha, provided an easily understood paradigm to distinguish among the textiles that I had analyzed and attempted to categorize.

Reconsiderations

Adding the circumstance of uncut or cut-and-stitched cloth to the other parameters contained in the textiles of Thai village society makes the meaning of all of them, and of the people who wear them, more complicated. Comprehending the totality of the attributes of women's skirts and of monks' robes makes their opposition more apparent than real.

Rather than a linear continuum moving from one extreme to the other – from women's clothing to monks' robes, with men's sarong somewhere in between – traditional Thai textiles may form a circle. Both women's skirts and monks' robes bear motifs representing important aspects of the world as either humanly or mythically constructed. Women's *sin* designs are often grouped into horizontal or vertical bands, with intervening stripes that impose a rigidity on the layout. Moreover, the design is woven in a geometric pattern, which is not absolutely necessary given the technology of *mat mii/ikat* resist-weft tie-dyeing (Gittinger, personal communication, 1988). *Mat mii* as conventionally produced tends to produce blocky figures with stepped, rather than smooth, diagonal lines. This is definitely a break from truly representational figures. Finally, a woman's skirt can be constructed of pieces, a main section and top and bottom borders, all with designs (*laay*). Even if the skirt is not made of three separate pieces, it is divided into those areas in terms of structure. Thus all women's skirts have a three part configuration. All of these attributes of *phaa sin* are in addition to the designs themselves, addressed earlier.

Grouped elsewhere on the perimeter of the circle, beyond the dress of men but leading back toward that of women, is that of monks. Monks wear an abstract motif stated by its creator to represent rice fields. Rice fields are one of the most important aspects of a tropical South Asian or Southeast Asian culture. In many of the languages of these regions, the word for "rice" acts as a gloss for "food." The division of land into sweeping vistas of rice paddies separated by bunds represents significant and continuing labor on the part of the people of these cultures.

In the Thai context, rice production is associated with women; it is through women that the family ownership of land continues over the generations. Women are preferentially responsible for processing rice and the foods that accompany rice.

Thus, while the motif of cut-and-sewn rectangles seen in monks' robes might be considered simple geometry in one context, another understanding is presented by considering these robes in their religious context. Moreover, the Buddha, when designing monks' robes, specifically used the reference of rice fields to make clear how robes of members of the Sangha should be constructed. Through the pattern of the robes, the Buddha clearly associated monks with the things of this world.

Finally, men's garments fit into this circular configuration as an intermediary. Like women's clothes, their clothes have color; the color darkens with the wearer's age, symbolizing men's decreasing attachment to this world. However, their textiles are without "design," with simply a pattern of colored checks or with stripes at the ends of an otherwise plain but finely woven textile. No relationship between the rectangular rice field motif of monks' robes and the squares and checks of men's clothing is reported by Thai village informants. These laymen inhabit an organizational space different from women, yet also of them. The dress of men clearly connotes their "shuttle cock" role between household, village, and *wat*.

Conclusions

This paper has expanded on several different themes. Its purpose was to use the continuing analysis of an aspect of material culture – dress – to understand a people's social organization. This continuing inquiry into material culture has revealed more ambiguity than clear-cut distinctions; material culture can express several different and even contradictory ideas.

In this formulation, Thai textiles express a much closer relationship between women, men, and monks than had heretofore been proposed. While monks renounce the things of this world, those things themselves subtly but overtly announce their presence in a monk's daily life. The robes of a monk recognize that which provides him with a life.

Without stretching the image too far, the rice field motif on monks' robes might be interpreted as evidence of the matrilateral emphasis in Thai culture. Rice fields represent one aspect of the women's contribution to the continuing existence of the individual monk and the Sangha, as evidenced by the maintenance of the village *wat* by the wealth of women's rice fields. Without women's consent in providing sustenance (rice), textiles, and sons, the religious system would die.

The existence of the rice field motif as a meaningful pattern also sheds light on the roles of Buddhist monks in Thai village life. Members of the Thai Sangha are not total renunciates removed from ordinary life. Through their expected behavior they participate in daily lay life. Their peregrinations around the community to receive alms, their roles as counselors and as storehouses of information, their usefulness as foci of a community, their daily intake – no matter how modest – of food supplied by women, and their dress temper a picture we might have of total renunciates.[12] Theravada Buddhist monks wear a modest uniform. They show through their appearance as representatives of the

Middle Way that the prevailing faith is neither flamboyant nor shocking. Through their robes they constantly reaffirm their relationship to the rice fields, one of the most basic artifacts of their world. Monks are involved in, and dependent on, the things, ways, and production of this world. A rice field motif for their robes, no matter how understated, signifies this.

In short, the dress of all persons in Thai village social organization indicates that they inhabit the world of desire. While dress may give hints of movement toward, and participation in, other worlds, women, men, and monks are beings of this world.

From this increased understanding of the place of monks' robes in the array of Thai village textiles, we also gain an increased understanding of that culture's conceptions of the world. In Thai culture, even those beings who are most removed from the things of this world carry the impress of that humanly constructed world. Women, on the other hand, represent not a simple consociation with nature, but nature controlled and modified by humans. For Thai, the natural world unmodified and therefore unusable by humans is uninteresting. Nature made usable by humans, however, is worth considering and appreciating. Traditional Thai textiles communicate this complex understanding graphically and clearly.

Notes

* This paper was first written while the author was teaching at Drew University, Madison, New Jersey, USA. Thanks are due to the Drew University Faculty Travel and Faculty Research Funds for supporting the travel to the workshop where this paper was presented. The paper was extensively rewritten, following the comments of the editors and other individuals, while the author was Research Associate at the Research Institute for Northeastern Art and Culture, Srinakharinwirot University, Mahasarakham, Thailand. Thanks are due to the Institute's Director, Ajan Akom Vorajinda, and the Vice President of the University, Dr. Veera Boonyakanchana, for their support during my research of Thai textiles.

1. I am indebted to Dr. David Szanton for initially pointing out this possible configuration to me after my first presentation on Northeast Thai textiles in 1978. He was particularly struck by the correlation of these textiles and traditional interpretations of Borobudur, the Mahayana Buddhist monument in Java.

2. Even after stitched clothing became common for everyday wear, first as a result of Muslim contacts and more recently as a result of European tailored garments, unstitched clothing (preferably of silk) was required for ritual activities.
3. The *Pali-Burmese Dictionary* published by the Buddha Sassana Organization (1970, Vol. 7:482–85) notes that an alternative tradition exists, in which it is said that the Buddha's stepmother, as a way to make merit, donated robes to the Blessed One within a year after his Enlightenment. Recognition of this alternative story, however, does not appear to change the basic point made in this paper.
4. According to the *Pali-Burmese Dictionary* (1970, Vol. 7:482–85) the kinds of yarn from which a robe could be manufactured are limited to those noted. Particularly prohibited are robes made from jute, human hair, animal hair (other than wool), leather, wood, the bark of trees, vines, banana plant fiber, and bamboo.
5. It is interesting to note that Thai describe the color of monk's robes as *sii luang*, meaning royal color. This has implications for the later discussion of the ambiguity inherent in these textiles.
6. Information about the background and composition of robes worn by members of the Thai Sangha is contained in a *Vinaya* commentary, Vol. 2, available for 15 baht ($1 US = 25 baht), that monks are urged to read. This includes the history of the derivation as recounted above (pp. 15–16), an illustration of the structure of a robe, giving the names of its various sections (pp. 17–18), and a series of photographs showing the proper ways to wear the robes (pp. 22–23) (Kromphrayawachirayanwaroorot 2459).
7. In cases of both *phaa sin*, women's skirts, and *phaa sarong*, men's skirts, the Thai refer to a length of cloth as a *phun*. Each *phun* is standardized at two *lah*, or 180 centimeters. This length is made into a cylinder for wearing by sewing the two ends together, but this simple seaming is not the stitching together of patches that form the body of the monk's robe. One kind of cloth, the man's *phaa chongkraben*, is much longer and is not sewn.
8. The sarong resembles a "Scotch plaid" skirt, something one would expect to see in the United Kingdom. However, this pattern occurs with great frequency not only in Thailand, but also in Malaysia and Indonesia. It appears to have been imported from India (Barnes, personal communication, 1989). This motif is not classified as *laay* by Thai. Whether these large plaids in some way replicate the cut-and-sewn characteristic of monks' robes remains to be investigated.
9. As of 1989, this ceremony still continues in certain parts of northeast Thailand and Laos.
10. Becoming a monk for a period of time less than one's lifetime is the norm for those Thai men who do become monks. However, it is also an accepted practice for a man to become a monk more than once, perhaps first when he passes the age at which ordination is possible (twenty), again when his

mother dies, and finally late in life if his wife has died and his children are on their own. This periodic involvement in the Sangha does not mean the man is any less Buddhist than a lifelong monk; one lives as one is able according to one's karma (Keyes and Daniel 1983).

11. See Lefferts 1989 for an interpretation of royal textiles and the roles they play in Thai social organization.
12. It has been suggested that it would be better to call Japanese Buddhist renunciates, who often act as foci of community life, "priests" rather than "monks." This might be especially appropriate considering that several Japanese Buddhist sects permit the marriage of their adepts. No one has yet suggested such a renaming for Thai members of the Sangha but, given their roles in village life, it would not be inappropriate.

References

Buddha Sassana Organization, *Pali-Burmese Dictionary*, Vol. 7, Rangoon: Buddha Sassana Organization, 1970.

Keyes, C.F., and E.V. Daniel, eds., *Karma: An Anthropological Inquiry*, Berkeley: University of California Press, 1983.

Kromphrayawachirayanwaroorot, S., *Vinaymuk, lem* 2 (Vinaya, Vol. 2), Bangkok: Mahamakhutratchawithayalay, 2459 (1916).

Lefferts, H.L., Jr., "The Kings as Gods: Textiles in the Thai State," *Textiles as Primary Sources*, Proceedings of the First Symposium of the Textile Society of America, Minneapolis, 1989, pp. 78–85.

———, "Textiles, Buddhism, and Society in Northeastern Thailand," presented at *Textiles and the Organization of Human Experience*, Wenner-Gren Symposium, 1983.

———, "Social Foundations of Rural Thai Buddhism," seminar paper, University of Chicago, 1977.

———, *Baan Dong Phong: Land Tenure and Social Organization in a Northeastern Thai Village*, Ph.D. diss., University of Colorado, 1974.

Reynolds, F.E. and M.B., trans., *Three Worlds According to King Ruang: A Thai Buddhist Cosmology*, Berkeley Buddhist Studies Series No. 4, Berkeley: University of California Center for South and Southeast Asian Studies, 1982.

Rhys Davids, T.W., and H. Oldenberg trans., *Vinayapitaka*: *Mahavagga I–IV (Part I)*; *Mahavagga V–X and Kullavagga I–III (Part II)*; *Kullavagga IV–XII (Part III)*, Delhi: Motilal Banarsidass, 1965–1969.

Tambiah, S.J., *Buddhism and the Spirit Cults of Northeast Thailand*, New York: Cambridge University Press, 1970.

4

Purse-Proud

Of Betel and Areca Nut Bags in Laboya (West Sumba, Eastern Indonesia)

Danielle C. Geirnaert

The Laboya are farmers who live on the south coast of West Sumba in eastern Indonesia. They cultivate mostly rice, maize, cassava, and coconut. They grow vegetables and peppers on a smaller scale. These crops provide their staple diet. Meat is consumed on ceremonial occasions only. Although perhaps less important from a western nutritional point of view, the Laboya consider two other plants to be essential for their physical and spiritual well-being, namely, betel (*kuta*) and areca nut (*katiba*). Betel and areca nut are mixed together with lime (*kapu*) and sometimes with tobacco (*baku*) as well. The sharing of a betel quid (*mama*) accompanies all social relationships. This activity entails a degree of trust and intimacy between participants. Men and women like to chew this mixture that dyes their teeth black in the long run. Formerly, white teeth were considered to be a characteristic of children, of foreigners and of animals only. Like dark hair, glistening black teeth enhance the beauty of a woman. Teeth stained by the betel quid are aesthetically pleasing and a sign of successful socialization.

It is highly improper for an adult to leave home without his or her purse containing all the necessary ingredients for a betel chew: betel fruit, areca nut, and the bamboo container (*wo*) for lime. This bag, called *kaleku mama* (bag for the betel chew) or more briefly, just *kaleku*, is plaited from pandanus (*pada*) leaves. The ornamentation on a *kaleku*, a major item of Laboya dress, expresses the wealth and the social prestige of the owner. Even when it is stowed away at home, a *kaleku* should never be left empty, a sign of utmost poverty and an ill omen for its owner. The purse must always contain at least some areca nut. Also, a betel and areca nut bag that is old and torn must be replaced by a new one. It is believed that wearing a tattered *kaleku* may lead to illness.

Every grown man and woman owns a *kaleku* befitting his or her gender and social status. When meeting someone, one must hand over his or her *kaleku* with a slow, formal motion of the arm to that person, who is expected to respond in the same manner. After having taken some betel and some areca nut from one another's bag, lime containers are exchanged in the same way as the *kaleku*. Age and status may determine who presents his or her *kaleku* first. But if the social difference is not too big, good manners require that both partners hand over their *kaleku* simultaneously. No conversation can start without this ceremonial greeting. The exchange of *kaleku* is nonverbal, yet is somewhat comparable to the exchange of compliments in Western society. It marks the beginning of a social relationship.

It is almost certainly no accident that in his book on Sumba, Onvlee devotes his second chapter to the habit of chewing betel and areca in several parts of the island (1973:27–45), just after having discussed cattle, the other major concern of the Sumbanese, in the first one. Although he does not always consistently specify the region he is writing about, nor when he worked in the different parts of Sumba (mostly before the war), many of his detailed comments illustrate the Laboya's attitudes toward betel chewing. Throughout Sumba, betel and areca nut are the most common food offerings to ancestors. A deceased person should be buried with his or her *kaleku*, for when the dead meet their ancestors, both parties exchange betel and areca nut.

In the region of Wejewa in West Sumba, Onvlee (1973:30–31) reported in the 1930s that uncircumcised boys and young people whose teeth were not yet filed were forbidden to enjoy a betel quid. To do so would have been an insult or *sobo* (in Wejewa, this word also means "prepuce"). If a boy persisted in this habit before he was circumcised, his wound would become infected after the operation. Onvlee also writes that after the filing of their teeth, boys and girls were encouraged to chew much betel and areca nut to prevent the swelling up of the gums. In Laboya, people record that before World War II, uncircumcised boys and untattooed girls followed the same taboos. Today this rule still applies to uncircumcised boys. Although teeth-filing and tattooing are no longer practiced, youngsters refrain from chewing betel until they reach puberty. Sharing a betel quid is reserved for adults only.

At large scale social gatherings, called *pesta* or "feasts" by the Indonesian speaking Sumbanese[1] (Geirnaert 1987), the first gift that guests receive on their arrival at their hosts' house is a portion of betel and areca nut. These ingredients, presented in a small basket, are slid into the visitor's *kaleku* that he or she holds open for this purpose. This welcome gift serves a practical purpose as well, for it helps the host to count the number of people who have actually responded to his invitations. The right amount of plates of rice and meat can then be prepared accordingly.[2]

All families must have an extra supply of areca nuts at least, ready for unexpected visitors. In Laboya, I was told that a woman's inability to offer areca nut to a guest brings shame upon her husband and all members of the family who live in their house. Having no *katiba* to offer is a sign that they belong to the poorest members of the society. Such an omission demonstrates that a man has either no garden to grow areca palm, implying that he is a descendant of slaves, or that he is unable to borrow from others because his social relationships are minimal. This last feature characterizes people of low status as well, who are too poor to entertain an important network of gift exchanges during feasting.

"Chewing until one's mouth is red/Eating until one's belly is full" is a Laboya phrase that expresses the wish for prosperity (Onvlee 1973:27, my translation). In modern times, the expression "he requires some betel and areca nut" is a metaphor for asking for money. When planning a night session during which ancestral spirits will be addressed, it is usual to offer them some betel, areca nut, and a few coins as well.

It is often said that one must not eat from the *kaleku* of an unknown person for fear that his or her ingredients might be poisoned, or worse, stolen. In this last case, the punishment for theft, to be hit by a thunderbolt, would fall upon the thief as well as his companion. On the other hand, to offer one's *kaleku* is a sign that one has no feeling of animosity toward others. For instance, the exchange of betel and areca nut marks all occasions on which a settlement between rival parties has been reached. It is also the conventional manner to open relationships with strangers, as the following example shows.

Laboya has but one main road for motorized transport. Riding a horse and walking remain the most important means of transportation. A network of trails covers the hilly land. Leaving their village early in the morning, men and women follow these narrow paths to go to their fields. Late in the afternoon, they take the same route to go back home. Walking in single file, people often meet farmers coming from the opposite direction. Verbal greeting is not a traditional Laboya custom. Both parties usually pass one another in total silence. However, with recent social changes, it may happen that a man or a woman decides to have a chat with a stranger, resulting in a temporary bottleneck along the trail as *kaleku* are exchanged.

Onvlee remarks that the purpose of the gift of betel and of areca nut is to honor someone. Also, he records that of the presents given in someone's honor, the Sumbanese say "it [betel and areca nut] is our soul" – *ndewandanja*, probably in Wejewa language (Onvlee 1973:35). Other authors have hinted that there is a relationship between goods such as betel and areca nut as well as their container, and the concept of "soul."

In the literature, information about the social role of the betel and areca bag is scarce. Yet a recent study on the significance of the betel quid in Indonesia pays some attention to the role of containers as an indication "of the social position of the owner" (Jordaan and Niehof 1988:172). The article notes that in Eastern Sumba, "a person's betel container is described as a *sign of the soul*" [my emphasis] (Jordan and Niehof 1988:172, quoting Forth 1981:74). The authors also mention Onvlee stating that "to leave behind one's betel container, machete, or cloth is to lose *part of one's personal vitality* [my emphasis]" (Jordan and Niehof 1988:172, quoting Onvlee 1973:11). Forth (1981:74) records that "in East Sumba, the betel container is brought to the grave of the deceased each day of the period of mourning, and if the dead person belonged to the nobility it is kept in the clan's ancestral house thereafter." In autumn 1982, I witnessed some of the preparations preceding the funerals of the Raja of Pau, and other members of his family in Rindi, East Sumba. A few of the sacred betel and areca nut bags of the Raja's wife-givers needed repair. Although usually not in view, they were taken out of the ancestral house's attic and I was allowed to take photographs of these beautifully beaded East Sumbanese bags. Most of these beads were formerly imported from Holland where they are known as *Amsterdamse kralen* (Amsterdam beads). In Sumba, people say that they come "from the ancestors." In Rindi, only noblewomen were allowed to work on the betel and areca nut bags that were to accompany the dead in their graves. Because of their aesthetic qualities, East Sumbanese betel and areca bags are the most well known in museum collections.

In contrast, West Sumbanese bags, including the Laboya type, are far less visually spectacular. But the analysis of the way they are made and of their ritual role may provide an explanation for the fact that they are "a sign of the soul" and that they represent "part of one's personal vitality," at least in Laboya. By its intricacy and its colors, the patterns of a Laboya *kaleku* tell the approximate age and the status of its owner. At one glance, the *kaleku* reveals the social position of one's interlocutor. I propose to explain the relationship of this visual information to the concept of "soul" in Laboya.

The *Kaleku Mama*: The Bag That Holds the Spiritual and Physical Components of Man

Kaleku means "bag" or "pouch." Other types of bags exist, such as the *kaleku baku,* "tobacco pouch," which is much smaller than the *kaleku mama.* The word *kaleku* without any other specification also refers to the crop of a cock or hen. One man explained to me that the *kaleku*, like the crop of a bird, cannot be separated from its owner without lethal consequences, just as no adult may leave home without his or her betel and areca nut bag. The loss of a *kaleku* endangers the life of its owner. If a person happens to forget his or her *kaleku* at someone's home, he or she will try to recover the bag as soon as possible. In some cases, a divination rite may have to be held during which the ancestors will be asked for help to discover the whereabouts of the bag. Once recovered, a pig must be sacrificed to the *marapu* (the spirits of the ancestors) to thank them for their help. The reason for such concern is that a *kaleku* contains some of its owner's *dewa* and *mawo,* the basic components of the human being.

Mawo can be translated as "the shadow" or "the breath" of a person; *dewa* as his or her "spirit." I have discussed *mawo* and *dewa* in other publications (Geirnaert 1987; 1989b; 1990). The body or *tau* is a recipient for *mawo* and *dewa.* At death, *mawo* and *dewa* follow separate paths. *Mawo* makes the body disintegrate and rot away. *Mawo* induces the process of decay; in many ways, *mawo* is putrefaction. The rotting fluids of all dead persons become clouds, and eventually rain. Clouds and rains are different aspects of *mawo;* they no longer belong to any individual in particular. They are the *mawo* of all deceased persons and belong to the society collectively. *Dewa*, in contrast, cannot rot. *Dewa* is closely related to the name of a person. After death, the *dewa* of the deceased is called back to live in the house of his or her descendants. *Dewa* is more connected to a specific lineage than *mawo.* The two concepts are crucial for discussing and understanding Laboya weaving and plaiting. Indeed, the Laboya say that "Moon," the half of the dual upper god called Wulla-Laddo (literally, Moon-Sun), is responsible for either spinning and weaving or plaiting human beings.

More precisely, while spinning, the action of the moon consists of joining together *mawo* and *dewa* in the body of the unborn. The role of the moon in relationship of *mawo* and *dewa* is more evident in textiles than in plaiting. Cotton, for example, is associated with breath, clouds, and hence with the *mawo* of the dead. When spinning, women, like the moon, collect *mawo* and join it to the *dewa* of their husband's house or lineage (*uma*) (Geirnaert 1990; 1990). Nonetheless, the *kaleku* brings specific additional information concerning the meaning of colors in plaited and in woven material. The *kaleku's* color scheme, its size, and its patterns indicate the stage of life of the bearer and his or her status. Some patterns are linked to the owner's gender.

The *kaleku mama* is conceived as a container for part of the *mawo* and the *dewa* of its owner. For instance, it is forbidden to turn one's *kaleku* upside down and shake it in order to clean it outside one's home, particularly in the fields. People say that they fear that part of their *mawo* might escape. If *mawo* is unable to find its way back, after a while *dewa* will leave as well, causing the death of the owner. However, one may clean one's *kaleku* at home, because the house is a protected area in contrast to the open fields (Geirnaert 1990).

Accidental death disturbs the normal transformations of *mawo* and *dewa* in the afterlife. In former days, the most dramatic form of violent death occurred during headhunting raids. In the case of sudden death, *mawo* in particular tends to disappear and disintegrate in the sky, under the heat of Sun, the other half of the deity Wulla-Laddo. To make the *mawo* return back to earth requires a special ritual, called *pogo nauta* (to cut the ladder), a major ceremony in former headhunting days (Geirnaert 1989b). During this ritual, the *mawo* of the deceased person, formerly often a victim of a headhunting raid, is asked to come down using the *nauta* or ladder, which is supposed to link the earth to the sky. After *mawo* has arrived, the *nauta* has to be destroyed to prevent *mawo* from escaping again. The *kaleku* of the deceased is one of the implements that is used to catch his or her *mawo*. Preferably, this *kaleku* must be the one he or she wore at the time of death. If that *kaleku* is not available, a new one will be made. The patterns on this new *kaleku* must correspond to the age and social status of the deceased at the time of his or her untimely death.

How to Read a Kaleku Mama

Let us now consider how a *kaleku* is made. The raw material is provided by pandanus (*pada*) leaves. Women usually cut them toward the end of March, when the rains are already diminishing. Although the association is less evident in the case of pandanus than for cotton, there is a belief that the leaves of the pandanus shrub are filled with as much *mawo* as possible at that time of the year.[3] The leaves are dried in the sun. Care is taken that they do not dry out too much; otherwise, they break easily when plaited. The dried leaves are then cut into strips and stored away. The thinner the thongs of pandanus, the finer the *kaleku* will be. Basically, plaiting (*mayana*) consists of intertwining the strips perpendicularly to one another. The beginning is crucial for obtaining a fine bag. The strips must be absolutely perpendicular to one another when one starts plaiting. If the strips are not absolutely perpendicular, the bag will be unaesthetically askew when finished. Inexperienced young women often make this mistake. The thinner the pandanus strips are, the more difficult it is to plait at right angles. The beginning stage of plaiting is comparable to that of weaving. The obligation is the same: to plait or weave as straight as possible. In the realm of textiles, this stage is sacred because it represents the weaving of a human being (Geirnaert 1990). Starting to weave askew is comparable to raising an abnormal child. Even if this association is not made explicitly in the case of plaiting a *kaleku*, the idea is latent. Only elderly, and preferably noble, women are thought to plait properly. It does indeed require much practice to plait a fine *kaleku*.

The finishing border, called *walita* (usually pronounced *wal'ta*) is just as important as the beginning. Technically, it must prevent the work from unravelling. Several patterns exist for plaiting the *wal'ta*. Once the *wal'ta* is finished, the bag may be embroidered. Men never plait, but they may embroider a finished bag. The *wal'ta* and the rest of the bag may or may not be decorated, depending on for whom the bag is meant. If it has been made for an elderly person, the *kaleku* must remain plain, without any decoration. The Laboya do not reckon age as we do. Their conception of age is a relative one. The elderly are people who have great-grandchildren. *Kaleku* for older people are larger than for younger men and women. Size is not dictated only by relative age of the owner; it also corresponds to a difference of gender. Men are entitled to larger *kaleku* than women. However, this rule applies more to the *kaleku* meant for married adults than for young unmarried people.

In contrast to the *kaleku* meant for the elderly, the bags for young people have to be embroidered with lavish patterns and they must be colorful (Plate 4.1). Embroidered *kaleku* are called *kaleku pahurata* (*kaleku* with drawings or decorations). Until the late 1950s, women used thread spun from locally grown cotton for their embroidery (*hubi*). Red, yellow, black, and sometimes dark blue threads were obtained by using natural dyes, the same ones used for textiles. *Curcuma domestica* provided yellow. Red was obtained from the bark of a tree called *yayu malli* (literally "red tree," perhaps brasilwood). A ferruginous mud preparation (*habbu*) dyed the thread black.

In Laboya, the dark blue color of indigo seems to have been little used for *kaleku,* in contrast to its prevalence in Kodi, the westernmost region of West Sumba. Visually, the contrast between *kaleku* from Laboya and those from Kodi is striking. Next to the East Sumbanese betel and areca bead bags, the Kodinese are the most common in museum collections. Whereas embroidered Laboya bags for young people are predominantly red, yellow, and black on a natural background, the designs on Kodinese bags are indigo blue only. The size of the Kodinese bag is also an indication of the wearer's relative age and status. However, in Kodi, only the very old have plain bags. Everybody else is entitled to wear embroidered bags. The color of the betel nut bags does not seem to communicate in formation about the

Plate 4.1 A *kaleku* for a young married girl, with *mamuli* motifs embroidered in red and black. Note the partition of the design in two *koro* or "walled rooms," a design restricted to the young. Coarsely plaited, slightly askew; corners with tufts. (Height: approximately 15 cm.; Length: approximately 20 cm.)

age and status of the wearer. Also, the Kodinese use a different raw material for their betel and areca nut bags, namely palm leaves (*lontar* in Indonesian) instead of pandanus. The Kodinese still prefer to use hand-spun, indigo-dyed thread to embellish their *kaleku*. They ply three or four threads together for that purpose. With rare exceptions, the Laboya have either abandoned this custom or never liked using indigo thread for their bags. At present they find the bright colors of imported thread less troublesome and far more attractive. Green, pink, and violet have been added to the traditional colors on Laboya bags for young people.

The horizontal embroidered lines on a Laboya *kaleku* are called *hurata japi*, the vertical ones, *hurata dede*. When they cross one another, they form squares, called *koro*, meaning "a room closed by walls." The most traditional pattern of Laboya *kaleku* consists of two *koro* in the center (Plate 4.1). However, such a design is not allowed for middle-aged people. The abundance of smaller *koro* in different colors is a design that suits young people only. As people grow older, the vertical lines and hence the *koro* gradually disappear from the design (Plates 4.2 and 4.3).

The last stage in embellishing the *kaleku* consists of embroidering the two bottom corners of the bag with a triangular pattern called

Plate 4.2 A *kaleku* for a middle-aged mother, with *mamuli* and *lolo lua* motifs in red and black. Expensive copper chain with Dutch coins attached to buffalo-horn pieces. Very finely plaited; corners with tufts. (Height: 20 cm.; Length: 26 cm.)

Plate 4.3 A *kaleku* for an elderly woman past childbearing age, usually a grandmother, or for an elderly man. Single *lolo lua* motif in black only. Copper chain without coins, attached to buffalo-horn pieces. Very finely plaited; embroidered corners in black, without tufts. (Height: 23 cm.; Length 31 cm.)

karibo kabihuna (Fig. 4.1). The corners are called *kabihu*, the same term as for clan. A tuft of hair (*wulu mata kabihu*: hair of the source of the *kabihu*) attached to each corner or *kabihu* gives a finishing touch to the bag (Fig. 4.1). The word *mata* means eye, source, water spring. Interestingly, just after death, the *mawo* of a deceased goes to the clan's sacred water spring to meet the ancestors. That spring is also the place where ancestors who wish to be reincarnated may refill themselves with water, that is, with life. Ancestors may inhabit the animals that swim in such springs. In many ways, a clan's sacred spring may be considered a source of life. Whether the *wulu mata kabihu* refers to that kind of source or spring remains speculation. This interpretation receives some support from the fact that elderly people who are approaching the time when their *mawo* will return to the clan's spring are not allowed to have tufts at the corners of their *kaleku*.

As people enter middle age and grow older, the color scheme of their *kaleku* becomes more subdued. Yellow is the first color to be omitted. Yellow and red refer to the solar cycle. Yellow is associated with the East, and red relates to the West. When rice ripens, it is said to pass from yellow to red. As people enter full adulthood, the yellow color turns into red in analogy with the passage of life. Vertical lines, *hurata japi*, no longer adorn the *kaleku* of middle-aged men and women. Horizontal lines only, *hurata japi*, decorate their bags (Plates

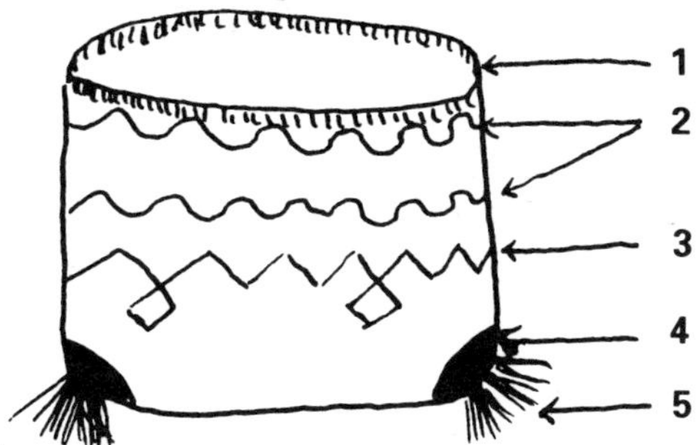

Figure 4.1 A diagram of a *Kaleku* for a middle-aged woman

1. *Kabolo Watu*
2. *Hurata Lolo Lua*
3. *Hurata Hamuli*
4. *Karibo Kabihuna*
5. *Wulu Mata Kabihu*

4.2 and 4.3). Again, unconscious references may be at work at this stage. For instance, a young man reaches full social membership only when he *kade*, that is when he "stands up," meaning that he is going to marry soon. It seems that as people are reaching the next stage in their life cycle, the attributes which correspond to their former status must be abandoned.

The most common patterns among the horizontal type of decoration are the *hurata mamuli* (drawing of the *mamuli*, a golden ear pendant: Fig. 4.1, Plates 4.1 and 4.2) and the *hurata lolo lua* (drawing of the cassava liana, a simple zig-zag line: Plate 4.3). The golden ear pendant or *mamuli* is part of the presentations given by wife-takers to their wife-givers. In Laboya mythical accounts, the *mamuli* is closely connected to the fecundity of women.[4] The *mamuli* pattern is reserved for the *kaleku* of women in their childbearing age. It is forbidden on men's *kaleku*. *Mamuli* are embroidered either in red or in red and black. *Mamuli* patterns are not thought suitable for a woman past childbearing age. Older women, like older men, prefer the *lolo lua* or cassava liana in black.

As people become grandfathers and grandmothers, the color red disappears from their *kaleku*. Black only is used. Patterns are greatly simplified. The *lolo lua* embroidered in black is the only pattern suitable for older people. However, it may be repeated two or three times on the same bag. As people grow older still, only one row of *lolo lua* is admitted. Then, the only decoration permitted is the *kabolo watu*, the top embroidered border on the *wal'ta* and embroidered corners, without tufts however. Finally, the *kaleku* is left plain (Plate 4.4).

We may conclude that the color scheme on betel bags is related to the life cycle of the individual. The presence of brightly colored patterns represents the promise of life such as it exists during youth. For the Laboya, like for all West Sumbanese, strong, contrasting colors represent life. The Laboya, however, conceive life in terms of the different stages *mawo* and *dewa* go through, from being united at birth to their coming apart at death. The contrast between white and black, in particular, is explicitly associated with life, whereas more subtle combinations of matching nuances are considered to be dead (*mate*). The Laboya associate the appearance of patterns as the result of using strong contrasting elements: bright threads upon a light background. This idea applies to their textiles as well. The fading of colors leads to the disappearance of the design. Therefore, it conveys the idea of declining life. The absence of colors, hence of patterns, relates to approaching death.

A succession of color schemes linked to the passage of generations

Plate 4.4 Old man pounding betel and areca nut in a buffalo horn, because he is toothless. His own *kaleku* is entirely plain, on his left. The decorated one belongs to a middle-aged female visitor. The borders of that *kaleku* are embroidered with traditional Laboya patterns, consisting of a black and yellow *lolo lua* variation. The decorations in the center are modern ones, copied from Lolinese betel and areca nut bags. The Lolinese live in the central highland of West Sumba, north of the Laboya. The pattern on the far right of the *kaleku* represents a Lolinese version of the *mamuli*. The man wears his loincloth in the traditional Laboya way, that is, without shorts. His shirt is a modern addition.

is not unusual for Indonesia. A recent study has shown that in East Java, to each generation of women, "from marriageable daughter to grand-mother past child-bearing age, corresponds an array of skirt and shoulder cloths with specific colours and patterns" (Heringa 1988:55–61). Although more research would be needed in order to avoid random comparisons, it is noteworthy to remark that in East Java, grandmothers wear dark blue-black skirts and shoulder cloths, whereas young marriageable girls are dressed in red motifs. Also, the Javanese word *ireng* means "black" as well as "lying fallow" (Heringa 1988:59), perhaps an implicit reference to women past their menopause. In other parts of Java, particular batik motifs relate to the past fertility of older women. Thus, a *sarung* decorated with a multitude of large fruits suits a mature woman, preferably a grandmother, with many children and grandchildren (Geirnaert and Heringa 1989:No. 1246).

Somewhat similar to these ideas, in Laboya the disappearance of the *mamuli* on women's *kaleku* is linked to being a grandmother who can no longer bear children herself. However, this short comparative excursion to Java cannot be pursued any further. Major differences between the two cultures forbid us to do so. For instance, the fading of colors in Laboya applies to both aging men and women.

In West Sumba, the Laboya alone seem to associate the color scheme and the intricacy of patterns of the *kaleku* with the process of life. The Kodinese hold similar ideas, but their *kaleku* do not appear to carry such information. Instead, the Kodinese express growth and decline in terms of different shades of indigo in some of their textiles. For instance, their checkered *gundu* cloths should include all shades of indigo, in reference to all stages of life. The Kodinese ceremonial *ikat* cloth for men (*wolo remba*) also relates the contrast between white and indigo-blue to life and death (Geirnaert 1990).

Remarkably, in Laboya, only the *mamuli* motif appears to be gender specific. All other motifs may be worn by both sexes. Likewise, gender does not rule the color scheme of the bags. "Relative age" appears to be a more essential criterion than gender for the choice of colors as well as that of patterns. Now let us examine how "relative age" relates to concepts of the "soul."

The Kaleku as an Item of Social Prestige

The *kaleku mama* does not only tell the phase of life in which the person to whom it belongs is situated, and it does not only relate to gender. The *kaleku* also expresses prestige. First, its fineness reveals costliness. A perfectly straight *kaleku* made of thin pandanus strips is highly valued. It may require a piglet to acquire it. Secondly, the strap to carry it on the shoulder is important. It may consist of plaited strips of pandanus or of twined colored threads. But it may also be a copper chain (*kalari ta wuru*) (Plate 4.2) that only the rich and the noble may actually wear. Copper chains are no longer sold in any of the Chinese shops in Waikabubak, the small capital of West Sumba. They are relatively rare nowadays because they date back to colonial times. They may have served several purposes in the past, totally unrelated to their present use as shoulder straps for betel and areca nut bags. Their length and the thickness of their links determine their quality and their exchange value. Furthermore, the chain needs to be embellished at each end by an old coin (*kalib*) with a hole in the middle (Plate 4.5). For this purpose, old Chinese coins may do, but pre-Independence old Dutch-Indonesian coins are more valued. The bag is worth more if both coins are old Dutch colonial pieces of money. One particularly fine example had two coins bearing the inscription: *Nederlands Indieë* 1922. Such coveted chains are not just attached to the bag. They are fixed with the help of a carved piece of valuable buffalo horn (*kadu kalari ta wuru*), through which small holes are

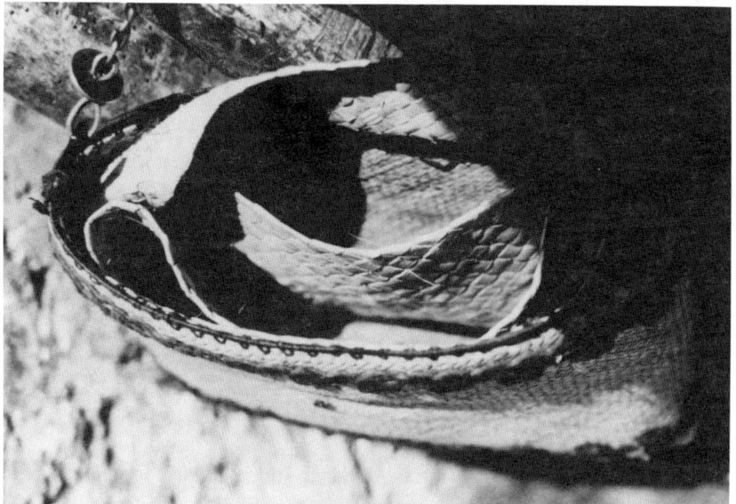

Plate 4.5 The photograph shows the space between the inner bag and the outer bag. This space is left open during the *Pogo nauta* ceremony in order to capture the "soul," that is, the *mawo* and the *dewa* of the deceased. (See Fig. 4.2)

bored. This intermediary piece of buffalo horn is sewn like a button on the upper corners of the *kaleku.*

A *kaleku* may be given away or may need to be replaced by another one. The chain is then removed and kept for the new *kaleku.* Although no rule forbids men to adorn a copper chain, during my fieldwork I only saw women wearing such items of prestige. I was told, however, that formerly men were proud to show off with such chains as well. Nowadays, they are often inherited from mother to daughter, but they may be given in exchange for a cloth, a pig or, if particularly beautiful, a young horse.

The chain and the coins may be attached to the *kaleku* after its owner is no longer entitled to wear many colors. They are items that represent his or her social status, gained throughout his or her life. A woman acquires prestige by bearing many healthy children. A man obtains authority by giving feasts, thereby developing a wide net of social relationships through which he can accumulate riches. This is how men and women acquire status during their lifetime. In Laboya, this acquired status is strongly linked to the *dewa* component of a person. However, prestige and wealth are not "owned" personally. After death, a person's *dewa* remains in the house of his descendants, whereas his *mawo* helps his body to decay. A person's *mawo* rejoins the *mawo* of all other ancestors, whereas his *dewa* remains bound to a specific lineage. The gradual disappearance of colors in the *kaleku* implicitly relates to this process. Multicoloredness refers to the period of life during which someone increases his or her *dewa.* In contrast, black, and eventually the absence of motifs, anticipate the stage when a person, no longer engaged in the process of acquiring more prestige and riches, becomes more putrefying matter, that is, more *mawo* than *dewa.*

The use of the bag during the *Pogo nauta* ceremony meant to recall the *dewa* and the *mawo* of those who died untimely deaths, shows the intimate relationship existing between the bag and the concept of the "soul," that is *mawo* and *dewa.*

The Secret Insides of the Kaleku

Simple *kaleku* have no inner bag. But more elaborate *kaleku* should conform to the ideal model, that is, they should contain a smaller inner bag (*tapena*). The latter is plaited separately from coarser pandanus strips than the outer bag. It is not decorated. The inner bag is made to fit the size of the *kaleku.* An extra flap is plaited on the top edge of the *kaleku* itself, taking the *wal'ta* as a starting point. This flap (*dani bali hadena*, "the back-flap" or "the flap that is turned back") is turned inside the *kaleku* and covers the upper border of the inner bag (Fig. 4.2). The flap hides and protects an inner space between the outer and the inner bag, which is called *dani larina*. This is a secret place that the Laboya compare to the intimacy of a couple's sleeping quarters. Nobody should ever lift the flap called *dani bali hadena* and take a look inside the *dani larina*. It is a serious offense to do so. In daily life, people keep some money and an extra supply of betel and areca nut in that space. The *dani larina* is actually the place where part of the *mawo* and part of the *dewa* of the *kaleku*'s owner dwell. I was told that during the *Pogo nauta* ritual, part of the *kaleku* of the deceased is left open in order to catch his or her *mawo* back. During this ceremony, the *kaleku* pictures the deceased with all the social attributes he or she had acquired at the moment of death: relative age position, gender, and status. The *kaleku* represents the reconstruction of the deceased as a social being. Once *mawo* has returned to earth, it may proceed further with the process of decay. As a consequence, the *dewa* of the deceased may return to the house and lineage to whom it belongs. From that time forward, the living may speak of the deceased and address him without risk. As the Laboya say, the deceased will not be forgotten and his or her *dewa* will have come to

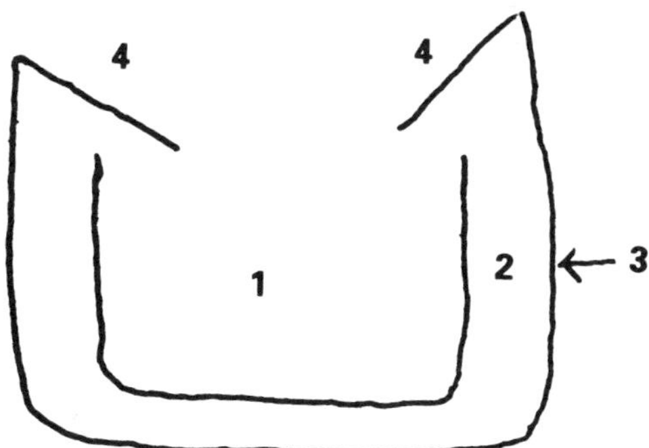

Figure 4.2 Section of a *Kaleku*

1. Inner Bag
2. Space between inner and outer
3. Outer Bag
4. Flaps

its final place (*hadau*), among the other spirits of the ancestors of the lineage, in the trapeze-shaped top of the house. Curiously, the word *wal'ta* means both "to, towards" and "from." *Wal'ta* always implies a movement to or from something. It is closely related to the idea of a place, situated between a beginning and an end. For the Laboya, it is essential to know "one's place" during ceremonies, so that partners with whom one exchanges ritual goods may easily find the spot where one stands. A geographical position during ceremonies implies definite social relationships and ritual roles.

The belief that a *kaleku* harbors some essential components of its owner, parts of his or her *mawo* and *dewa,* explains the intimacy that characterizes the exchange of *kaleku* between people. It also helps to understand some customs that are puzzling at first glance. When a young unmarried couple exchanges *kaleku,* it is understood that they are lovers. This supposition is strengthened by the physical characteristics of betel and areca nut. The Sumbanese use the fruit of the betel and not the leaf, as in other parts of Indonesia. By its shape, in Laboya, the fruit is associated with a phallus and represents "man." Similarly, the round areca nut is "woman." Identical associations are found in East Sumba as well (Jordaan and Niehof 1988). Once, an elderly Laboya man asked me to bring back "medicine" from Europe so that a young girl with whom he had fallen in love might welcome him as a husband. He planned to use it in the same way as traditional herbal medicine. He intended to make an invisible type of glue that he would smear underneath his *kaleku.* He and the girl would exchange *kaleku.* By holding his bag on her lap, she would be impregnated with the medicine that would seep through her *ye* or tubular skirt. The charm, by influencing her *mawo* and her *dewa,* would make her fall in love with him.

Conclusions

As seen, the *kaleku* is a personal item that contains part of the owner's vital components: *mawo* and *dewa*. However, it would be wrong to consider *dewa* and *mawo* as exclusively personal components. The Laboya concept of "soul" is not based on the individual, but on the social. A particular combination of *dewa* and *mawo* defines a person as long as he or she is living, that is, able to entertain and to intensify the total amount of social relationships. In this respect, Laboya society should be compared with Melanesian systems, in which so-called "big men" build up extensive social relationships.[5] To summarize, one could say that for the Laboya, from a social point of view, death is not the loss of life in general, but the loss of a particular combination of *mawo* and *dewa*. These are the main principles of life that are continuously exchanged between the living and the dead, circulating between the various lineages. Within this continuous cycle of exchange, it appears that gender plays a relatively subdued role. Prestige and authority, so often ostentatiously expressed during feasting, not in the least through dress, appear to be the participant's main concern.

Not only the bag itself, but the implements that it contains – all being necessary for the betel quid – stress social prestige, and to a lesser degree, gender. The traditional lime container for a Laboya man is a calabash. The cork is made of a small piece of wood, carved until it fits the opening of the container. Women should have a container made of bamboo. Nowadays, both men and women prefer the bamboo type. Some people adopt the most modern variant of lime containers: an empty plastic bottle that is particularly handy during the rainy season. But other implements are not gender-specific. They relate only to the status of the noble and of the rich. As people grow older, they are expected to use a larger bamboo container, and men always have a bigger one than women; the rich and the powerful being entitled to the largest of all. The lid of the bamboo lime container is made of wood. It is often shaped into buffalo horns, a source of prestige.

Additional implements suit the toothless elderly only, regardless of sex or status: a small iron spoon to scoop out the meat of coconuts, an iron pounder (*alu*), and a buffalo horn, in which the betel and the areca can be pounded together with lime. Sometimes a small brush made of coconut fibers for cleaning the implements completes the outfit. Because it is made of iron, a scarce product obtained mostly from motor car parts, the pounder is a valuable item. At home, young children are entrusted with the *alu*. As a mark of respect, they pound the betel quid for their grandparents. Once it is finely mashed, the elderly man or woman is able to enjoy the quid, if possible, in the company of other people. Holding some of the mixture on one tip of the *alu*, he or she may silently present it to a guest before resuming a conversation. The betel quid is a first step to exchange, toward the continuity of social relationships, and hence of society.

Notes

* The fieldwork in Laboya was carried out between 1982 and 1984. It was sponsored by the Netherlands Organization for the Advancement of Pure Research (ZWO, now called NWO). In the autumn of 1986, I spent a few weeks in Laboya, a trip that I financed myself.

1. Sumba is divided in several ethnolinguistic communities. The word *pesta* covers several indigenous names given to ceremonies consisting mainly of a communal meal. The size of the gatherings is variable; from as few as twenty people to as many as hundreds of participants. Although rare nowadays, there are occasions when guests number more than two thousand or even three thousand people.
2. In Laboya, like elsewhere in Sumba, the organization of "feasts" has a competitive character and they are planned by men only.
3. Cotton is filled with *mawo* most in October and November, when it is ripe and ready to be plucked.
4. For a discussion of the significance of the *mamuli* in Laboya rituals, see Geirnaert 1989b.
5. I am well aware of the challenging and potentially fruitful comparison between the Laboya with certain aspects of Melanesian societies, a problem evoked during the conference by H. Morphy, whom I wish to thank for his suggestions. I would also like to cite the work of A. Iteanu, who, apart from writing a monograph on the Orokaiva, a Melanesian society (1983), gave a lecture on the components of an Orokaiva person at the Institute of Cultural and Social Studies in Leiden (1988). His work has been a source of inspiration for some of my comments on the relationship between *dewa* and *mawo*. I also wish to mention that on many aspects of dress in relationship to headhunting and feasts of merit, comparison with non-Austronesian societies such as the Naga of northeast India (R. Barnes in this book) is an inviting subject for future work.

References

Forth, G.L., *Rindi: An Ethnographic Study of a Traditional Domain in Eastern Sumba*, Verhandelingen van het Koninklijk Instituut voor Taal-, Land-, en Volkenkunde, Martinus Nijhoff, The Hague, 1981.

Geirnaert, D.C., "Hunt Wild Pig and Grow Rice," in R. De Ridder and J.A.J. Karremans, (eds.), *The Leiden Tradition in Structural Anthropology. Essays in Honour of P.E. de Josselin de Jong*, Leiden: E.J. Brill, 1987, pp. 106–22.

———, "Textiles of West Sumba: The Lively Renaissance of an Old Tradition," in M. Gittinger, (ed.), *To Speak With Cloth: Studies in Indonesian Textiles*, Los Angeles: University of California Museum of Cultural History, 1989a, pp. 56–79.

———, "The Pogo Nauta Ritual in Laboya (West Sumba): of Tubers and Mamuli," in C. Barraud and J.D.M. Platenkamp (eds.), *Rituals and Socio-Cosmic Order in Eastern Indonesia*, Bijdragen tot de Taal-, Land- en Volkenkunde, Vol. 145, No. 4, 1989b, pp. 445–63.

———, "The Kijora: a thing for lost soul," in Pieter ter Keurs and Dirk Smidt (eds.), *The Language of Things: Studies in Ethnocommunication*, Leiden: E.J. Brill, 1990.

———, "The Snake's Skin: Traditional Ikat in Kodi, West Sumba (Eastern Indonesia)," *Indonesian Textiles, Symposium 1985. Ethnologica NF* 14 Cologne: Rautenstrauch-Joest Museum für Völkerkunde, 1991, pp. 34–42.

———, *The Woven Land of Laboya: Socio-cosmic Values in West Sumba (Eastern Indonesia)*, Ph.D. diss., Rijksuniversiteit Leiden, In press b.

———, and R. Heringa, *The A.E.D.T.A. Batik Collection/La collection de batik de l'A.E.D.T.A.*, trans. Annette Berra, Paris: Association pour l'Etude et la Documentation des Tissus d'Asie, 1989.

Heringa, R., "Textiles and Worldview in Tuban," in R. Schefold, V. Dekker, and N. de Jonge (eds.), *Indonesia in Focus: Ancient Traditions-Modern Times*, Meppel: Edu'Actief, 1988, pp. 55–61.

Iteanu, A., *La ronde des échanges. De la circulation aux valeurs chez les Orokaiva*, Cambridge and Paris: Cambridge University Press/Editions de la Maison des Sciences de l'Homme, 1983.

Jordaan, R.E., and A. Niehof, "Sirih pinang and symbolic dualism in Indonesia," in D.S. Moyer and H.J.M. Claessen (eds.), *Time Present, Time Future. Essays in Honour of P.E. de Josselin de Jong*, Dordrecht and Providence: Foris Publications, 1988, pp. 168–77.

Onvlee, L., *Cultuur als Antwoord*, The Hague: Martinus Nijhoff, 1973.

5

Gender Boundaries in the Production of Guatemalan Textiles

Cherri M. Pancake

For centuries, textiles have been an integral part of the economic and social life of the Guatemalan highlands. This can be attributed in large measure to the role of the community as the focus of cultural life. After conquering Guatemala in the mid-1500s, the Spaniards found that gathering their Indian subjects into towns greatly simplified the activities of religious conversion, the organization of forced labor, the collection of tribute, and the quelling of uprisings. Indian towns were allowed a considerable degree of autonomy as long as they met the demands of the governing regime. Over time, the communities evolved inwardly, each developing its own language dialect, weaving techniques, ethnic costume, religious and agricultural cycles, and craft specializations. A strong sense of community is still the salient characteristic of Guatemalan Indian culture.[1]

Handwoven textiles play a dual role in community life: they serve as the basis of local costume and also represent a source of cash income. For many years, research efforts centered on the identification and classification of garments and other handwoven cloths. Published results underscored the radical differences – in construction, color, design, materials, and even the manner in which textiles are worn or used – from one community to another.[2] More recent publications have focused on the use of ethnic dress as an expression of cultural identity.[3] In contrast, little information has emerged on the economic importance of textiles in Indian life. A handful of studies have analyzed textile-related activities in towns whose craft specializations include weaving for sale to outsiders.[4] Textile production is not documented, however, for the many regions where agriculture and other occupations take economic precedence. This lack of documentation is unfortunate because textile-related work, providing an outlet for seasonal or intermittent hourly labor, represents a critical source of income for many Indian families. Furthermore, although neither gender can be said to dominate textile production, textile activities represent the sole source of cash income for most Indian women.[5]

This essay explores gender boundaries in the production of Guatemalan textiles. The significance of present-day patterns cannot be fully appreciated without some understanding of the general cultural setting in which they occur. Therefore, the discussion begins with a historical overview of Guatemalan textile traditions.[6] This is followed by a survey and critical evaluation of prevailing notions concerning the relationships between textile production and gender. Previous assessments of gender roles are based largely on circumstantial evidence, and future studies would benefit from a more structured and objective approach.

Historical Overview

Guatemala's textile heritage has evolved over more than two millennia, with most of today's techniques representing direct continuations of pre-Columbian traditions. Manuscripts surviving from the era of the Spanish conquest reveal that vegetable fibers, principally cotton and maguey,[7] were the mainstay of a flourishing textile industry. Strict sumptuary laws governed the production and use of ceremonial and utilitarian cloths as well as garments. Spinning, weaving, and textile use are well documented in the *codices*, the pictorial manuscripts that represent the primary source of historical information on daily life among the Mesoamerican cultures.

Raw cotton was prepared for spinning by spreading it on a skin-covered frame or cushion and beating it with smooth forked sticks to remove impurities and to align the fibers. The spinner then pulled an end from the mass of fibers and attached it to a spindle (spinning stick). A clay or wooden whorl was attached to the lower end of the spindle to provide tension and momentum. To facilitate twirling and avoid undue pressure on the thread, the apparatus was rested in a gourd or pottery bowl. Spinning entails two actions carried out simultaneously: the spinner draws out the fibers into a thin strand and then, by twirling the spindle, imparts a twist to the strand that holds it together and gives strength to the thread. With a supported spindle, the process of drawing and twisting continues until the thread reaches arm's length; the spinner then winds it on the spindle and repeats the process. Stronger fibers, such as maguey, obviate the need for spindle support.

The spinner can stand or kneel, suspending the spindle from the thread being spun. This so-called drop spindle offers three advantages over the supported spindle: a longer length of thread can be spun before it is wound on the spindle, both hands are free to manipulate the fiber, and tension and momentum are regulated more easily.

Weaving was carried out on the Mesoamerican stick loom,[8] an extremely simple apparatus consisting of a handful of sticks, a cord, and a strap to gird the weaver's body. Sticks at the top and bottom served to keep the warp threads evenly distributed. To provide tension, the top bar was bound to a sturdy support, such as a tree or house post; the loom was then drawn tight by fastening the lower bar to the weaver's hips with the strap or belt. The loom elements were held together only by the threads being woven. In terms of textile development, the greatest advantage of the stick loom over other loom types was that it allowed the weaver to exercise complete control over the work in progress. Loom tension was regulated by the position of the weaver's body: leaning forward loosened the tension on the warp threads and leaning back tightened it. Small changes in body position thus effected changes in the texture of the cloth, and subtle variations in spacing and tension were possible. A skilled stick-loom weaver could produce combinations of weaves that would be difficult or impossible to achieve on a rigid warp loom.

Extant historical manuscripts indicate that both spinning and weaving were female occupations, associated with the deities of femaleness, birth, and fertility. Basic textile skills were taught by mother to daughter at an early age as part of the socialization process. Although a certain degree of proficiency was considered indispensible, weaving and spinning expertise were respected; in some cases they were honored with contests and prizes.

Pre-Columbian garments required a minimum of sewing and cutting. One characteristic of the stick loom is that it lends itself to textiles with four selvedges, or finished woven edges. Fabrics with four selvedges tend to be dimensionally stable, making hems or protective seams designed to prevent unravelling unnecessary. A second characteristic is that the stick loom imposes strict limitations on the size of the finished cloth. The majority of textiles woven on the Mesoamerican loom measure under twenty-four inches across and between one and five yards in length. These factors had a profound effect on Mesoamerican dress. No fitting and very little cutting were needed for most items of dress; instead, rectangular or square cloths were seamed to form simple, flat garments. Sashes, headdresses, and kilts were long single webs. *Huipiles* (blouse-like upper garments), skirts, and cloaks typically made use of two or three narrow pieces joined lengthwise. Virtually all garments were wrapped or draped about the body rather than fitted to encase the limbs.

By 1524, the year of the Spanish conquest of Guatemala, a long and well-established textile tradition had evolved. Few changes came about during the first years of Spanish rule, but by the close of the sixteenth century the first of several key events had occurred: the introduction of wool. There is no direct evidence on how the fiber was originally processed, but some technological transfer must have accompanied the raw material, since the beating method used for cotton would not have served for the scaly wool fibers. It is likely that wool cards (for fiber preparation), teasel fans (for brushing the finished cloth to raise a nap), and the spindle wheel[9] arrived in Mesoamerica quickly. The fact that the implements used today resemble the crude versions common in medieval Europe rather than their more recent counterparts lends credence to an early introduction. The innovations were notable because they reduced significantly the amount of time needed to prepare yarn for weaving.

The Spaniards also introduced the European treadle loom, which was to have radical and pervasive affects on Guatemalan textile production. The stick loom was certainly more than adequate for creating traditional Indian garments woven of cotton, maguey, or even the new wool, but it was not suitable for producing the yard goods then popular in Europe and required by the Spanish colonists. A new textile industry came into being, centered around a simple, heavy style of treadle loom common in sixteenth- and seventeenth-century Europe. The salient advantages of the new loom were increased speed and greater dimensional capabilities. Fabrics woven on treadle looms were commonly between 100 and 150 yards in length, and undecorated textiles could be produced in less than 5 percent of the time required on a stick loom (even if it were possible to accommodate long webs on the latter). Because more parts of the loom were rigidly controlled, the finished cloth also exhibited more homogeneity in size and texture. On a treadle loom, however, the panels of a garment could no longer be woven to the exact size needed, nor could major structural variations be incorporated in a single piece. Since weaver control over individual patterns was hampered by the monolithic treadle loom, an improved model borrowed from the Chinese textile industry was also introduced during the Spanish colonial era. The draw loom had a virtually unlimited pattern repertory, allowing the weaver to pick and choose among many elaborate design repeats.

Although fiber preparation, spinning, and weaving were traditional female roles in pre-Conquest Mesoamerica, men took over these responsibilities for Spanish wool. The Spaniards established large-scale weaving workshops, where male Indians were forced to labor under appalling conditions. Women continued to produce textiles at home, but they too were affected by colonial rule, forced to spin cotton fiber distributed by the authorities and weave it into fabrics for shipment to Spain, often with no remuneration for their work.

Two other technological innovations occurred at undetermined points prior to the end of the nineteenth century. First, another spindle type, the whirl spindle, came into use for maguey fibers. This implement consisted of a small hook rotating on a hand-held shaft; although related spindles were known in Europe, it is possible that it evolved independently in the New World. The second innovation was a small loom combining structural aspects of the treadle loom with the strap-controlled tension of the stick loom. It was probably developed in Guatemala, but as yet no evidence has been found concerning its origins.

Acknowledged Gender Boundaries

The concept of gender boundaries in the production of Guatemalan textiles is not a new one, although the term is. Virtually all published studies have commented informally on the sexual division of textile activities, most recognizable in the strong correlation between gender and weaving technology. Thus, women are exclusively associated with the indigenous stick loom – surviving virtually unchanged from the pre-Conquest era – while men are linked to European-inspired treadle looms.[10] Most authors extend the division to include fibers, observing that men weave with wool and women with cotton. As outlined in the preceding section, these ideas seem to have a historical basis. When new techniques were introduced from Europe during the colonial era, their use was typically confined to that portion of the community interfacing with the outside world: adult males. Females continued to employ the traditional pre-Columbian methods and materials.

The spinning of particular fibers has been acknowledged as a similar gender boundary: men are reported to spin wool but not cotton, while the opposite is often cited for women. Personal field observations lead me to believe that gender roles may actually be related more to the implement than the fiber: men seem to use the spindle wheel (for wool), drop spindle (wool), or whirl spindle (maguey), but never the supported spindle. Women, on the other hand, rarely use a drop or whirl spindle, opting for the supported spindle (cotton) and occasionally the wheel (wool). A similar tool-oriented explanation appears to apply to the hand-plying of threads into yarns, considered by most sources to be a strictly feminine activity. My field data suggest that the reason is because the yarn strength obtained through plying is important for women's backstrap loom technology, but not for male-dominated looms. That men can and do use the same technique when necessary is clear from examples in maguey-producing regions – where strength is required, men hand-ply the fiber using a whirl spindle.

Within a given community, additional gender specificity has been found to apply to particular techniques or subtasks. In most cases the distinction is drawn along the lines of individual products. Women might weave *huipiles* and sashes, for example, while men might crochet bags and weave blankets. On occasion both sexes contribute to the production of a single item, and here the activities of each are more clearly delineated. Women may do one type of embroidery and men another; alternatively, women may weave the cloth and men stitch the seams or knot the fringes. In terms of task division, however, there do not appear to be any discernible patterns from one community to another.

Table 5.1 summarizes these and other gender boundaries that have been noted in the literature. Note that textile segregation is perceived in terms of *technological role*. No hierarchy of activities is implied, nor can either sex be characterized as dominant to the other. As in many other aspects of traditional Indian life, the sexes are seen to collaborate in a more or less equal partnership, each responsible for certain needs and relying on the partner for others.

Table 5.1 Traditional Gender Boundaries

	implements	fibers and dyeing	techniques
female	stick loom supported spindle	handspun cotton hand-plied yarns	single-faced brocading double-faced brocading gauze weaves
both	*spindle wheel*	*commercial cottons* *silk and rayon*	*plain weaves* *two-faced brocading*
male	treadle looms whirl spindle drop spindle	wool maguey ikat dyeing	crochet, knotless netting tapestry weave twill weaves

Most authors have extended the technology model further, suggesting that men weave items destined for sale, while women's textiles are for personal and family use. Since the nature and cost of their respective products (treadle-loomed yard-goods vs. stick-loomed piece-cloths) preclude any real commercial rivalry between the sexes, this is perceived as an extension of the equal partnership concept. Although there are some historical antecedents, the notion more probably derives from prevailing attitudes concerning gender economics. In positing distinct professional roles for male and female weavers, one cash-oriented and the other subsistence-based, we imply the production-reproduction model of occupational segregation: men see the outside world and "produce" textiles to meet its demands, while women weave to "reproduce" the necessities of domestic life.[11] Although the concept is never concretized in writings on Guatemalan textiles, its presence is implicit in remarks about female weavers, women's use of ethnic dress, and their adherence to traditional ways.

A Closer Look at Gender Roles

There are several problems with the prevailing gender-technology synonymy for gender boundaries in textile production. In the first place, the number of contradictions to the scheme is disquieting. Consider, for example, two recent anthropological studies: Laurel Bossen states unequivocably that "Mam women do not use wool" and "the men do not know how to weave using the backstrap loom," while Sheldon Annis affirms in equally strong terms that "there is nothing unusual or unacceptable about a man doing backstrap weaving" (Bossen 1984; Annis 1987).

Similarly, the universally accepted notion that women do not use treadle looms is contradicted by data collected in towns throughout Guatemala.[12] Comparable discrepancies can be found in the area of spinning. Women do spin wool in many communities, using both the drop spindle and the wheel, and some employ the whirl spindle for maguey.

The confusion may be due in part to semantic subtleties. In field studies of tapestry, Mia MacEldowney and I found that the male head-of-household was invariably named as "the weaver," even though the entire family – including women and young girls – participated in weaving and related activities on a regular basis. In general, my experience has been that almost every community exhibits exceptions to the supposed traditional gender roles.

A second difficulty is that the traditional conception of gender technology does not adequately explain recent changes in the division of textile labor. This is particularly problematical in terms of the "crossing" of gender boundaries. No one disputes the fact that Guatemalan Indian life has changed dramatically over the past thirty years. An unprecedented level of political violence has extended to even the most remote areas, and economic and religious upheavals have provoked factionalism in many communities. In recognition of these social forces, authors who note a blurring of male and female roles in the production and marketing of textiles are apt to attribute it to a generally declining interest in ethnic traditions.[13] The position may be justified with respect to some changes in textile production patterns, such as an apparent decrease in the number of weavers of both genders. It is not compatible, however, with the clear evidence that women now participate actively in the production of items once considered the exclusive province of male weavers.[14]

A third problem stems from the fact that the production-reproduction model appears to be based on largely circumstantial factors. First, the assumed differences in loom technologies make it appear that only men weave in quantity. It is true that males are likely to "mass-produce" textiles in the sense that multiple items are woven with just a single-loom setup, whereas the backstrap loom requires individual preparation for each item. There are also significant differences in the technical complexity of loom-related weaving techniques, so that a woman backstrap weaver may invest several orders of magnitude more work in a single piece than a male treadle weaver. Therefore, the yard-goods typically made by men are more likely to be perceived as trade items than are women's pieces, particularly since it is easier to track the market distribution of bulk products. Moreover, men typically weave in a mini-workshop setting where two or more looms are in use simultaneously and earnings can be calculated on a daily or piece-by-piece basis. They also follow a regular full-time schedule (at least on a seasonal basis). Most women, on the other hand, weave alone or in pairs in a setting redolent of domesticity: the privacy of their family living compound. Since they alternate weaving with a variety of other activities, it is difficult to estimate the real extent of their textile-related commitments. Thus, circumstances conspire to make it appear that it is only men who engage in commercial textile ventures, while women weave as a domestic chore. A closer examination of textile production patterns, however, reveals that women invest substantial amounts of time and raw materials in weaving for sale or exchange, and that many women have given up weaving items for family consumption.[15]

An Alternative Approach

It is clear that technology is not a sufficiently strong foundation on which to base the notion of gender-specific roles. By limiting our viewpoint to the artifacts of the weaving process, we ignore the intent of the weaver. In particular, the production-reproduction viewpoint must be challenged. I contend that this interpretation of Guatemalan textile patterns is based largely on details of the weaving environment: the physical locale where textile activities take place, the proportion of daily time devoted to weaving, the uniformity of the products, and the number of items produced within a given period. It ignores the fact that women – left out of census calculations because they weave part-time and in the seclusion of their homes – account for a disproportionately large share of textile production in terms of overall value. This can be explained by two factors. First, women represent an overwhelming majority among Guatemalan handweavers, both in number and in terms of the hours invested in weaving-related activities. Second, differences in the techniques employed by men and women mean that the average value of a textile product varies significantly by gender; the complexity of stick-loom *huipil* is reflected in a selling price ten to one hundred times that of a comparable piece woven by a man.[16]

Like many other aspects of traditional life, textile production has witnessed a gradual realignment from a subsistence to a cash economy. As individuals and communities find that they can no longer exist in self-sufficient isolation, occupational roles are changing for both sexes. Most authors comment that the number of weavers has decreased, yet fail to note that the women who persist seem to weave more often and for a wider audience of consumers. Bossen, for example, found that 69 percent of the women in Todos Santos wove commercially in 1975, although just thirty years before not a single instance had been recorded.[17] In other recent studies, Annis reported that 83 percent of weavers surveyed in San Antonio Aguas Calientes produced items for sale, and Barrios noted similar results for Comalapa.[18]

The increasing commercialization of women's textile-related activities is not an accident. Most female weavers with whom I have spoken are aware of the importance of marketing and are surprisingly knowledgeable about the ultimate destination of their work. They realize that

Table 5.2 Patterns of Textile Consumption

domestic	*intracommunity*	*intercommunity*	*interethnic*	*international*
weaver immediate family extended family	commissioner barterer purchaser	non-local purchaser non-local commissioner itinerant vendor	Ladino tourist Ladino retailer Indian retailer	foreign tourist foreign retailer Ladino wholesaler

they have access to several potential markets for textiles. This information is generalized in Table 5.2 (although the classifications are mine, the concept is based on field interviews with weavers). At the domestic level, a woman weaves for personal or family use, either without remuneration or in exchange for other domestic chores. Within the larger context of the community, she may accept materials on commission, weaving a specific item "made-to-order" in exchange for cash or services, or she may choose to invest time and materials in a textile for later sale to another community member. At the regional or intercommunity level, a woman may accept commissions from Indians living in other towns or weave items for direct or indirect (via an intermediary, typically an itinerant vendor) sale to other communities. In addition, the past fifty years have seen the development of substantial new markets outside the Indian population. Consequently, a woman now may weave textiles for sale to tourists, either foreigners or *Ladinos* (Guatemalans of non-Indian or mixed origin). Indirect outside markets may be reached through various retail or whole sale alternatives.

The fact that women weavers are aware of a hierarchical network of markets belies their role as simple domestic reproducers. Most importantly, the weavers recognize distinct consumer preferences not only in color, pattern, and raw materials, but also in the techniques and level of skill demanded for each market. Many textile production decisions are based on these perceptions.[19] A more realistic approach to establishing gender boundaries in textile production, therefore, might be to examine the relationship between gender and product. If the production-reproduction dichotomy were valid, textiles produced by women would be uniformly destined for domestic or perhaps intracommunity use, while men's work would fill the intercommunity and other "commercial" levels.

Table 5.3 Recent Gender Boundaries

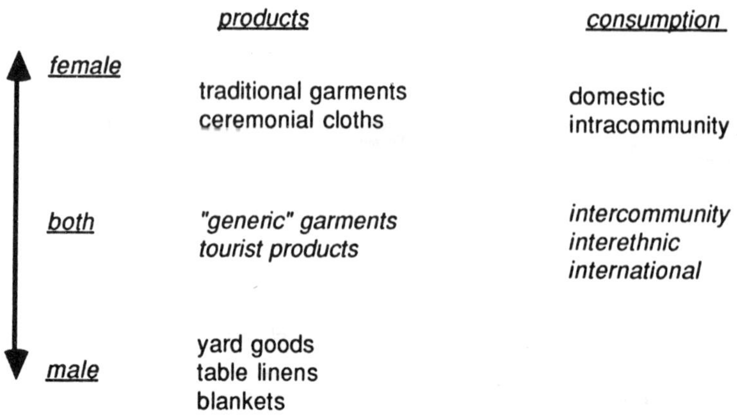

	products	consumption
female	traditional garments ceremonial cloths	domestic intracommunity
both	*"generic" garments* *tourist products*	*intercommunity* *interethnic* *international*
male	yard goods table linens blankets	

As Table 5.3 demonstrates, this is simply not the case. Two patterns can be observed. The first relates to the type of textile produced by each sex. Male weavers typically generate quantities of repetitive items, such as yard-goods, linens, and blankets. Women, on the other hand, are likely to weave highly individualistic garments or decorative cloths. Gender integration occurs in the case of tourist products and what might be termed generic garments: shawls, skirt lengths, and utility cloths. A second set of boundaries operates at the same time, but on the level of consumption patterns. Here we see that the production of the local ethnic dress is in the hands of women, while textiles destined for sale outside the community are woven by both sexes. If it appears that women enjoy a wider latitude than men in selecting products and markets, this corresponds with my observations among Guatemalan weavers. Many women expressed a sense of personal pride and satisfaction that they were technically capable of generating a broader range of styles, fabrics, and elaborate decorative techniques than could their male counterparts.

Conclusions

The prevailing notion of technology as a basis for interpreting gender boundaries is inadequate to explain observed patterns in the production of Guatemalan textiles. Three factors have been identified as problematical: (1) there are too many contradictions to reported gender roles to permit any confidence in the scheme; (2) the concept of gender technology can not account for recent changes in the division of textile labor; and (3) extension of the model to a production-reproduction dichotomy, a common trend in the literature, appears to be largely unfounded.

An alternative approach has been outlined, emphasizing the reasons why a person engages in textile-related activities rather than focusing on the environment within which the activities are performed. Obviously, a considerable amount of field research remains to be done before the issue can be confirmed or denied. It is to be hoped that a more economic orientation will buffer the influence of traditional assumptions on occupational segregation. The fact that many authors applaud the Indian woman's role as maintainer of culture does little to ameliorate the implication that she looks to the past while her man looks to the future. Such a viewpoint is inaccurate as well as unflattering. Guatemalan Indian women, like their Bolivian counterparts, "are proud of their activities, possess a positive self-image, and have high aspirations."[20]

In closing, I would like to suggest that the term "boundary" carries connotations that may be inaccurate in the Guatemalan context. A boundary circumscribes or restricts actions, relegating the object – here, the Indian weaver – to a passive role. This is in keeping with the popular interpretation of cultural persistence in Guatemala: that the Indian withdraws into traditionalism as a means of surviving the incursion of external forces. Yet recent studies indicate that Guatemalan Indians are not just objects of change, but in fact are agents who deliberately act to preserve their ethnic uniqueness, adapting to change from within their own culture as well as from outside influences.[21] Perhaps our preoccupation with delimiting boundaries obscures the real content that lies beneath.

Notes

1. The persistence of the Guatemalan Indian community has intrigued researchers for the reason encapsulated by Sol Tax more than fifty years ago: "From the point of view of the Indians themselves, the people of each *municipio* constitute a unique group, united by blood and tradition, and

differing from all others in history, language and culture" (Tax 1937:433). This is not to say that Indian communities are simple or particularly unified in makeup. As Sheldon Annis recently demonstrated, religious and political factionalism has profound effects on village life: "The cultural stability of the past . . . has been fractured . . . by population pressure, growing landlessness, environmental deterioration, and military repression . . . by land windfalls, new technology, development programs, and expanding primary education. Both kinds of pressures have contributed to a surprisingly skewed distribution of wealth within the ostensibly homogeneous Indian community" (Annis 1987).

2. See, for example: Anawalt 1975; O'Neale 1945; Osborne 1935, 1965; Delgado Pang 1963; Pancake and Baizerman 1981; Rowe 1981; and Schevill 1985.
3. Notable examples include: Barrios 1985; Castellanos 1986; Pancake, 1991; Maynard 1963; Pancake 1988; Morrissey 1983; and Rodas and Polanco 1987.
4. See, for example: Annis 1987; Pancake and Annis 1982; Hagan 1970; and McEldowney 1982.
5. Bossen 1984; and Annis 1987. Morrissey mentions the importance of textile production and sales to women from the Lake Atitlàn area (Morrissey 1983). The relationship between the economic and social roles of Indian women has been dealt with only peripherally in most studies. Two recent works, however, have underscored the importance of an economic basis for gender distinctions among Guatemalan Indians: Bossen 1984, and Ehlers 1980.
6. A more comprehensive treatment of this topic may be found in Pancake 1977.
7. Maguey is the generic name for a variety of coarse fibers obtained from the leaves of *Agave spp.* and *Furcaea spp.* Today, maguey fibers are generally used for cordage; examples include sisal (*Agave sisalana*) and henequin (*Agave fourcroydes).*
8. The stick loom is also referred to as the backstrap, hipstrap, waist, belt, or girdle loom. In Guatemala the term stick loom is most appropriate because (1) it allows for the fact that the sash or strap is actually worn around the waist, hips, or buttocks rather than the back; and (2) it draws a distinction between this simple loom and a special-purpose loom that combines elements of the table and floor looms while at the same time employing a belt or backstrap to provide tension.
9. Although frequently referred to in the literature as a spinning wheel, the Guatemalan device simply makes use of a wheel drive to turn the spindle, and therefore is more properly a spindle wheel.
10. O'Neale goes as far as to classify them as "men's looms" and "women's looms;" (O'Neale 1945: *passim*).
11. The production-reproduction dichotomy has been used in a variety of

contexts. Here, I use the term "reproductive" to refer to activities for subsistence, while "productive" work generates exchange value, typically cash income. In asserting that Guatemalan weavers feel their work is much more important than "commercialized housework," I am particularly indebted to Florence Babb's observations on Peruvian marketwomen: "When they told me 'Without marketers, Huaraz couldn't survive,' they were expressing themselves, perhaps, as sustainers or social reproducers, but they were also recognising their productive contribution to the economy and society" (Babb 1986).

12. Personal field notes, especially from surveys conducted with Mia McEldowney, Jill Ashman, and Barbara LaPera.
13. See Osborne 1965; Morrissey 1983; Rodas and Polanco 1987; Pettersen 1976.
14. My field notes are replete with examples of women who have "crossed over" into the production of supposedly male-dominated items. similar occurrences were noted by McEldowney 1982, and Barrios 1985.
15. Attempts to quantify the number of hours women invest in weaving have not been particularly successful; see Pancake and Annis 1982. Annis, however, documents some substantial changes in product destinations (Annis 1987); similar examples may be found in Bossen (Bossen 1984).
16. Figures on the domestic sector of Guatemala's handweaving economy are conspicuously absent in the literature. The only census dedicated to handicrafts deals almost exclusively with workshops registered with the government – male treadle-loom establishments (Dirección General de Estadística 1982). Hagan's work suffers from a similar limitation in scope, although he also includes registered "firms" of backstrap weavers (Hagan 1970). This lacuna is surprising in view of the magnitude and economic importance of domestic weaving – an estimated 45,000 persons engaged in part-time commercial weaving in 1976 (Annis and Pancake 1977). Nevertheless, most studies of Guatemalan textiles focus on changes in the textiles themselves or the technology used to produce them, rather than on the role of weaving in community and household economies.
17. Bossen 1984.
18. Annis 1987, and Barrios 1985. Barrios's treatment is unique in providing transcriptions of field interviews with male and female weavers.
19. See Pancake and Annis 1982; Annis 1987; and Pancake 1991.
20. Beuchler 1986. Although not all weavers enjoy weaving, the vast majority take pride and pleasure in their work and feel a strong affinity with weavers from other cultures.
21. Watanabe presents a convincing argument for this (Watanabe 1984). A social historian's perspective can be found in Smith's critical commentary (Smith 1987).

References

Anawalt, P., "Pan-Mesoamerican Costume Repertory at the Time of Spanish Contact," Ph.D. diss., University of California, Los Angeles, 1975.

Annis, Sheldon, *God and Production in a Guatemalan Town*, Austin: University of Texas Press, 1987.

———, and C.M. Pancake, "Improving the Supply of Dyes and Fibers to Artisanal Weavers," presented to USAID/Guatemala, 1977.

Babb, F., "Producers and Reproducers: Andean Marketwomen in the Economy," in June Nash and Helen Safa (eds.), *Women and Change in Latin America*, South Hadley, Massachusetts: Bergen and Garvey, 1986.

Barrios, Asturias de L., *Comalapa: Native Dress and Its Significance*, Guatemala: Museo Ixchel del Traje Indígena, 1985.

Beuchler, J.-M., "Women in Petty Commodity Production in La Paz, Bolivia," in June Nash and Helen Safa (eds.), *Women and Change in Latin America*, South Hadley, Massachusetts: Bergen and Garvey, 1986.

Bossen, L.H., *The Redivision of Labor: Women and Economic Choice in Four Guatemalan Communities*, Albany: State University of New York Press, 1984.

Castellanos, G.M. de, *Tzute y jerarquía en Sololá*, Guatemala: Museo Ixchel del Traje Indígena, 1986.

Delgado Pang, H.S. de, "Aboriginal Guatemalan Handweaving and Costume," Ph.D. diss., Indiana University, 1963.

Dirección General de Estadística, *I Censo artesanal 1978*, Guatemala: Dirección General de Estadística, 1982.

Ehlers, T.B., "La Sampedrana: Women and Development in a Guatemalan Town," Ph.D. diss., University of Colorado, 1980.

Hagan, A.J., "An Analysis of the Hand Weaving Sector of the Guatemalan Economy," Ph.D. diss., University of Texas at Austin, 1970.

Maynard, E., "The Women of Palin: A Comparative Study of Indian and Ladino Women in a Guatemalan Village," Ph.D. diss., Cornell University, 1963.

McEldowney, M.R., "An Analysis of Change in Highland Guatemalan Tapestry Hairribbons," M.A. thesis, University of Washington, 1982.

Morrissey, R.C., "Continuity and Change in Backstrap Loom Textiles of Highland Guatemala," Ph.D. diss., University of Wisconsin at Madison, 1983.

O'Neale, L.M., *Textiles of Highland Guatemala*, Washington, D.C.: Carnegie Institution of Washington, 1945.

Osborne, L. de Jongh, *Guatemalan Textiles*, New Orleans: Tulane University Middle American Research Institute, 1935.

———, *Indian Crafts of Guatemala and El Salvador*, Norman: University of Oklahoma Press, 1965.

Pancake, C.M., "Communicative Imagery in Guatemalan Indian Dress," in M.B. Schevill, J.C. Berlo and E.B. Dwyer, (eds.), *Textile Traditions of Mesoamerica and the Andes: An Anthology*, New York: Garland, 1991.

———, "Nuevos métodos en la interpretación de textos gráficos: aplicaciones de la 'teoría del lenguaje' a los tejidos autoctonos de Guatemala," *Mesoamérica*, Vol. 16, 1988, pp. 311–34.

——— "Textile Traditions of the Highland Maya: Some Aspects of Development and Change," presented at International Symposium on Maya Art, Architecture, Archaeology, and Hieroglyphic Writing, Guatemala, 1977.

———, and S. Annis, "El arte de la producción: Aspectos socio-económicos del tejido a mano en San Antonio Aguas Calientes, Guatemala," *Mesoamerica*, Vol. 3, No. 4, 1982, pp. 387–413.

———, and S. Baizerman, "Guatemalan Gauzes: A Description and Key to Identification," *Textile Museum Journal*, Vol. 20, 1981, pp. 1–26.

Pettersen, C. de, *Maya of Guatemala: Life and Dress*, Guatemala: Museo Ixchel del Traje Indígena, 1976.

Rodas, I.M. de, and R.M. de Polanco, *Cambio en Colotenango: traje, migración y jerarquía*, Guatemala: Museo Ixchel del Traje Indígena, 1987.

Rowe, A.P., *A Century of Change in Guatemalan Textiles*, New York: Center for Inter-American Relations, 1981.

Schevill, M.B., *Evolution in Textile Design from the Highlands of Guatemala*, Berkeley: University of California Lowie Museum of Anthropology, 1985.

Smith, C.A., "Ideologías de la historia social," *Mesoamérica*, Vol. 14, 1987, pp. 355–366.

Tax, S., "The Municipios of the Midwestern Highlands of Guatemala," *American Anthropologist*, Vol. 39, 1937, p. 433.

Watanabe, J., "We Who Are Here: The Cultural Conventions of Ethnic Identity in a Guatemalan Indian Village, 1937–1980," Ph.D. diss., Harvard University, 1984.

6

The Jewish *Kippa Sruga* and the Social Construction of Gender in Israel

Suzanne Baizerman

In the early 1980s I lived in Israel and in the course of my daily life I became aware of the array of skullcaps, *yarmulke* in Yiddish, *kippa* in Hebrew, worn by orthodox Jewish Israeli men (Plate 6.1). One widespread variety, the *kippa sruga* (plural *kippot srugot*), is small, often multicolored, and crocheted, with a range of patterns around its border. It is usually handmade by women friends and relatives of the wearer. Unlike the dress of many other orthodox males, the dress of those who wear the *kippa sruga* could in other respects be classified as Western dress, from business suits and casual college sportswear to bus company and military uniforms. Gradually I came to understand the multiplicity of personal, social, and political meanings contained in the *kippa sruga*, which serve to identify wearers as members of a particular subculture. In particular, I came to appreciate the way in which this small item of apparel and its associated technology played a part in the social construction of gender. The making and wearing of the *kippa sruga* reinforces gender categories and ideologies in a subculture where gender distinctions are highly important. While the *kippa sruga* is a very well-defined item of dress, an analysis of its production and function has implications for the study of more complex forms of technology related to apparel fabrication and gender.[1]

In this discussion, serious consideration is given to the technology involved in the production of the *kippa sruga*, which includes the social context of the object's production, the materials and processes of production, as well as the object itself. Such an approach focuses on the way in which, in Lechtman's words (1977:15), "people elaborate technological behaviour along lines that are meaningful socially, economically and ideologically." In their terms, technology serves as "a

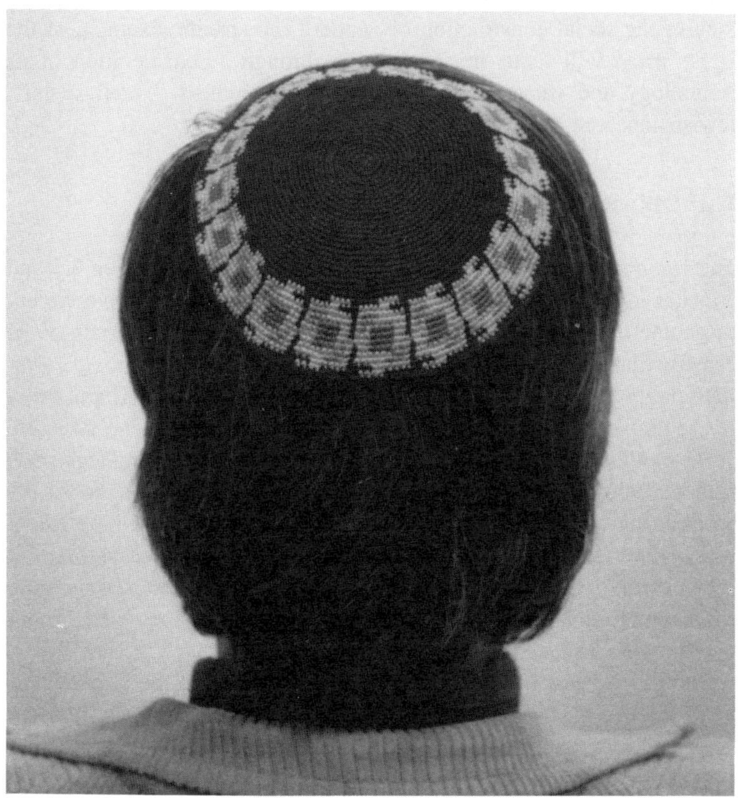

Plate 6.1 The *Kippa Sruga*

vehicle for maintaining a symbolically meaningful environment" (Lechtman 1977:17). Such a view of technology is echoed in a more recent article by Pfaffenberger, where he discusses the "social vision woven into technology" (1988:241). Technology, to Pfaffenberger, is a "set of social behaviors and a system of meaning" (1988:241); technology is "simultaneously material, social and symbolic" (1988:236).

Even though Pfaffenberger deals with technological systems on a vastly different scale – irrigation systems, in fact – his approach has relevance for what have traditionally been classified as "feminine technologies," the domestic arts, the textile or fiber arts. Worldwide we can observe a certain connection between fiber art, specifically domestic dress technology, and women. Rejecting a biological explanation of this correlation, we will instead consider a explanation that relates technology to the social construction of gender. The specific example of the *kippa sruga* will focus this discussion through a consideration of its technology and various aspects of its social context: Israeli society, Jewish law, the home, and the community.

The Object and Its Technology

The *kippa sruga* (Plate 6.1) is a shallow, circular cap, between 3.5 and 5 inches in diameter, the outer border of which is patterned in a variety of geometric and representational designs. Tools and materials of its construction are simple: fine, plied, mercerized cotton and a correspondingly fine crochet hook. Thus the production of the *kippa sruga* is a portable activity, which fits into odd bits of time. The structure of the cloth is also simple – a vertical and lateral interlooping technique (Emery 1980:43) popularly known as "single crochet." Designs for the border range along a continuum of complexity, the most intricate of which may take many hours to execute. The stitch is easy to learn, but to create intricate multicolored patterns, especially those involving dark colors, and to fabricate the slightly convex shape of the *kippa sruga* takes skill and practice.

The cap is worked in a spiral fashion beginning at the very center. New stitches are worked in previous rounds with increases made to keep the fabric flat. Increases may be made at regular intervals creating a textural pattern; however, it is more usual to have the increases made almost invisibly at random at the crocheter's discretion. While the diameter of the caps varies in size from 3.5 to 5 inches, most caps fall into the larger end of the range. One rule cited that the size of the *kippa* must be at least the width of four fingers.

For the border designs, crocheters work from patterns on graph paper (Plate 6.1 and Figs. 6.1–6.4). These patterns can be from pattern books sold for this purpose, adaptations of patterns from other sources (cross-stitch patterns, for example), or original (innovative) patterns. Often patterns are traded with friends or relatives. The patterns vary from five to twenty-three rounds, averaging between ten and thirteen rounds. The crocheter begins the pattern to fit with the projected final diameter of the *kippa*. When working the border pattern, no increases are made. By working the border without increases and then gradually decreasing the circular form, the maker creates the convex shape of the cap.

Figures 6.1–6.4 Examples of *Kippot* Patterns on Graph Paper

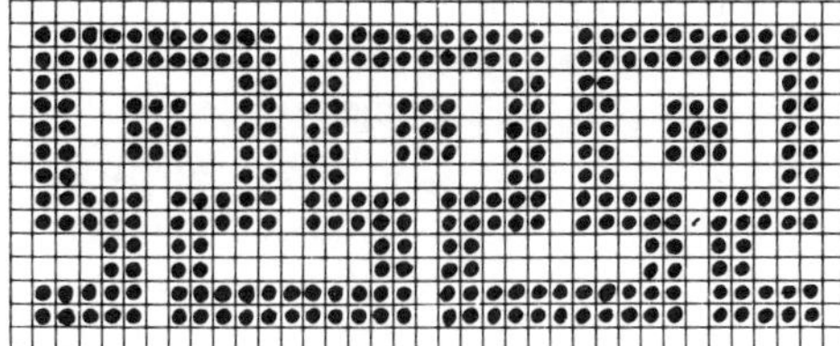

Figure 6.1

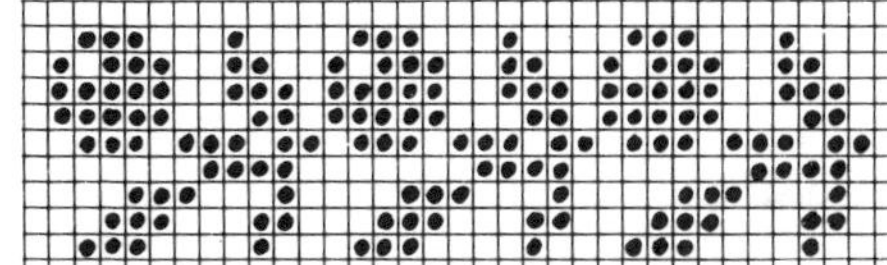

Figure 6.2

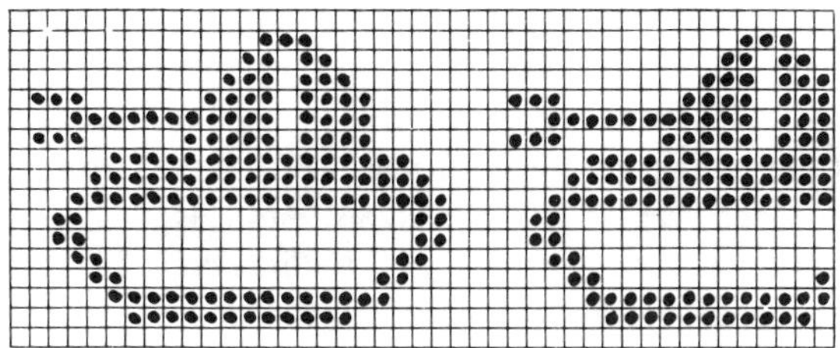

Figure 6.3

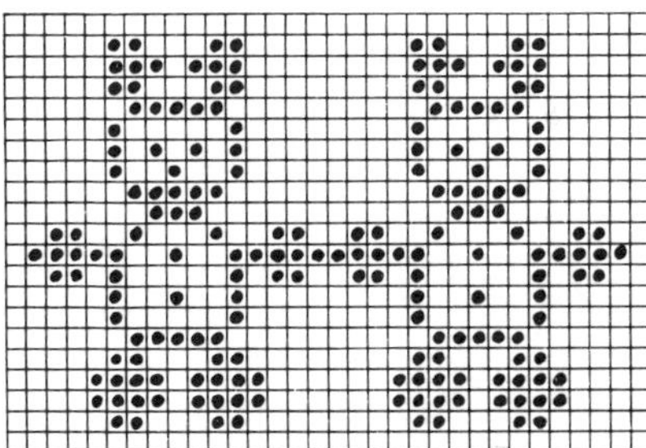

Figure 6.4

Among those who crochet kippot, there are various levels of skill based on the number of colors employed in a single cap, and, to a lesser extent, on the complexity of the design. Beginners form their patterns of a single color on the background color. Complexity increases as three and four colors are used in the patterned border. Skill is also measured by speed of output. Informal contests to see who can crochet a *kippa* the fastest have been reported. Crocheters who work with many colors and complex designs at a high rate of speed are held in high regard. Some crocheters become "professionals" and sell their work – usually not the most complex patterns – in retail shops.

The *kippa sruga* is secured to the head with either a metal bobby pin or a metal clip that snaps into place. Men's haircuts often accommodate the shape of the *kippa*, fuller in front, more cropped further back. While there is a typical positioning of the *kippa sruga*, variations can be observed. For example, *kippot* can be worn askew, reminiscent of the French beret.

Designs on the patterned borders can be divided into geometric, stylized plant, letter, and animal designs, among others. Geometric designs and plant designs are the most frequently found (Figs. 6.1 and 6.2). These may also include the wearer's name or a group to which he belongs, a place name such as "Jerusalem," political slogans such as "Golan is Ours!", or even the name of his employer. Other occupational themes are depicted graphically. For example, small tanks might make up the border design for a man in the Israeli Army (Fig. 6.3). There are other graphic representations. Animals such as bunnies or teddy bears are used on "kiddie *kippot*" for little boys (Fig. 6.4). Another popular design is the word "Jerusalem" written so as to form the silhouette of the walled Old City.

Designs relate to various personal characteristics. Caps made for a businessman are worked in subdued colors (mainly black and white) and geometric designs, creating a kind of "grey flannel *kippa*." Informants indicated that for a sensitive, artistic type of man, floral patterns are used. Extroverted men select brighter colors. Attempts to construct a more detailed typology of designs were frustrating. Innovation of design is highly regarded. Therefore, it is difficult to find two *kippot* that are exactly alike.

Kippot appear to be regarded as part of a dress ensemble. They generally match what a person is wearing, especially in color. Some men will request a new *kippa* if they buy a new shirt or sweater and have no *kippa* in their wardrobe to match it. This ensembling of *kippot* with other aspects of attire is reflected in special *kippot* worn with uniforms, such as those for the army or the bus company. Men may be involved in the selection of color or designs for *kippot* if they have the interest.

Kippot in Social Context: Israeli Society

The *kippa sruga* is worn by male members of one segment of Israel's orthodox Jewish subculture. Like many other Israelis, they are mainly descendants of European (Ashkenazi) Jews. Most people associate the rise in popularity of the *kippa sruga* with the early days of Israeli statehood, more than forty years ago. More specifically, the *kippa sruga* is said to have risen in popularity within the B'nai Akiva Youth Movement. The B'nai Akiva developed as the youth arm of the Mizrachi, an organization which aimed to promote *aliyah* (immigration to Israel) from Europe. Unlike so many secular Jewish-European (Ashkenazi) pioneers who immigrated, these immigrants were religious Jews, pioneers who wanted to combine their orthodoxy with work in the fields, who wanted to combine religious study with manual labor, who wanted to be fervently religious and part of the modern world. During the 1950s B'nai Akiva became a worldwide youth movement.[2] Today, world television viewers may catch glimpses of the *kippa sruga* in televized accounts of activities taking place in the Jewish settlements on the occupied West Bank. Many settlers are members of Gush Emunim, a group fervently dedicated to the continued occupation of this area, and they typically wear *kippot srugot.*

Israeli men can be divided into two broad categories on the basis of headcovering. The first is the roughly 80 percent of the population of men who wear no headcovering in public, though they probably wear headcoverings for ritual purposes. The remaining 20 percent who do wear a *kippa* in their daily routines can be divided into three subgroups. The first group is the orthodox Hassidim. They usually wear a black *kippa*, covered when outside by a large-brimmed black hat. The best-known version is the fur *shtreimel* worn for ritual occasions. (This hat and much of the man's garb have their origins in eighteenth-century Poland.) Members of this group are sometimes referred to as "The Black Hats" or "Black Jews." They do not serve in the military and may not even acknowledge the existence of the State of Israel. The second group of *kippa*-wearers are those who visibly display the *kippa sruga*. These men will serve in the military and are highly nationalistic. They are associated politically with the National Religious Party. The third group wears a variety of other embroidered, crocheted, printed, and plain *kippot* (not *kippot srugot)* and are not easily categorized on the basis of political, religious, or other beliefs.

To the very orthodox "Black Jews," the men who wear the *kippa sruga* and other decorated *kippot* seem frivolous, not serious enough about their religion. To those who wear no *kippa,* the men who wear the *kippa sruga* often seem too zealous, particularly in military matters (although their comparatively moderate religious zeal is more acceptable than that of the "Black Jews").[3] In donning the *kippa sruga* the man makes a statement about his position on a religious continuum and about his political beliefs, and can often give clues about his occupation and personality. In a complex nation such as Israel, the *kippa sruga* helps define a certain segment of the population. Women in Israel do not wear the *kippa*, although there is no specific injunction against it.

Kippot in Religious Context: Jewish Law

Life for the orthodox Jews, including those who wear the *kippa sruga*, is governed by the body of traditional Jewish law known as the *halacha*. At the core of the *halacha* are the 613 *mitzvot* or commandments that penetrate every aspect of Jewish life, from religious ritual to cooking to sexual activities. There are daily prayers, weekly Sabbath observances, and yearly ceremonial obligations, as well as other ritual events that occur during the life cycle: at birth, the coming of age of religious responsibility (usual at the age of thirteen), marriage, and death.

One prominent theme of *halachic* law is separation, for example, the separation of the sacred from the profane, the Sabbath from the rest of the week, the kosher from the nonkosher, the Jew from the Gentile, and the men from the women. This emphasis on separation was adaptive for preservation of cultural boundaries as Jews dispersed throughout the world during the Diaspora. There is a strict separation of men and women in Jewish law, most visible in the segregation of men from women during religious services. By law, women are exempt from any religious duties that are time-bound or public, such as praying or attending religious services at a specific time. The resulting apparent inequality is often difficult to understand from an outside, feminist perspective. An emic interpretation points to the different yet complementary roles played by males and females. "The private spiritual act is enjoined for both men and women, but for women it is the approach to the divine as the public is for males" (Prell 1981:424). "While the male role may, because of its public nature, seem more glamourous, the female role is equally important and equally valued" (Meiselman 1978:62). The center of the Jewish woman's religious expression is the home. "The family has always been the unit of Jewish existence, and while the man has always been the family's public representative, the woman has been its soul. . . . The Jewish woman is the soul and inspiration of the Jewish home. . . . The highest ideal to which a human being can aspire is to dedicate his life completely to the service of God. For a woman this means the creation of a Jewish home" (Meiselman 1978:16, 26). Thus, "a woman makes a Jewish home and enables her husband and son to pursue study" (Prell 1981:424) for, as Meiselman notes (1978:32), "The Talmud tells us . . . the enabler of an act is greater than the performer. Enabling is a fundamental Jewish act and not a secondary level of performance."

Dress technology, too, is affected by religious edicts. In terms of *halachic* law, the Bible issues a prohibition on cross-sex dressing and a prohibition against the mixing of flax and wool (*sha'atnez*) in the construction of fabrics for clothing. Talmudic law, the result of the interpretation of Biblical law, adds further injunctions, for example, specifications about tying *tzizit* (corner tassels) on the prayer shawl or *tallis*. The practice of covering the head comes from neither *halachic* law nor Talmudic law, but rather from *minhag* (usuage or custom). Hence, there is controversy surrounding the matter of males covering their heads. To some it is a custom, to others it is a law, to still others it is a custom that has become law.[4] Within the context of Jewish law, then, the making and giving of *kippot* allows a woman to perform the *mitvah* of enabling male relatives and friends to fulfill their obligation to cover their heads and, in general, to meet their spiritual responsibilities.

The matter of women covering their heads, or more particularly their hair, is another matter dictated by custom rather than law. Some Orthodox women cover their hair only in the synagogue. Others cover their hair whenever they leave the home. Within certain Orthodox communities, married women will shave their heads and wear wigs, in some instances even glamourous ones, when out of the home. Others will cover their hair with scarfs. The rationale for this covering of the hair is given different interpretations. To some, it is an expression of modesty. To others, "exposed hair equals nudity, and seeing it would therefore be sexually provocative to men" (Schneider 1984:236).[5]

Kippot in the Context of the Jewish Home and Community

A girl's first efforts to crochet a *kippa sruga* may take place within the home, by producing *kippot* for brothers and fathers. A *kippa* is offered as a gift, as a token of affection. The fineness, attention to detail, and time investment make this an appropriate symbol of caring. (Indeed, a man in public with a crocheted *kippa* lacking in detail suggests an isolated person with insufficient social ties).

The *kippa sruga* also plays a role in the socialization of younger members of the community. The daughter of the family may learn to crochet from her mother, female relatives, or female peers as part of her socialization into the role of an observant woman. A son learns to wear the *kippa* at home. As soon as he is old enough to keep one on his head, probably around two years, he will begin to wear one. His mother, no doubt through concerted effort, keeps the *kippa* on her two year old, helping him to fulfill the injunction to cover his head. The men of the family may have a special *kippa sruga* for the Sabbath and Holy Days. Traditionally, this one is white with blue or black border designs. When the boy arrives at the age of religious responsibility and becomes a *bar mitzvah*, he will likely have a special new one. For his wedding, too, a special new *kippa* would be made, likely by his fiancee. When he is old enough to join the B'nai Akiva youth organization or some similar group, he will want especially fine *kippot*.

Within the religious community the adolescent subsystem is a very active area of *kippot* exchange. Young boys and girls do not engage in the same dating rituals known in more secular adolescent communities. *Kippa* exchange becomes a means of communication. A young girl will offer *kippot srugot* to her male friends. Later she will begin making *kippot* for her more serious suitors. In fact, she will probably reach her peak output of *kippot* during this courtship phase of her life. A girl can show a young man her interest (in a socially acceptable way) by crocheting him a *kippa*. A young man can indicate his interest by asking a girl if she would make him a *kippa*. It is an item of exchange in the courtship ritual. During their teens, girls will get together and trade designs. Crocheting takes place everywhere – at home, riding the bus, during classes at school. After marriage there is a decline in the woman's *kippot* production, except perhaps when she has small sons. Then she waits until her daughter is old enough to learn.

In the course of this research, little information was provided on the origin of the *kippa sruga*. Most informants guessed that its techniques were brought by European immigrants to Israel. It is likely that the *kippa sruga* developed out of the folk needlework tradition of Europe, sustained and augmented in Israel because of its similarity to the many similar folk needlework traditions brought by Jews entering from all points of the Diaspora. Like Israeli folk dancing, it is a synthesis of technical and symbolic features from a wide geographic domain. And like Israeli folk dancing, it is easy to learn and execute. It is a "democratic" technique. The development of the technology of the *kippa sruga* also appears to be related to the nineteenth-century Western ideology known as the "cult of domesticity" (Bose 1987:267), which elevated the social activity of mothering to an important task and women's homemaking to a profession. Within this ideology, needlework was a highly appropriate activity for women.

Conclusions

The example of the *kippa sruga* has provided an opportunity to study the relationship of domestic technology to gender. The *kippa sruga* is a remarkably simple example of technology that produces apparel. An unusually small item of dress, it requires only a simple tool and a small amount of ordinary materials to execute, and it can be mastered with ease. Yet even in this simple example, technology plays a role in the reproduction of gender and serves to reinforce gender boundaries within a particular subculture.

In various cultures throughout the world there are examples that show how technology, specifically fiber arts, reinforces gender boundaries. These examples are most often found in agricultural societies, where the fiber arts have been well appreciated for their metaphoric depiction of transformation: fiber from nature (plants and animals) is transformed into culture (cloth). The resulting cloth can then be a vehicle for further symbolic elaboration on themes of an even cosmic significance. Consider the relationship of rain clouds and cotton (both symbols of fertility) among the Pueblo Indians, or the brocaded "prayers for rain" embellishing the *huipiles* of some Maya Indians. Although women are usually associated with these fiber arts, sometimes men occupy this place. Among the Pueblo Indians, for example, traditionally the men were the weavers, and the symbolic power associated with cloth was in their hands. Perhaps it is agricultural life that links the *kippa sruga* to other fiber art traditions. It is as if the *kippa sruga* is a vestige of these earlier connections between fiber and fecundity, passed on to needleworkers from the Diaspora, foremothers of Israeli immigrants.

It would be tempting to offer the example of the *kippa sruga* as a classic example of what is referred to as "dual spheres." This maligned phrase has come under criticism in recent years as the overly simplistic relegation of men to public spheres and women to private spheres of life. In this conception, women, relegated to the private, domestic sphere, are thought to gain "psychological security and a firm sense of self worth and importance" despite their "secondary social and cultural status" (Chodorow 1974:66). However, a deeper examination reveals that the concept of dual spheres is of limited utility here: the *kippa sruga*, while an item of primarily domestic manufacture, reflects many meanings in the public sphere, both in the orthodox community and the world at large.

For a woman, the making of the *kippa sruga*, like many of the everyday activities engaged in by the skillful homemaker, may help define gender identity and fulfill a role as enabler of men in her family. Within the boundaries of home and community gender is reproduced as the young girl learns skills for a gendered repertoire. Her *kippot* may distinguish her as one who fulfills a *mitzvah* to beautify. She may show her competence, and gain personal satisfaction in performing this creative act. The activity is not strictly homebound. It is an activity that can be conducted "in the world" – on the bus, at school. The qualities that this activity symbolizes can be seen by the public. The *kippa sruga* becomes a visual metaphor for creative, resourceful domesticity. Within the context of women in the community, the technology of *kippa*-making reinforces social bonds through the exchange of patterns. In addition, it provides opportunities for status enhancement as skills of individual performers are recognized for their speed, level of technical competence, or innovation.

The exchange of *kippot* strengthens the bonds between males and females within the community as part of the courtship ritual as well as within the family, and thereby strengthens the community. The wearing of the *kippa sruga* establishes the distinction in gender; it helps to define the observant male, one who can identify himself as an individual through his dress style and complementary *kippa*. Within the subculture as a whole, it distinguishes those who belong from those who do not. It is analogous to March's finding concerning weaving and the Tamang of Nepal: the crocheted *kippa* is "a representation of ethnic and religious solidarity" (1983:739). But the *kippa sruga* clearly separates the wearer from the ultra-Orthodox, signifying a special kind of individual – religious yet nationalistic and individualistic.

In recent years in the United States there have been women who have donned the *kippa*, including the *kippa sruga*, as well as the *tallis* or prayer shawl, during synagogue services as a way of signifying their more active participation in ritual. Such challenges to dress customs have been subject to debate. Are the *kippa* and *tallis* distinctly male items of attire? Does the donning of a *kippa* or a *tallis* violate the biblical injunction against cross-sex dressing? What does the donning of the *kippa* have to do with feminism and women's rights? Such questions about the meanings of the *kippa* suggest further avenues for investigation.

In summary, the technology of the *kippa sruga* reflects the "social vision," in Pfaffenberger's terms, which calls for the strict separation of men and women, the reinforcement of male individuality, and an attitude of modernity. The technology also reflects the woman's responsibility to create a Jewish home where family members learn and are helped to fulfill religious obligations. The object and its technology have been used as one way to help "maintain a symbolically meaningful environment."

Notes

1. In this paper I use "gender" following Hess and Ferree to mean "a principle organizing social arrangements, behavior and even cognition," "a system for dividing people into distinct, non-overlapping categories despite their natural variability on any particular characteristic" (1987:16).
2. Spread of the *kippa sruga* most likely came about as a byproduct of this youth movement. In the United States, the Conservative Synagogue Youth organization was active in sponsoring trips to Israel and generally stimulating enthusiasm for Zionism among young Jewish Americans. Teenagers traveling to Israel brought home *kippot srugot* and learned to crochet them. Their parents traveled and brought back these *kippot*, too. The *kippa sruga* enjoyed a surge of popularity after the victory in the Six-Day War in an outburst of Jewish pride.
3. Outside of Israel, the meaning of the *kippa sruga* appears to be different. In South Africa, for example, the *kippa sruga* seems to indicate a more orthodox person than it does in Israel. A man who wears a *kippa sruga* in South Africa and then emigrates to Israel may literally have to "change hats." He may have to don a plain black *kippa* in Israel to communicate the same degree of religiosity that the *kippa sruga* indicated in South Africa.

   In the United States, the *kippa sruga* seems to indicate a person of lesser religiosity than it does in Israel. The man wearing a *kippa sruga* in the United States might, for example, drive to the synagogue on Saturday, unthinkable to the Israeli who wears a *kippa sruga*. An American who wears a *kippa sruga* in the United States who visits Israel may be embarrassed because he is "read" as more observant than he is. It does not appear that political beliefs are communicated by the *kippa sruga* in the United States or South Africa. However, there does seem to be a message, at least in the United States, that the wearer is a modern religious person and one who supports the Zionist cause.

It is likely that the experiences of wearers outside of Israel (where they would be in a minority) would be different in certain ways. The general population might not know how to evaluate this item of apparel; it might not even be read as a religious symbol.

4. The *kippa* is worn constantly by some, even in sleep. As one man put it, "A Jew covers his head as a sign of respect for God. . . . And – tell me, please – am I not still a Jew when I'm sleeping?" (Arden 1975:284). Like other religious articles, a worn-out *kippa* would receive special burial, perhaps in a synagogue.
5. See Schneider 1984:234–41 for a more complete discussion of women's dress and Orthodoxy.

References

Arden, H., "The Pious Ones," *National Geographic Magazine*, Vol. 148, No. 2, August 1975, pp. 276–298.

Bose, C.E., "Dual Spheres," in B.B. Hess and M.M. Ferree (eds.), *Analyzing Gender: A Handbook of Social Science Research*, Newbury Park: Sage Publications, 1987, pp 267–285.

Chodorow, N., "Family Structure and Feminine Personality," in M.R. Zimbalist and L. Lamphere (eds.), *Woman, Culture and Society*, Stanford: Stanford University Press, 1974, pp. 43–66.

Davis, E. and E., *Hats and Caps of the Jews*, Jerusalem: Massada Ltd. Publishers, 1983.

Emery, I., *The Primary Structures of Fabrics*, Washington, D.C.: The Textile Museum, 1980.

Encyclopaedia Judiaca, "Dress," Vol. 6, Jerusalem: Keter Publishing House, 1971, pp. 213–25.

Hess, B.B., and M.M. Ferree (eds.), *Analyzing Gender: A Handbook of Social Science Research*, Newbury Park: Sage Publications, 1987.

Krauss, S., "The Jewish Rite of Covering the Head," *Hebrew Union College Annual*, Vol. 19, 1945, pp. 121–68.

Lechtman, Heather, "Style in Technology – Some Early Thoughts," in H. Lechtman and R.S. Merrill (eds.), *Material Culture: Styles, Organization, and Dynamics of Technology*, St. Paul: West Publishing Co., 1977.

Levi, S.B., and S.R. Kaplan, *Across the Threshold: A Guide for the Jewish Homemaker*, New York: Farrar, Strauss and Cudahy, 1959.

March, K.S., "Weaving, Writing and Gender," *Man*, Vol. 18, No. 4, 1983, pp. 729–44.

Meiselman, M., *Jewish Woman in Jewish Law*, New York: Ktav Publishing House, 1978.

Metzger, T. and M., *Jewish Life in the Middle Ages*, New York: Alpine Fine Arts, 1982.

Pfaffenberger, B., "Fetishised Objects and Humanised Nature: Towards and Anthropology of Technology," *Man*, Vol. 23, 1988, pp. 236–52.

Prell, R.-E., "The Dilemma of Women's Equality in the History of Reform Judaism," *Judaism: A Quarterly Journal of Jewish Life and Thought*, Vol. 30, No. 4, Fall 1981, pp. 418–26.

Schneider, S.W., *Jewish and Female: Choices and Changes in Our Lives Today*, New York: Simon and Schuster, 1984.

Siegel, R., and M. and S. Strassfeld, comps. and eds., "*Kippah*," *The Jewish Catalog*, Philadelphia: The Jewish Publication Society of America, 1973.

Straus, R., "The 'Jewish Hat' as an Aspect of Social History," *Jewish Social Studies*, Vol. 4, 1942, pp. 59–72.

7

Quilted Apparel and Gender Identity

An American Case Study

Catherine A. Cerny

Social life for the individual is multidimensional. In American society, one interacts with many different individuals, social groups, and subcultures during the course of one's life, if not during the course of the day. These social contacts yield diverse opportunities for individual action and expression. Each becomes an arena in which society potentially mediates individual consciousness of self. These interactive contexts include communities united by social, religious, or political ideologies; neighborhoods based on ethnic origins; and social groups unified by occupations or leisure interests. Each group might be characterized by some distinctive clothing patterns; for example, the business suit of the corporate world or the uniforms of the Little League baseball team. In each case, we, as outsiders, generally assume that distinctive dress – a "uniform" of sorts – functions to demarcate the group from others in larger society and to suggest the sharing of particular values and attitudes among the membership. At the same time, dress performs a socializing function for the participant: dress facilitates the person's identification with the values of the collective body and mediates integration as member of the community (Hamilton and Hamilton 1989). Widely acknowledged is the former – the capacity of dress to communicate the social identity of the wearer. Less widely explored is the latter – the function of dress as a "vehicle" of culture. From this perspective, dress mediates the rationalization of self and society.

Can observation of a predominately female community and its social discourse yield insight into the means by which some women utilize dress to mark selfhood? Lenz and Myerhoff (1986) have described a "feminine culture" that, in spite of its substantial overlap with the more dominant "masculine culture," is distinctive. It is a culture centered in women's friendships; feminine "values, behavioural style, world view" become apparent through social interactions (Lenz and Myerhoff 1986: 6). This paper addresses this question by focusing on the wearing of quilted apparel by members within an American quilt guild.[1] Specifically, I expand the meaning of quilted clothing beyond its function to reference the individual as a "quilter" and question how a woman's production and use of quilted apparel become means of characterizing gender.

Women and Textile Expression: Quilt Guilds and the Quilt Tradition

Recent studies have addressed women's occupation in the fabrication and use of textiles. From a cross-cultural perspective, Schneider and Weiner (1986) outlined the powerful ways that diverse textiles have manifested cultural values and social relationships. More specifically, investigators of American society have examined the significance of the domestic art (needlework) tradition as an expression of female experience and as evidence of her creativity (Dewhurst, MacDowell, and MacDowell 1979; Maines 1974–1975; Parker and Pollack 1981). Parker (1986) identified a relationship between the history of Euro-American embroidery and the social construction of femininity. Recently, particular attention has been given to quiltmaking (Farb 1975; Radecki 1982; Stewart 1974). In their study of a rural quilt club, Ice and Shulimson (1979) noted that the members' quiltmaking served to reaffirm values toward family and community, as well as qualities of independence and interdependence in the quilter.

Throughout the United States, quilt guilds have built upon strong friendships between quilters within an urban or rural community. Each quilt guild is part of a broadening network of guilds nationally and internationally, stimulated by the American Bicentennial in 1976 and supported by a proliferation of quilt magazines and books, quilt museums, and quilt symposiums and exhibitions during the 1980s.

Integral to modern quiltmaking has been quilt tradition. Quilt manuals, written during the early half of the twentieth century, documented this tradition. These books presented not so much a factual record of quiltmaking during the nineteenth century but a sentimental account of the women who quilted and the meanings that quiltmaking had in their lives. Webster (1928 [1915]) identified the dual values of community and individuality as central to women's quiltmaking.

> The dominant characteristics of the quilt making are companionship and concentrated interest. Both of these qualities, or – better yet – virtues, must be in evidence in order to bring a quilt to successful completion. The sociable,

> gossipy 'quilting,' where the quilt is put together and quilted, has planted in every community in which it is an institution the seeds of numberless lifelong friendships. . . . Content with life, fixity of purpose, development of individuality, all are brought forth in every woman who plans and pieces a quilt. The reward of work lies, not only in the pleasure of doing, but also in the joy of possession – which can be passed on even to future generations, for a well made quilt is a lasting treasure. (Webster [1915] 1928:149)

At the same time, these authors established the significance of the quilt. It was a visual record – "the precursors of the photograph album" (Ickis 1949:267) – that commented on a woman's perceptions and experiences, especially as they concerned family life. "The American patch quilt and the woven coverlet became documents revealing the character, temperament and activities of women (and sometimes the men) who designed and made them. Not only new names for traditional designs, but new patterns, were created which, sometimes structurally, sometimes pictorially, but more often merely by name, reflected the hardships through which families passed in the epic experience of making a new home in a new land" (Peto 1939:xiv–xv). By elaborating on the technique and social context of quiltmaking, these quilt "historians" provided modern women with one means of putting daily life in perspective.

One way a traditional view of female identity has reinforced modern values is evidenced in the members and activities of American quilt guilds. A former president of Minnesota Quilters Inc. commented to the guild membership in her monthly column: "Yesterday, I was playing a familiar role, superwoman! I don't exactly fill out the costume like Lynda Carter, but I was accomplishing four tasks at one time. . . . I sighed wearily and then took a deep, deep breath and thought, *Priorities*. . . . I'm looking forward to a cold, dull January. It will give me time to curl up under a quilt and slow down and make firm my resolution to take time for my family, friends, and quilting" (Bradford 1983:2). The late twentieth-century quilt has built upon this tradition and become a context in which women can reaffirm traditional roles within the family. At the same time, the guild is a community outside of the family that provides support as the woman establishes autonomy in modern society. One member of the quilt guild characterized the organization[2] as "a group of people who can appreciate your interest and have understanding for the sorts of problems you may encounter. . . . There is comfort in knowing you are not alone and the support and encouragement of those with similar interests is more meaningful than groundless praise of those who have never had the experience" (as quoted from questionnaire in Cerny 1987).

Minnesota Quilters Inc.

Minnesota Quilters Inc. has a membership of more than eight hundred quilters and is located in the urban communities of Minneapolis and St. Paul. The typical member is female, married with adult children, between forty and fifty years of age, employed in full- or part-time work and with household income between $30,000 and $50,000. While the majority of the members enjoy quiltmaking principally as a leisure activity, some women gain income through quiltmaking, directly – by selling quilted items, or indirectly – as storeowners, salesclerks, or teachers.

Quilt events are scheduled to allow selective participation within the subculture, as well as to maximize periods of individual quiltmaking. Whereas the regularity of monthly meetings sustains the quilter's interest throughout the year, the fall retreat and spring symposium encourage total immersion in a "quilt culture," with two to four days of workshops, lectures, exhibits, and conversations with friends. At the same time, guild events guide the member as she focuses her quilting interests and refines technical and design skills necessary for expression. The guild enables each woman to learn more about quiltmaking techniques and historic traditions, and provides opportunities for her to share her insights and talents and gain recognition for accomplishments.

Today, as in the past, quiltmaking is a social activity that draws upon cooperative action to enhance individual achievement and self-esteem. Values of independence and interdependence, of family and community, are continually recalled through stories about the isolated pioneer quilter and her quilts; at the same time, the values are redefined through modern discourse and action. In this respect the modern guild is reminiscent of the nineteenth-century quilting bee, in which women gathered to quilt and finish a neighbor's quilt. The community supports the individual member. According to one president, "*full* benefits of membership depend on willingness of individual members to participate. We can create quality and substance in our organization by sharing our special skills, opportunities and talents. . . . we have a tremendously diverse body of experiences from which to draw" (Sidebottom 1985:3). From the member's perspective, the friendship and stimulation gained through contact with other quilters are central to her participation in guild events. Each quilter "shares" with and is "inspired" by other quilters. Members emphasize the importance of common interests and understanding, of "speak[ing] the same language" or of having "a kindred spirit." One quilter summed up what was special about being a Minnesota Quilter: "The fellowship with women of all ages from which inspiration flows."

Quilted Apparel: Scope of Apparel Use

The examination of dress among quilters in a large quilt guild in Minnesota posed an initial dilemma. The significance of a quilter's dress, if indeed there was a characteristic dress, was not immediately apparent. There appeared to be no pattern of wearing apparel as a "uniform" of quilter identity. At any monthly meeting, a small percentage of members wore some form of quilted apparel as part of a clothing ensemble. Most frequently this garment was a vest or jacket – less frequently, a dress or skirt. Cooler weather or meeting in an air-conditioned building might account for some seasonal fluctuations, as members might select a quilted vest or jacket rather than a sweater.

Yet, there were factors that correlated with increased visibility of the garments. The wearing of quilted apparel by the membership became more widespread during special events, especially the annual quilt exhibit and symposium (Plate 7.1). At the same time, quilted apparel was seen in other contexts: women displayed quilted garments, along with other quilted items, in show-and-tell segments of monthly meetings. Style shows of quilted apparel were held both as an alternative for monthly meeting programming, as well as part of evening program-

Plate 7.1 Women, each wearing a quilted vest, examine quilts on exhibit during the guild's spring symposium. (Photograph by Catherine Cerny)

ming for the annual symposium (Plate 7.2). Workshops on design and construction techniques for quilted apparel were popular educational alternatives (Plate 7.3).

Furthermore, responses to a questionnaire suggested the extent of quilted apparel, not otherwise apparent in observation of guild activities. The majority of the respondents (69 percent) owned at least one quilted patchwork garment and/or had made a quilted garment (72 percent). Yet, as backed up by observations, the members tended not to wear quilted apparel to Minnesota Quilters Inc. activities. Only 2 percent of the respondents noted that they wore quilted garments all of the time, whereas 28 percent responded that they wore such garments half or most of the time. Wearing quilted apparel was not limited to Minnesota

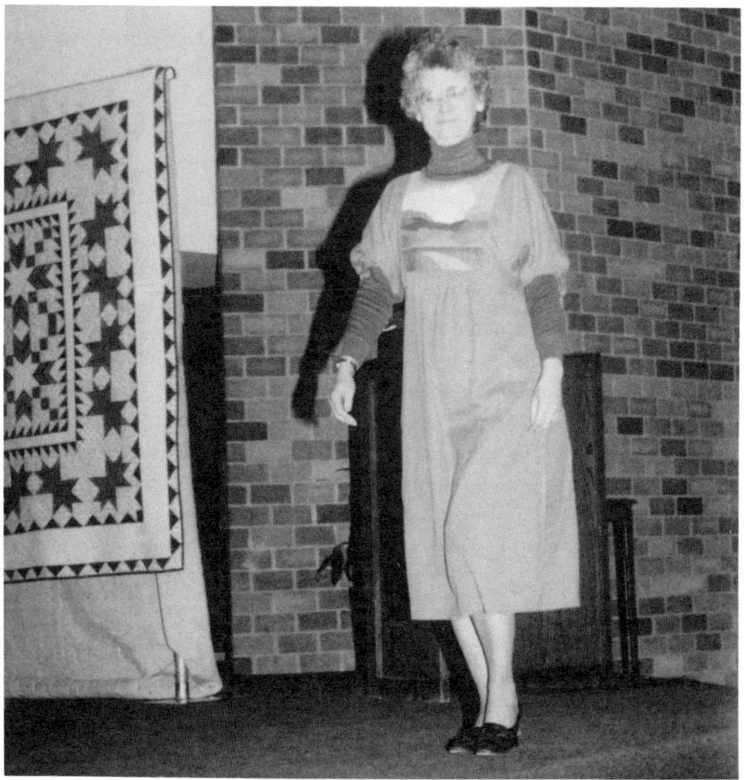

Plate 7.2 Guild member wears a quilted dress during the style show of the guild's spring symposium. (Photograph by Catherine Cerny)

Plate 7.3 Guild member demonstrates the use of hand-dyed fabrics in quilted apparel at a monthly meeting. (Photograph by Catherine Cerny)

Quilters Inc. activities; the women also noted wearing quilted apparel for socializing, shopping and running errands, work and professional duties, church activities, and recreational activities.

Making quilted apparel appeared to be more extensive than wearing quilted apparel. Over the years, 71 percent of the members had made at least one garment; within the previous year, 50 percent of the respondents had either worked on or completed a garment. These garments were made for personal or professional use (64 percent for themselves, 12 percent for teaching display), as gifts (44 percent for immediate family, 18 percent for distant relatives, and 8 percent for friends), or for sale or commission (9 percent).

What we start to see is a pattern in which the quilted vest is more than simply something to be worn. Equally if not more important is the garment's use as gift. I am suggesting that to understand the significance of quilted apparel, we must view it on parallel terms with other items made by the quilter; that we view quilted apparel as one type of quilt. This necessitates noting the circumstances of quiltmaking in the guild, with special attention to quilted apparel. Quilted apparel is embedded in the quiltmaking idiom; it acquires meaning largely from this cultural context. Correspondingly, members understand the significance of the garment in large part from their participation in quiltmaking and guild activities.

Presence of Quilted Apparel in "Quilt Culture"

Educational and display activities are the principle contexts in which quilters collectively formulate the expression and then communicate meaning both to self and others. The woman's participation in the quilt community, either through defined activities or informal interactions, enables her to develop quiltmaking skills and to integrate creative pursuits as part of her lifestyle and as complementary to outside social responsibilities. Educational activities, including workshops and programs, develop the student's artistic and technical skills initially necessary for quiltmaking, and then for translating the traditional two-dimensional quilt format to one designed to fit the body and complement the person. (For example, the log-cabin pattern, a popular style of bed quilt, has been adapted to quilted jackets.) At the same time, instructors stimulate and direct individual creativity. Samples shown by the instructor demonstrate ways of personalizing design to suit a range of individual preferences and expressive objectives. In such cases, a student can see how changes in scale, block arrangement, color, and placement on a garment can produce a unique log-cabin jacket.

Display activities include show-and-tell, quilt exhibits, and style shows. Show-and-tell has been cited as a primary reason for membership. Show-and-tell segments during the monthly meetings and workshops encourage each member to share her work, be it in progress or completed. At the same time, with applause from other quilters, a member gains a sense of social approval for her accomplishment. In her comments about the quilt, the woman elaborates on several different factors about the quiltmaking process or on the use of a completed garment. In garments made for personal use, the woman points out the source of the design, technical process, or coordination of the garment within an outfit, and thus emphasizes her creativity in problem solving. At the same time, she makes references to others, including acknowledgment of inspiration from an instructor, technical assistance from peers, and support from family. Since many garments are made as gifts to relatives, much of a quilter's characterization of the garment relates back to the recipient. The quilter comments on the significance of the quilt pattern (the appliqué sailboat represents a boy's interest in sailing), the selection of certain fabrics (the fabrics were scraps left over from dresses made for her daughter), or the garment's use as gift (a Christmas present for a grandchild).

The style show becomes a more formal setting in which quilters, known for their skills, stimulate their peers with new ways of adapting quiltmaking to apparel design and use. The commentor points out certain aesthetic features or technical innovations, and also notes the context in which the garment was made – such as a personal artistic exploration, a gift to a son, a garment to be sold on commission, or an example to be used in the workshop. Just as guild members gain ideas for future projects, they can recognize the capacity of quilted apparel to mark the particular skills, interests, and attitudes of the quilter.

Finally, the day-to-day activities of the spring symposium become an opportunity for the member to model her own work informally. The aesthetic diversity of the garments characterizes widespread interests and points to the individuality of each quilter. Motivations vary: a teacher is likely to wear a garment that exemplifies her quilting expertise, a store owner might wear her quilted apparel to promote garment patterns, while others might demonstrate an acquired skill or express style preferences. The prevalence of quilted garments heightens the ambience of the special event, in which the woman's day is consumed by attending workshops, visiting the quilt exhibit, and meeting old or making new friends.

Special Characteristics of Quilted Apparel

Guild members were asked in the questionnaire to comment on the special nature of the quilted garment. (As indicated in note two, all uncited quotations are taken from written responses to the questionnaire.) These comments yield insight into the personal significance of garment making and use, in which garment and quilt are parallel; both are creative outlets and opportunities for expression. Four themes are apparent: (1) the experiential effect of wearing a quilted garment; (2) the distinctive form of quilted apparel; (3) its capacity to identify and differentiate quilters; and (4) the sentimental value inherent in making the garment.

The experiential effect of wearing a quilted garment is both visually and tactually pleasing on the quilter's body. One quilter writes: "I like the feel of cotton fabric, the look of pieced patterns and the texture and warmth of quilted layers." Yet, at the same time, the women are concerned with clothing that enhances body and coloring. Whereas the garments "can be designed for the wearer" and "can suit individual tastes," not all quilters look good in the garments. Quilters insist that well-designed garments "complement figure and other garments being worn with them."

Many of the respondents comment on the quilted garment's distinctive form, "individuality" or "uniqueness." It offers an alternative to ready-to-wear apparel because it is "unique, evidently hand made (actually, I think making something by hand, one can put things that mean something to oneself into it – symbols, colors ideas, pictures) . . . it becomes more like a "sacred object" – something as a reminder . . . something to stand between consumerism, mass production, the fashion industry. It personalizes." It is "not off the rack at K. Mart [sic]" or "not seen on the street every day." Furthermore, it is an "opportunity to use creativity" and stresses the communicative capacity of the artist. The quilter's choices are integral to the garment's uniqueness; design, fabric, and colour choices reflect its maker: "the individuality of the garment [lets] each maker select her/his own colors, fabric, patterns, style according [to] individual tastes. There's a pride in wearing a garment you feel you designed and crafted even if it's from a pattern, because as the maker you have made the choices." The garment becomes a means for the quilter to "display" her "workmanship," "interests," and "personality." The garment marks the woman's identity as a quilter: "I really believe it makes a personal statement about my quilting and being a quiltmaker." Others add that the garment "proclaim[s] yourself as a quilter" and shows "another aspect of my life related to quilting to wear what I live."

Finally, sentimental value mediates the creative process. "Love and care" go into the garment's creation and the garment is "very personal to [the] wearer." It is made with the "personal touch." This is especially important to quilted garments made as gifts. One person notes, "So personal, they 'say' I made it especially for you." Others added that the garments were "made with love."

Like the quilter herself, the garment is a unique product, handmade rather than ready-made. Her creative input marks it as special. Not unlike the antique quilt, the quilted garment potentially documents "her character, temperament and activities" (Peto 1939:xiv). Moreover, satisfaction comes from both garment making and from possession. As Webster noted, the historic quilt provided "the pleasure of doing" and "the joy of possession" (Webster [1915] 1928:149). These sentiments about the quiltmaking, recalled in the antique quilt, are attributed to modern versions of the quilt, including quilted apparel.

Significance of Quilted Apparel: Apparel as Quilt

Quilted apparel should not be considered a distinctive clothing sign/symbol system, but part of the larger quilt aesthetic/meaning system bounded by a "quilt culture." The meanings associated with apparel and derived from the quilt meaning system are activated through the quiltmaking idiom, which includes both the process of making quilts or like items and the social activities of the guild.

From this perspective, the idea of the quilt is the "key symbol" (Ortner 1973) from which innovations of use, technology, and design occur. Apparel represents principally an innovation of use. The quilted garment is a quilt form adapted to fit and be transported by the body. Quilt technology and design are modified to concur with the criteria of clothing design.

The quilted garment fulfills the functions of the quilt; it provides warmth and decoration. However, the context of apparel use differs from that of the quilt. For the most part, the modern quilt serves a decorative purpose as bedcover or wallhanging. The quilt (except when displayed in quilt exhibits and show-and-tell) remains within the domestic setting, in proximity to the family. The affection exemplified by the woman making the quilt remains private, shared within the family. Many of these quilts have been made to commemorate special events in the maker's or recipient's life (for example, birth, wedding, anniversary). Care is taken in its daily use; some are preserved as family treasures for the next generation.

In contrast, quilted apparel is clothing worn on the body; the quilter coordinates the garment with other aspects of dress according to her expectations about the social setting. Use extends beyond the family to encompass the quilt guild and the surrounding urban or rural community. The garment explicitly presents the wearer's identity as quilter to those with whom she interacts. However, the quilted garment's use is not limited to the quilter's personal wardrobe. Like other quilted items, apparel becomes gifts to family and friends, instructional examples to illustrate quiltmaking techniques, merchandising examples to promote classes or kits sold through a quilt or fabric shop, handcrafted vests or jackets to be sold through "Christmas boutiques," and/or wearable art to be exhibited in quilt and art shows. Whether part of the quilter's or the recipient's dress, its meaning is activated and perpetuated by regular use in the public setting.

Cultural Vehicle

Taking this analysis to a further point of abstraction, the semiotic perspective offers an opportunity to speculate on a semiosis of self-hood. Meaning is interpreted as a process that takes into account sociocultural context. The significance of the quilted garment is characterized in terms of concurrent metonymic and metaphoric relations that place the guild member in juxtaposition with quilt tradition and American society. In the quilt guild, the women "speak the same language." They share an understanding of tradition and its relevance in modern society. In turn, the meaning of any quilted item is generated through the women's participation in the "quilt culture" and their involvement in quiltmaking.

The metonymic aspect of quilted apparel is two-fold. The quilted garment, by virtue of its construction, stands for all quilts. Simultaneously, the quilted garment, by virtue of its use on the body, stands for the person; it defines identity as quilter and presents this role to others, within and beyond the quilt community. The garment denotes the person's presence as quilter; yet its features elaborate on her specific skills and orientation in quiltmaking.

The metaphoric aspect bridges the metonymic resemblances. The quilted garment, by its definition as quilt, associates one's character as a quilter to one's identity as a woman. The meanings central to "quilt culture" extend to the identification of the quilter's role in American society. While the woman's fabrication of quilted apparel qualifies her orientation to quiltmaking, her use of the garments points to how she wants society to perceive this orientation.

Quilt tradition is understood by the quilter through the quilts of previous generations of American women. The modern woman's role in society is derived from America's past – in the characterization of a "pioneer" identity, centered on the family and community (that is, interdependence), but demonstrating individual initiative and expression (that is, independence). Today, a traditional versus contemporary orientation toward quiltmaking is demonstrated by choice of item (bed cover vs. garment), technique (hand vs. machine piecing or quilting), pattern (established vs. innovative block design), and style and subject matter (literal replication of pine tree pattern vs. original interpretation of landscape). The quilt, designed and made according to nineteenth-century traditions, recalls women's responsibility to family and community; whereas the quilt that innovates upon traditional form focuses on the inventiveness of the quiltmaker in adapting to new and changing social circumstances. While both aspects are associated with the "pioneer quilter," emphasis on one or the other suggests the priority that a modern quilter places on interdependence (traditional) or independence (contemporary).

In the Minnesota case, the guild membership prefers either traditional quilts or traditional and contemporary quilts equally (Cerny 1987). Choices of quilt type, technique, style, and subject matter emphasize the value of interdependence (hand-pieced and quilted log-cabin quilt) or demonstrate a balance between the two values (machine-pieced and quilted log-cabin vest; hand-pieced and quilted dress with inset of original floral design). Correspondingly, the women's participation in the guild, as well as their comments on quiltmaking, point to the value of interdependence. This predominantly female community is a context in which they can reinforce their role in sustaining the extended family as a cohesive unit.

How the quilter uses quilted apparel can activate a more immediate impression of self. As part of dress, the garment identifies the woman as a quilter, with a character commonly associated with quiltmaking (resourceful, creative, artistic, purposeful). Correspondingly, the woman can use quilted apparel to specify certain relationships, ambitions, or attitudes that are important in her social life. As gift, the garment marks the friendship or kinship (qualities of warmth and affection) between quilter and recipient. As instructional sample, the garment exemplifies the quilter's concern with relating the relevance of the quilt tradition to modern women. As merchandising sample or ready-to-wear item, the garment presents the woman's entrance into a business community, not necessarily limited to women. As wearable art, the garment demonstrates a view that quiltmaking is part of mainstream Western art.

Conclusions

Mark Johnson has proposed a theory that meaning is "not merely a matter of how some *individual* might happen to understand something but rather how some *individual as embedded in a (linguistic) community, a culture, and a historical context* understands" (emphasis in original) (Johnson 1987:190). In the case of quilted apparel, the meaning is referenced by a meaning system and elaborated by a quiltmaking idiom. Related to the quilt in terms of technology and design, other quilted items function in parallel symbolic capacities. These quilted items, including the quilted garment, reflect the woman's perceptions of self. In their making, quilts perform a mediating role by exacting meaning from a now timeless domain of female culture, that of the nineteenth-century quilter, to a second, actual domain of twentieth-century life, that of the modern woman. The quilt guild stands at the coincidence of the two realities. Guild events involve the woman in symbolic action of a "quilt culture" and consequently motivate and shape creative expression. As she learns how to manifest her female experiences and relationships through quiltmaking, she expresses a selfhood that values interdependence and independence.

Rather than a single representation of American female identity, we have multiple variations upon this image, be they ideal, normative, or deviant. Quiltmaking is one case in which women can draw upon a cultural "tradition," largely defined by women, to shape a self-hood. Banner (1983) and Freedman (1986) have documented the importance of beauty ideals to gender identity. Likewise, fashion preoccupies the interests of many women as they make their clothing choices. There is a need for researchers to integrate knowledge of its sociocultural basis if a comprehensive understanding of dress and gender is to be achieved.

Notes

1. Major fieldwork of the Minnesota quilt guild was carried out in the United States from October 1984 to September 1985, with additional observations through July 1986. Methods included participant observation of guild activities, review of guild publications, and interviews with members.
2. Comments by members cited in this article are drawn from a questionnaire distributed at the guild's spring symposium in March 1985 (Cerny 1987).

References

Banner, L.W., *American Beauty*, Chicago: University of Chicago Press, 1983.

Bradford, L., "From the President," *Minnesota Quilters News*, Vol. 5, No. 6, 1983, p. 2.

Cerny, C.A., "Quilted Apparel: A Case Study of a Cultural Vehicle," Ph.D. diss., University of Minnesota, 1987.

Dewhurst, C.K., and B. and M. MacDowell, *Artists in Aprons: Folk Art by American Women*, New York: E.P. Dutton, 1979.

Farb, J., "Piecin' and Quiltin': Two Quilters in Southwest Arkansas," *Southern Folklore Quarterly*, Vol. 39, No. 4, 1975, pp. 363–375.

Freedman, R., *Beauty Bound*, Lexington, Massachusetts: Lexington Books, 1986.

Hamilton, J.A. and J.W., "Dress as a Reflection and Sustainer of Social Reality: A Cross-Cultural Perspective," *Clothing and Textiles Research Journal*, Vol. 7, No. 2, 1989, pp. 16–22.

Ice, J., and J.A. Shulimson, "Beyond the Domestic: Women's Traditional Arts and the Creation of Community," *Southwest Folklore*, Vol. 3, 1979, pp. 37–44.

Ickis, M., *The Standard Book of Quilt Making and Collecting*, New York: The Greystone Press, 1949.

Johnson, M., *The Body in the Mind: The Bodily Basis of Meaning, Imagination, and Reason*, Chicago: University of Chicago Press, 1987.

Lenz, E., and B. Myerhoff, *The Feminization of America: How Women's Values Are Changing Our Public and Private Lives*, Los Angeles: Jeremy P. Tarcher, Inc., 1986.

Maines, R., "Fancywork: The Archaeology of Lives," *The Feminist Art Journal*, Vol. 3, No. 4, 1974–1975, pp. 1–3.

Ortner, S., "On Key Symbols," *American Anthropologist*, Vol. 75, pp. 1338–46.

Parker, R., *The Subversive Stitch: Embroidery and the Making of the Feminine*, London: The Women's Press, 1986.

———, and G. Pollack, *Old Mistresses: Women, Art, and Ideology*, New York: Pantheon Books, 1981.

Peto, F., *Historic Quilts*, New York: The American Historical Company, 1939.

Radecki, P., "The Kinship Quilt: An Ethnographic Semiotic Analysis of the Quilting Bee," in Rosan A. Jordan and Susan J. Kalcik (eds.), *Women's Folklore, Women's Culture*, Philadelphia: University of Pennsylvania Press, 1985, pp. 540–64.

Schneider, J., and A. Weiner, "Cloth and the Organization of Human Experience," *Current Anthropology*, Vol. 27, No. 2, 1986, pp. 178–184.

Sidebottom, C., "President's Letter," *Minnesota Quilters News*, Vol. 7, No. 7, 1985, p. 3.

Stewart, S., "Sociological Aspects of Quilting in Three Brethren Churches in Southeastern Pennsylvania," *Pennsylvania Folklife*, Vol. 23, No. 3, 1974, pp. 15–29.

Webster, M.D., *Quilts: Their Story and How to Make Them*, New York: Doubleday, Doran and Co., Inc., 1928 (1915).

8

Lacemaking in Venetian Culture

Lidia D. Sciama

For a class to be ripe for hegemony means that its interests and consciousness enable it to organize the whole of society in accordance with those interests.

—Georg Lukacs,
History and Class Consciousness

This imposed consciousness is a false consciousness for those who are dominated, since it serves the purposes of the superiors but not of the inferiors. It hides from the inferiors the sources of domination and the processes by which it has come about.

—Maurice Bloch,
Marxism and Anthropology

A 'southerner': and what else? But the whole world is South – and especially in its worst aspects.

—Leonardo Sciascia, *1912+1*

Like lace, which is made of separate parts joined to fashion a larger pattern, this paper consists of different sections, some based on anthropological fieldwork, and some on a number of scholarly works. In the first part I describe how lace is made. The second part is a brief account of its history, and in the third part I discuss changes both in the workers' attitudes to the craft and in the symbolism of lace.[1]

My fieldwork was carried out mainly in 1982 in the lagoon island of Burano. Situated about six miles northeast of Venice, Burano forms a small estuary with Mazzorbo, Torcello, Sant'Erasmo, and San Francesco del Deserto. In contrast to Torcello and Sant'Erasmo, which are very sparsely populated, Burano, a cluster settlement with an area of about one square mile, has a population of just under five thousand. It used to be part of a separate commune, but since 1924 it has become an integral part of the Venetian municipality, and is now classified as a *quartiere*. As we shall see, while lace has traditionally been made throughout the city, Burano always has been known as one of the most active lace-making centers, and is particularly noted for its *punto in aria* (needle lace).

To understand the significance of lace in European fashion, as well as the moral values attached to its making, I have followed Roland Barthes's distinction between "image" and "written" clothing, that is, between the visual representations of garments in fashion magazines and the descriptive passages that usually accompany them:

> The sociology of Fashion is directed towards real clothing; the semiology of Fashion is directed towards a set of collective representations. The choice of oral structure therefore leads not to sociology but rather to that "sociologiques" postulated by Durkheim and Mauss in their essay on "Primitive Classification" (*Année Sociologique*, Vol. 6, 1901–2:1–72). . . . The function of the description of Fashion is not only to propose a model . . . but also, and especially, to circulate Fashion broadly as *meaning* (my italics, 1985:10).

However, while Barthes's analysis covers a one-year cycle, and focuses on whole sets of clothing, my study of lace is a historical one. The main starting point for my research is fieldwork, but a diachronic approach is consistent with the cast of mind I have observed in my informants, who generally see their lives in terms of past and present, and who associate their handicraft very strongly with history. Indeed, lace relates to fashion cycles that last far longer than one year. It is regarded as entirely outside the contingencies of fashion, since it acquires great value from antiquity. In contrast to other items of clothing, which are often ephemeral, as they are subject to the caprice of fashion, lace is then considered a "durable."

Concerning the meanings (in Roland Barthes's sense) that emerge from the cultural discourse that in the past accompanied Venetian lacemaking, an important aspect is its connection with female virtue, and particularly with values and norms we generally associate with Mediterranean notions of honor. As numerous ethnographers have shown, such notions of honor – and their supposed feminine counterpart, shame – are very difficult to render in a concise and definitive way, since they clearly have different contents at different times and in different areas. In order to clarify their relevance to lacemaking, however, I should like to provisionally describe "honor and shame" in the Venetian context as an informal code of moral, sexual, and social behavior, which is essentially secular, but is, at the same time, strongly influenced by religious belief and ideology. "Honor-and-shame" folk psychologies are generally based on strong gender oppositions; they view men and women as complementary, in both material and moral terms, and they generally imply that men should be strong defenders of their own and their family's honor. On the other hand, women, for whom Eve is the prototype and the Virgin Mary the unattainable ideal model, are considered fallible and morally frail in ways that could put their men's honor at risk.

"Shame" primarily designates the social and emotional consequence of sin and dishonor, but in this context it also connotes qualities like modesty and reticence, and is viewed as the brake by which women may prevent themselves from sinning. "Shame" is then sometimes equated with "female virtue." However, in this picture, virtue is viewed as almost entirely negative, in as far as women's attainment seems to be mainly that of avoiding dishonor for themselves and their families. That conception of women, in particular the view that they need constant protection, was a strong contributing factor in the organization of female work, and especially, as we shall see, in Italy's Catholic institutions.[2]

Lacemaking and its Origins

The following account of the way lace is made is based on a demonstration by one of Burano's workers, Lucia Costantini, at a craft exhibition in Venice. That she should have been encouraged to speak about her work, reversing the hierarchical control over knowledge and the flow of information (usually from Venice to Burano) is itself a sign of change.

In keeping with a traditional poetics, by which Venetians often assert the "interdependence of environment, tradition and craftsman," Lucia thinks that lacemaking is indissolubly tied to the lagoon landscape. An important aspect of the craft is its continuity between generations of women, and she is very proud of the fact that her simple tools – a needle, a pillow, and a wooden cylinder (*murello*) – once belonged to her grandmother.[3] The basic materials are paper, some cheap cotton cloth, and very fine cotton thread. A design is first drawn (traditionally by a male designer) on the paper, and then is sewn on to a piece of cloth by a stitch that will follow the outlines of the drawing and that will be removed when the work is finished.

The first basis of the lace proper is a buttonhole stitch, called *sacola'*, a Venetian word that bears a very close resemblance to the term for "fisherman's loop," *sagola'*. This forms the part of the textile known as *guipure*, which itself includes several different stitches. A second

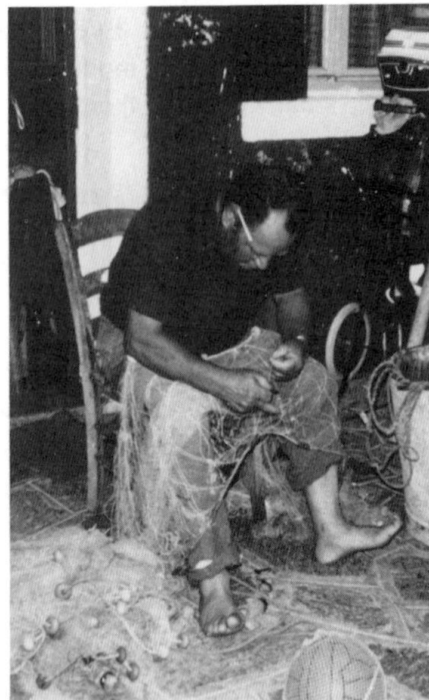

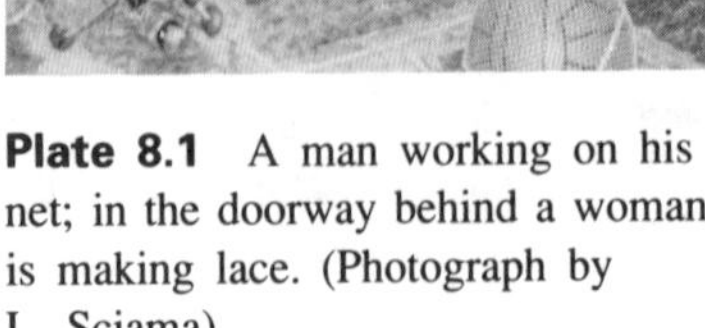

Plate 8.1 A man working on his net; in the doorway behind a woman is making lace. (Photograph by L. Sciama)

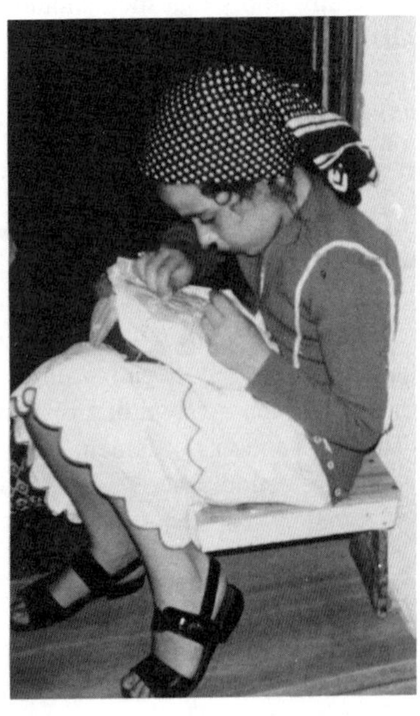

Plate 8.2 Little girl learning to make lace from her grandmother. (Photograph by L. Sciama)

group of stitches form the connecting tissue of lace; these, called *sbari* or "bars," according to the women, are like the bridges of Venice, since they join different "islands" – different parts of the lace, like leaves, flowers, or any other abstract or figurative elements. Finally there is the stitch known as *burano*, which is also called "net" because, as Lucia explains, women included it in their lace after observing the nets made by fishermen. At the last stage in the work, called "relief," a thick thread, which gives the finished work a striking three-dimensional quality, is applied at the edges and at the outlines of designs, then both the paper and the cloth are removed: the lace is completed.

One essential fact to remember is that *burano* is entirely different from bobbin lace, since it is made just with a needle.[4] That, plus the fact that it is "created" by its makers – since the cloth on which it is elaborated serves merely as a support – is considered symbolically meaningful by the women. Before returning to the symbolism of lace, however, I shall present a few historical landmarks.

Since lace, like all textiles, never survives as long as other archaeological remains, discussion of its origins is often based on tiny fragments and on labile arguments. But, while historical speculations, like some of the legendary versions they produce, may give little real knowledge, they are often themselves very rich in meaning. The main questions addressed by historians can be grouped under two headings: first, where, and under what conditions did lace begin, and, if it did not start in Italy, from where did it arrive? Second, in what spheres of Renaissance society did it first become widespread?

To summarize ruthlessly, since the literature is vast: no certainty has been reached about the earliest origin of lace, nor is there any reason to suppose that it had just one beginning. About its diffusion, however, it is now the general view that the craft may have been brought to Italy, or generally to the European Mediterranean, by Moslems in the ninth century.

Concerning the history of ideas on lace, and, in particular, its association with the religious life, some writers have seen a direct connection between the craft's organization in medieval Europe and biblical injunctions about the making of holy textiles for the Temple. Most of the relevant passages are in that part of Exodus which narrates the flight of the Jews from Egypt: before leaving, and following instructions imparted by Moses, the Jews were to ask of the Egyptians "jewels of silver and jewels of gold, and rayment" (Exod. 3.22). These, as well as all manner of rare and precious materials would be used for building the Ark or Tabernacle, that is, a movable Temple in which the Ten Commandments would be carried through the desert. The Tabernacle, as God ordered Moses, was to be covered with a top of pure gold, and screened with ten curtains of "fine twined linen," while, a veil, "made with blue, purple and scarlet linen" would cover the Ark, and thus "divide . . . the holy place and the most holy" (Exod. 26:31).

In addition, Moses ordered the Jews to make "holy garments for splendour and beauty" for Aaron and his sons, whom God had elected to be his ministers. And the task of making such garments was to be assigned to "the wise-hearted" and to those "filled with the spirit of wisdom" (Exod. 28). Here, then, the separation between sacred and profane textiles and the association of the former with the piety of their makers, as well as the corollary that materials and dyes should be given them in a spirit of trust, "without measuring," all begin to outline the main symbolic paradigms which were to become a strong inspiration for much early Venetian lacemaking. But another important aspect of the passages in Exodus is the association of sacred textiles with veiling.

In this case it is the Tabernacle that is ordered to be veiled, but under some circumstances persons, too, must be shielded from view, or from seeing. For example, in Jewish marriage rituals, as in numerous others, brides are veiled and can only be gazed at by their bridegrooms after the wedding ceremony is completed.[5] It is then possible to wonder whether fear of a completely unimpeded vision may have also characterized human relations, especially at important and ritually marked transitions. In particular, underlying analogies between different contexts of veiling, that is, veiling as separation of persons from God, and veiling of brides to symbolize the separation of the two kinship groups about to be joined in the wedding, seem to have become deeply rooted in Christian consciousness in the Middle Ages, when the metaphorical equation of "tabernacle" and "human body as a temporary abode for the soul" became quite a commonplace of devotional literature.

Another hypothesis is that lace may be derived from the knotted fringes at the corners of prayer shawls (tallith), which the Jews were ordered to make after a man was found gathering wood on the Sabbath. Their purpose was, as God said to Moses, "that ye may look upon it, and remember all the commandments of the Lord, and do them; and that ye go not about after your own heart and your own eyes, after which ye use to go astray. . . . And be holy unto your God" (Num. 15:32–41).

Association of that passage with lacemaking connotes ideas like expiation of sin, memory, striving for goodness, and, above all, the need to keep both the heart's desires and the eyes firmly in check – ideas with which the norms of the honor-shame code has already made us

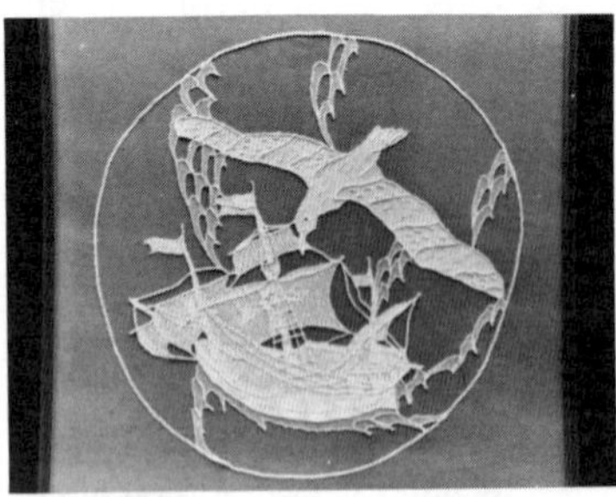

Plate 8.3 The ship of Christopher Columbus, made by Lucia Costantini. (Photograph by L. Sciama)

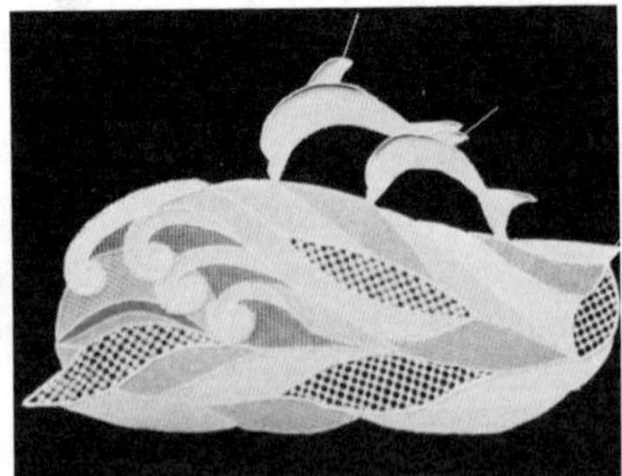

Plate 8.4 "Water," one of a series representing the Four Elements, by Lucia Costantini. (Photograph by L. Sciama)

familiar, and which are often implied or even explicitly related to lacemaking. A related fact is that Burano lace is entirely built on a sequence of knots. This, too, has vast symbolic echoes, relating to magical notions of loosening or binding.[6] These are sometimes just hinted at in folk versions of the origins of lace, but are almost never mentioned in its official or "School" lore. Indeed, according to their various organizers, and until quite recently, the lacemakers' ideal model has been heavily based on the notion that they should be devout, modest, and wise – this is, at least, the image constantly kept alive by their teachers and employers.

History of Lace in European Fashion

A short digression on the product itself, before we discuss the history of its production, may help us to understand some of its symbolic meanings as well as its changing place in gender-related clothing, and its gradual specialization as a supplement to feminine attire.[7] In general, history shows that this delicate and expensive textile is not only connected to the ritual and devotional aspects of life, but is also intimately tied with political change, and its uses often reflect the contrast between conservatism and liberal innovation, and clearly reveal the influence of politics on dress and on "good taste."

Historians agree that lace was first used in liturgical linens and over the vestments of priests, and only later was it widely worn by highly placed and powerful people. Even as it became part of dress, however, it never lost its early religious associations, and, particularly in its use with wedding dresses and veils, it clearly was (and is) meant to underline the body's ritual state, and to exalt the high worth of privileged virginity. The development of its symbolic aspects is also related with empirical facts, like the diffusion of cotton throughout southern Europe during the thirteenth and fourteenth centuries, as well as with changing attitudes toward the body and its health and hygiene (Vigarello 1987:53–94). Indeed, it was in this period that the use of bedsheets and underwear became increasingly widespread, and cotton and linen garments were initially worn *over*, rather than *under*, heavy wool or silk clothes, lace began to acquire great popularity as a decorative elaboration that distinguished the luxurious from the poorer textiles.

As we can see in numerous Renaissance and Baroque portraits (especially by Palma il Vecchio, Titian and Rubens), from about the end of the fifteenth century onward, lace always bordered the necklines and cuffs of women's dresses as well as men's shirts, and it thus marked the borderline between those parts of the body that were always clothed and those that had to be left uncovered. Variations in fashion also reveal important differences in attitudes toward the body; Italian and French styles generally favored upright collars at the back of the neck, which left the throat free and somewhat exposed; but Spanish etiquette required that the collar, usually pleated or roughed, should entirely surround the face. Large high collars thus isolated the head from the body by giving it a frame and a precious background (Olivari in Mottola-Molfina and Binaghi Olivari 1977:14 and ff.).

Spanish dress also heavily differentiated the male from the female figure: luxury and power were always displayed in the apparel of women. And, although power itself was conceived as divinely inspired, on a temporal plane, the women's display of riches clearly reflected the power of their men. Moreover, Spanish male dress, which generally derived from military models, allowed the display of physical prowess through the proud show of muscles and sexual attributes held in an external sheath, while the dress of high-class women tended to obliterate the female bodily structure through the flattening of the breast and the strict covering of the neck and feet, so that any hint of sexuality was suppressed and removed. The only parts of the body that could not be covered, the face and hands, were thus emphasized and detached from other parts of the body by the precious circle of latticed lace collars.

In contrast to Spain and its zones of influence, French fashion favored the use of lace collars only at the back of the head, while the throat was left uncovered and hints of female sexuality were never entirely removed. By about 1630 French necklines became very low, and female dress lost the characteristics that traditionally connected it with devotional images. French fashion – which, following changes in the balance of political power, began to lead that of other European countries – included superabundant use of lace. Masculine collars, lowered over the shoulders, became increasingly wide. The expression of power and the display of wealth through dress were no more only the prerogatives of women. For example, Louis XIV now presented himself as the symbol of his own power, rather than delegating that expressive function to his wife and mistresses. The image of the king as warrior thus gave way to that of the king as "the only person who could afford the most expensive and luxurious things" (Olivari in Mottola-Molfina and Binaghi Olivari 1977:16).

The close relation of lace with political events was clearly shown

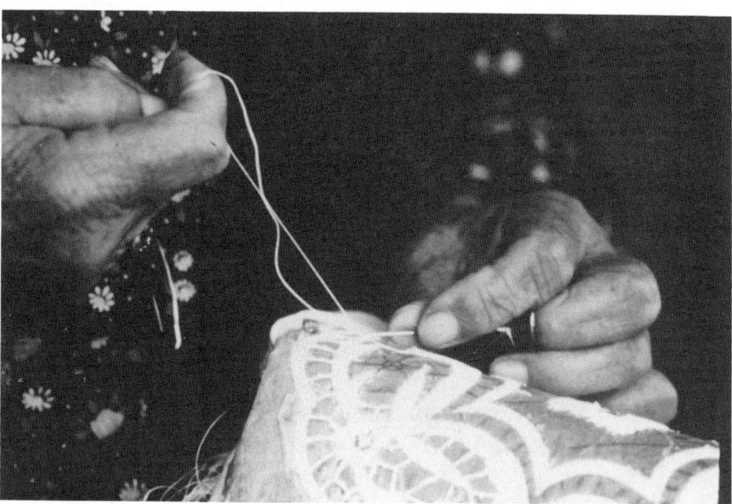

Plate 8.5 Practiced hands. (Information Department, Media Library of the Veneto Region)

Plate 8.6 Lace. (Information Department, Media Library of the Veneto Region)

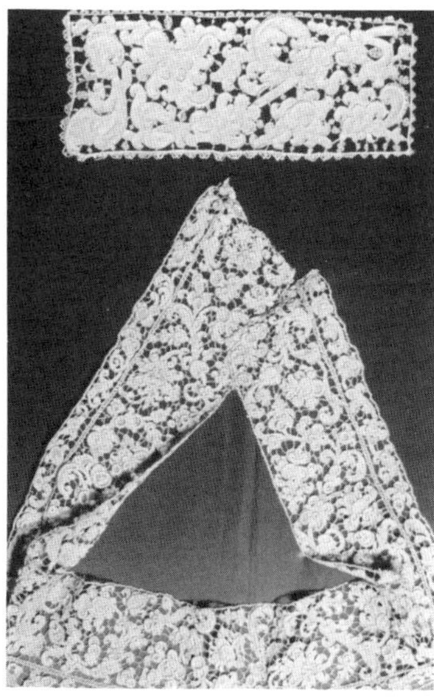

Plate 8.7 More lace. (Information Department, Media Library of the Veneto Region)

during the French Revolution, the Napoleonic period, and the nineteenth-century Restoration. Lace, which had already become less conspicuous in the last quarter of the eighteenth century with the spread of neoclassicism and simple "Greek" dress styles favored by English fashion, was viewed by revolutionaries as an ignominious manifestation of the ancient regime. Lace, however, was brought back into use rather rapidly in the very person of Napoleon I, who wore an elegant *jabot* at his coronation in 1804. Around 1811 it began to come back into general use, mainly as a complement to women's dresses. It was very widely used again between 1830 and 1835 in bourgeois clothes, but by then it had been removed from male attire, and was much used in women's underwear and in household linens.

Lacemaking in Venice from the Renaissance to the Eighteenth Century

It is interesting that the designs and fashions of lace are amply documented in countless portraits of the members of the dominant classes who wore it, but very little is known about its makers. Indeed the predicament of lacemakers, as well as problems met by their historians, is incisively summed up in the description of lace craft as "this celebrated black labour . . . which concerned a large part of Venice's female population, but which was not in any way protected by the then valid corporate system." For, unlike weaving and embroidery, which were predominantly practiced by men and located in workshops, lacemaking never came under the protection of a craftsman's guild (Gambier 1981:21). (Although, as one of my informants wryly observed, there certainly was a guild for Venice's prostitutes!)

One of the main problems regarding the history of early Venetian lacemaking – and especially when critically reconsidered in the light of my fieldwork – is its social origins. Given that Renaissance society was sharply differentiated, it is natural to wonder whether the craft was initially an aristocratic pastime, or whether it was in origin a truly "popular" skill. In other words, were its basic stitches, as some of my informants would say, "invented" in Venice's outlying islands, or were they taught to poor women by ladies, and especially nuns, as they were three or four centuries later throughout the Third World?

Historical data on work conducted informally by women at home are almost universally scanty, and references to the fact that Burano's women were famous for their lace are, in fact, as numerous as they are vague. An early mention of "two nuns overlooking the workers," in 1596, would suggest that work was organized, wholly or, at least in part, in convents (Gambier 1981:33). Additional evidence rests on the fact that the island had a relatively large population of Franciscan tertiaries, or *pizzocchere*.[8] Thus, while very little is known about work conducted informally in the island's cottages, historians, on the whole, assume that conditions of work in Burano's convents may have been similar to those that obtained in Venice. In either case, principles and regulations by which the work was organized show deep concern with those sections of the female population which, according to the dictates of honor, clearly needed protection. However, the perception of a need to cloister unattached women, like nubile girls, or young widows, was not motivated only by concern for their salvation, but also by the fact that they were themselves viewed as a potential threat to the good order of society.

Concerning the problem of the social origins of lace then, historians generally favor a view of early lacemaking as an aristocratic pastime and their evidence is the mention of two palace schools organized by the wives of doges in the fifteenth and the sixteenth centuries,[9] as well as the fact that Renaissance pattern books (in which lace is often confused with embroidery) are always dedicated to those aristocratic women in whose homes young girls would learn the craft before getting married or entering convents. The most frequent examples cited in their dedications are those of Penelope and Lucretia, who are therefore conceptualized as supreme examples of female virtue.

According to recent versions, therefore, lacemaking, which had its beginnings in Venice's palace workshops and rich convents, percolated down to more humble homes, and informal working groups became widespread throughout the city. At the same time, it was taken up in poorer convents, where at first it was practiced informally, but it was subsequently organized with increasing strictness, as it gradually became one of the main sources of income. During the initial period lace was made rather casually, so that women and nuns, "worked here and there, or sat in their cells," but by the seventeenth century, they did start to work in formally organized groups, "one of them read a book of devotion or they all together sang prayers and psalms so they could pass the time with greater spiritual comfort" (Gambier 1981:22).

Lacemaking, however, was most highly organized in a number of institutions, founded mainly for the protection of young women, or for the recovery of those who had already fallen into sin.[10] These were, in fact, lay foundations but they, too, were generally supervised by nuns. As is stated in their Founders' Acts, "virtue had at all times many fierce enemies, but never was it as threatened as when it was a companion to poverty and to beauty. . . . Our plan was to found . . . a place suitable to welcome those girls between the ages of twelve and eighteen, who, endowed with beauty, but lacking the means for an honest subsistence, either through the loss or through the wickedness of their parents and relatives, were on the brink of losing themselves forever" (Savio 1977:39).

Regulations were thus in keeping with a dominant concern about modesty and shame: dress was to be "young-looking," but "altogether positive and demure . . . with no frill, lace or other ornaments," and their veil was to be made of "severe close-woven cotton, not transparent . . . as was fit for the poor girls of that pious hospital." For their "holidays" – one day a year – the girls would be taken on a trip "all together on a boat, and a closed one, if possible. They were to behave at all times with modesty and reserve and they would be assisted on their journey by three of the school's deputies on their gondolas" (Savio in Motolla-Molfino and Binaghi Olivari 1977:40).

Each girl's earnings were divided into three parts; two-thirds went to the Institute for her support while one-third was saved for her dowry (whether she wished to get married or become a nun). The girls were given their daily task by the Mother Superior, and if they missed work for no good reason, they were quite mercilessly made to pay out of their subsequent earnings. Echoing Exodus, regulations also stated that the works executed had to be "slow, honest, and made for honest people." Orders and deliveries had to be arranged through the Mother Superior, so as to avoid "unnecessary friendships," since the nature of the craft itself tended to lead to the creation of networks of women, which, as it was feared, could be potentially corrupting if they extended outside close family or neighborhood circles (Gambier 1981:22).

One theme that emerges quite strongly is the struggle for the privilege of selling the lace, and the determination of the state, the merchants' guilds, and the convents to retain full control over the workers, as well as over their products. Despite the institutes' prohibition, however, attempts were often made by some presumably older and more experienced women to offer their handicraft for sale directly to the public. An eighteenth-century official thus angrily reports

> the ill-born novelty and the pernicious abuse recently introduced by several women who go about the town selling haberdasheries . . . in large quantities and involving considerable capitals. These women sell lace of all kinds white and black veils . . . needle point . . . yarns from flanders. . . . And they certainly

> damage the haberdashers whose capitals are all taken up in the running of shops, while they, with the freedom of their sex, introduce themselves into the homes of nobles, as well as into monasteries, where, on the occasion of novitiates, they do sell large quantities of goods (Gambier 1981:26).

Indeed, women from the lagoon's islands must have figured very prominently among such illegal street traders. But what is of great interest here is that the government's dislike of competition is clearly mixed with a concern over pollution. As the official's indictment implies, "because as women they are not feared, their sex grants them the freedom to knock at peoples' doors, but, as they do so, they certainly put their honour and their reputation at risk, for who is to say whether they are not, in fact, too free with their sexuality?" Street vendors, like gypsies, are thus always touched with a suspicion of shamelessness, or, as in an episode told me by an informant, with allegations of witchcraft.

Such a breakdown of discipline was in any case the prelude to radical change; by the eighteenth century, Renaissance institutions were in a state of decline. Several convents were dissolved by Napoleon in 1797, and, according to numerous historians, in the first half of the nineteenth century, lacemaking skills were almost entirely lost.

The Nineteenth-Century Revival

It is against the background of Renaissance history and of a sense of loss among Venice's aristocracy that we may best approach a period much closer to the present, and one that has left a strong mark on Burano's collective memory. Lacemaking after the French Revolution, the fall of the Venetian Republic, and the closure of numerous monasteries, always had the character of a revival. Indeed, it coincided with a period of reactionary restoration, and, by means of repeated attempts to reintroduce past monastic rigors in the organization of work, it inevitably brought about the reinforcement of shame as a normative and repressive ethos.

After the fall of its republican government, Venice had been occupied first by French then by Austrian armies, and only in 1866 was it at last joined to Italy. Meanwhile, the Italian peninsula had almost achieved political unification, but its aristocracy and Catholic middle class were still gravely troubled over the Roman Question, that is, the debate on territories thus far administered and owned by the Vatican. It was just at this period that, having lost all hope of maintaining its temporal power, the Church strove in all ways to reinforce its spiritual hold. Belief in the Immaculate Conception was thus declared a dogma in 1854 by Pope Pius XI, and, in 1864, in the famous papal bull *Syllabum Errorum*, the Pope at once condemned "liberalism, socialism and rationalism." Nineteenth-century Venetian lacemaking as well as the character of one of its most famous organizers, are, then, best understood in the context of the conservative reaction that followed unification.

During that same period, Venetian lacecraft in general was described as "languishing" and "in a state of decay," and, although Burano's lace was often mentioned, reports were vague and contradictory. For example, according to the Venice Chamber of Commerce, while "two thirds of Burano's women make lace," as another writer points out, "the number of workers cannot be stated with any degree of certainty," since due to "the absence of any formal factory," almost all the women work by themselves at home (Gambier 1981:32–33). But it may be precisely due to the isolation of Burano, and to the fact that, after the collapse of institutions, lace continued to be made by the women at home, that *punto in aria* was not entirely forgotten.[11]

Throughout the nineteenth century all references to Burano evoke a picture of poverty and isolation. In 1850 the island lost its privileges as a free port, and subsidies from Venice ceased altogether in 1860. When in 1872 the lagoon was entirely frozen, and fishing which was the island's main productive activity came to a complete halt, Burano sunk to such a point of destitution that an appeal for funds was made through the press (Pasqualigo 1887:40–42). The revival of lace making and the foundation of a school (the *Scuola Merletti di Burano)* then, must be studied in the context of nineteenth-century philanthropy, since they were brought about in an attempt to alleviate severe need.

The initiative was due to a Member of Parliament, Paulo Fambri, and to an aristocratic Venetian family, while organization was placed in the care of a committee of society women – whom Fambri, with the gushing Romanticism and class consciousness typical of his time, describes as "good, intelligent, rich, high placed, and possibly beautiful." Several of the women involved – some of them ladies-in-waiting to Italy's Queen, Margherita of Savoy who was the School's main patroness – very soon lost interest, but Countess Marcello (1839–1893), a hardworking and authoritarian figure, became increasingly dedicated to the running of the School. A study of her life history would by itself bear witness to the conservative attitudes that informed her philanthropic work. Like her husband,[12] she was committed to the

Plate 8.8 The Burano Lace School in its early days. (Information Department, Media Library of the Veneto Region)

Plate 8.9 Men mending nets. (Information Department, Media Library of the Veneto Region)

Plate 8.10 One of the heads of the Institute of Zitelle. (Information Department, Media Library of the Veneto Region)

cause of Italian national unity, but she was, at the same time, deeply attached to the church, and, during the long years of her widowhood, she saw her work for Burano's Lace School as a true mission.

She was convinced that piecework would give the women far greater freedom and dignity than work in factories. If a piece of work was not perfectly executed, she would cruelly cut it with her scissors, destroying a week's labor, but she would, at the same time, refer to the lacemakers as her "three hundred daughters." As her friends remembered, it was a great joy to her to see that, since the School had been founded, the numbers of illegitimate births had gone down considerably, and that she had helped not only raise the material standards of life, but, above all, improve the islanders' morals. But, far from introducing any new ideas in the organization of work, the School's governors explicitly stated that its rules were to be based entirely on those of Renaissance institutions. Girls would be admitted at the age of twelve on the conditions that they already knew the rudiments of the craft, they knew how to read and write, and they were in good health and of good character. Their education would come to an end, but they would continue to receive religous instruction.

Here we may very well ask by what rights such an institution should call itself a school, except that the use of that term was, as Karl Marx has shown in *Das Kapital* (1952:229), a very common device for evading laws on child labor. Indeed attendance at the School can be compared with a long unpaid apprenticeship, since between the ages of twelve and eighteen the girls worked with no payment, and only at eighteen would they begin to receive some meager compensation. Furthermore, work was minutely parcelled out, and each worker was encouraged to specialize in only one or two stitches so that speed would be gained rather than versatility.

As was pointed out by one enthusiastic observer, who was probably well aware of the Catholic opposition to the work of women in Lombardy's silk mills (which, it was feared, would put an end to the family), the island would become a rather singular type of factory – one in which married women could be employed almost on a full-time basis without leaving their homes and children at all.[13] The benefit this would bring the population in terms of control over women is always spelled out in great detail. Thus, paradoxically, at the same time that women were given an opportunity to gain some measure of economic independence, the feeling that they had to be kept ever in check was continually reinforced. This was coherent with the premises on which work was first organized, that is, to alleviate poverty and to counteract the predisposition to shame and dishonor, which were usually held to be its almost inevitable corollaries.

A rhetoric of poverty was exploited on both sides: lacemakers, although they were forbidden to sell their own handicraft for as long as they retained a connection with the School, would often take their wares to Venice, and sometimes even plead with passersby for a sale. As worthwhile buyers of lace were traditionally the very rich, however, great emphasis was placed by the School's organizers on the fact that the ability to sell the product was almost more crucial than its actual manufacture, since as Countess Marcello never failed to stress, its sale depended on social networks that Burano's lacemakers, or even Venice's bourgeois traders, could never hope to penetrate.

In purely commercial terms, Burano's lace always had ups and downs, and, not surprisingly, one of its most successful moments in recent history – perhaps its last – was in the 1930s, when, under the protection of the National Committee for Fashion (*Ente Nazionale della Moda*) the School was commissioned to make a precious lace surplice to be presented by the Fascist government to Pope Pius XI for the Jubilee of 1930, the year after church and state were officially reconciled and relations taken up again after the rift that followed the Vatican's loss of temporal power in 1870 (Clark 1986:254–56).

Subsequently, the School was also charged with making cot furnishings for the Princess Royal Maria Pia of Savoy, as well as an exquisite bridal veil for Mussolini's daughter Edda, which was to be the gift of the Senate on her wedding to Count Ciano. Some of my informants still remember the time when, at a very young age, the best among them worked on Edda's veil:

> Twenty whole meters of wonderful lace. We worked at it for months. Then, when it was finished and pressed, we laid it out on the table for the authorities to see, and it looked as light as a cloud . . . they gave us a vermouth and biscuits. . . . They even allowed us an afternoon off, and we all went for a walk in Mazzorbo, laughing and singing <ahi, ahi, my veil is broken, my veil is bro-o-o-ken / oh, cruel traitor, you have broken my veil!>[14] . . . . So much work, and just to cover her backside! (1982 fieldwork).

For a brief period, then, again the School's order books provide interesting glimpses into significant national events, but the craft once more sank into inactivity during and after the Second World War. Its running was left entirely to the nuns, and, according to documents of 1973, it appears that by that date, it had already been closed for some time (Davanzo Poli 1981:3).

Present Conditions

At the time of my first fieldwork in Burano, the island was, as it has always been, indissolubly tied with images of lacemaking. In most other respects, however, life was very different from anything I had been led to expect from vague but frequent references to it in the press or in general literature. Buranelli are no longer riddled with poverty. Thanks to a number of factors – like Italy's expanding economy, the employment of women in Murano's glass factories, a lower birth rate, improved education, and the higher prices of fish – they are now relatively prosperous. But they still smart under their old wounds, and their political interaction with the city is often characterized by a keen awareness of the wrongs they suffered in the past.

Under those circumstances, the economy and organization of lacemaking were naturally bound to change. Numerous lacemakers were (and still are) deeply resentful about the way the nuns had simply wound up the School when in the 1970s they got into financial difficulties. This action left them unemployed and without any pension, at a time when no other employer would have been able to ignore trade union rules. On the other hand, amid a general feeling that lacemaking skills are about to be forgotten and abandoned in favor of more rewarding occupations, many women continued informally to make lace.

A new phase in the history of the craft was about to begin in 1981, when, following a general awakening of interest in textiles, it was proposed that Venice should have a permanent museum of lace. Buranelli, who had seen that many of the items shown at prestigious exhibitions had been made in their island, firmly demanded that the museum be in Burano. It was then decided that the School should be reopened as well, and that its archives be organized for public consultation. In addition, it was proposed that lacemakers should at long last form their own cooperative and sell their lace directly to the public. Surprisingly, such plans were not by any means unanimously welcome. On the one hand, the workers who had become keenly aware of their past exploitation had little confidence that forming a cooperative would bring them any advantage; and local traders, who had rapidly filled the vacuum left after the Second World War by Venetian wholesalers, were very much concerned that bureaucratic interference would be detrimental to their businesses.

A further complication was that a large part of the lace sold in Burano since the 1960s and 1970s is not made locally, but is imported from the Far East. The idea that a cooperative would now both take important commissions and produce small items to sell on the souvenir market was thus bitterly resented, especially by shop owners. At the same time, although some of the workers were ready to recognize that the great influx of Far Eastern lace was very unfair competition, they nonetheless maintained that they found the going system acceptable. "I don't want to complain," they would say, "I like to work freely, as much as and when I please."

Attendance at the newly revived School was rather poor at the beginning, but courses are now regularly taught with some degree of success, and teachers have generally encouraged pupils to make their own drawings and to break down the strict adherence to tradition, which they had been forced to follow in the past. At the same time, the Museum has led to an increase in the numbers of day tourists and in the sales of imported as well as locally made lace. Thus the long-standing association of Burano with the craft certainly continues to hold, but trading, as distinct from making, is now the most desired activity, and those who have no capital often obtain some goods to display on their stalls on credit from prosperous wholesalers.

As one of the women explained to me, the relation between "real *burano*" and imported lace is similar to the relation between "costume" and "real" jewelry: there is room for both. "Real *burano*," they say, is a collector's item, and, while assertions that the women now only make lace for themselves and their families were sometimes meant to forestall any damage I might make regarding the tax authorities, they were often quite true. Pleasure in at last being able to keep for themselves a handicraft, the value of which had been traditionally sanctioned by royalty, but which previously they had almost never been in a position to own, has now made lace very desirable as both a household and a personal ornament, and its possession has become a symbol of economic success. As a result, framed lace Madonnas, flowers, and butterflies, in the rather kitschy styles and reduced sizes of the 1950s and 1960s, were displayed in almost every home I visited.

Conclusions

I started this paper by making a connection between ideas of virginity and purity and the organization of lacemaking in convents and schools. I have related their discipline with the deliberate reinforcement of feelings of shame, which, already present in the culture, were further instrumentalized by well-intentioned outsiders. However, among other aspects of recent social change in Burano, as everywhere else in Italy, not least are changes in women's lives that were brought about especially with the legalization of abortion, divorce, and the widespread acceptance of contraception (as numerous informants said to me, "the best thing that was ever invented!"). Many women are beginning to wonder if "shame" is really just some deeply ingrained form of false consciousness. As a result, while virginity is still valued, it is no longer the be-all and end-all of a woman's sense of personal worth. In everyday life, behavior, and conversation, sexual virtue is somewhat less marked, both in its exaltation and in negative statements of transgression, and families, as well as individuals, are in general less dependent on the judgments of neighbors than they were in the recent past.

Lace has partly changed from "stuff to sell" to "stuff to keep," that is, property to be kept as heirloom or used in gift exchange, and, above all, worn at christenings, confirmations, and weddings. On such important ritual occasions, lace still communicates most of the meanings I have described through its history. Symbolic associations, however, are now less univocal and narrow, and the states of mind and body they should signify are somewhat less obligatory. The wearing of white for brides and the making of lace, which in the past might have absorbed the whole of a woman's adolescence and youth, are no longer as indissolubly tied with purity as to make their use where virginity is known to have come to an end a double shame. At the same time, the devotional aspects of lacemaking are almost forgotten, and so are (almost) the virginal and the "prude" connotations of its wearing: the idea of honor is still present, but some of its basic tenets have greatly changed.

Meanwhile, however, new symbolisms have developed: lace is still related to notions of purity, but in the 1980s, that is no longer the sexual purity of its makers and wearers, but the purity of an entirely preindustrial product, unsullied – like Burano itself – by machinery, and completely untouched by modernity, truly antique, uncontaminated; created, as my informants tell me, almost miraculously from nothing: the archetypal female craft.

Notes

1. I wish to thank Dr. Doretta Poli, Dr. G. Ellero, Director of the I.R.E. Archives, and Count Girolamo Marcello, whose personal recollections offered some precious insights into the history of Burano's Lace School. My strongest gratitude goes to the women and men of Burano for their generosity and their warm hospitality.
2. "Honor and shame" have been studied by numerous British and American anthropologists throughout the Mediterranean. It would not be possible here to introduce a full bibliography, but some of the main features of honor codes, and especially those related to conceptions of gender, are in Campbell 1964; Peristiany 1965; Friedl 1967; Davis 1977; Herzfeld 1980; Sciama 1981. However, most scholars have focused on "honor" in relation to family organization and patterns of authority, but, to the best of my knowledge, honor in the institutional sphere has not been as widely studied. A possible development of this work is comparison of Venetian institutions with missionary schools and workshops in the third world, one example of which is *The Lacemakers of Narsapur* described by Mies 1982. For an interesting comparison with uses of "shame" in English girls' public schools, see Okely 1978.
3. In some ways, however, Lucia is anxious to leave tradition behind: she considers that the craft is a vehicle for expressing both her feelings and her capacities for abstraction. Unlike the lacemakers of the past, she makes her own original drawings. Given the poor rewards generally obtained, Lucia says that, like other artists, she only works out of *passion*.
4. According to some historians, needle lace is the most primitive form of the craft, thus, for example, as N. Cuthbert writes, "Early hand lace was produced by needle work, but ultimately this was superseded by pillow or cushion lace, whereby threads were twisted around pins inserted in the face of the pillow" (1960:1).
5. See Crawley 1902:2, 25–59; and Van Gennep 1960:117, 166.
6. See de Martino 1972; Di Nola 1983; Eliade 1952; and Lienhardt 1961:282–83.
7. Except in traditional Scottish costume. In Eicher/Roach-Higgins' Table 1.1 (p. 18), lace would appear to be sometimes "wrapped" or "suspended" round head or/and shoulders, and either inserted in or adhered to clothes, and occasionally hand-held.
8. In a contemporary definition, these were "women, mostly widows, who having withdrawn from the world, either through devotion or through necessity, reduce themselves to live in certain places which are specially set aside for them, and, thus retired, they live on alms and on some small exercise of their own. . . . Because they do not observe the strict rules of the cloisters, they cannot be called nuns. Their tasks are to accompany the dead to their burials, to pray and to perform other pious works" (Vecellio

1590). Several streets both in Venice and in Burano are still named after them. Their name itself may have derived from *pizzo*, lace.

9. Giovanna Dandolo Malipiero and Morosina Morosini Grimani, respectively.
10. Zitelle, Penitenti at San Girolamo, Derelitti at San Giovanni e Paolo, San Lazzaro dei Mendicanti, and Incurabili. (But see Semi 1983). My recent finding, with the director of the Archives of Venice's I.R.E., Dr. G. Ellero, of manuscripts concerning the foundation of a charitable trust by a native of Burano, the priest Francesco Rossi, to benefit the island's orphaned or very poor girls' sheds new light on the history of its laceworkers (Capitoli della Compagnia Delle Donzelle Periclitanti 1749; and Will of Don Francesco Rossi 1757, with Codicils 1760 and 1762).
11. As R. Williams has shown for the English word "industry" before the industrial revolution, *fabbrica* and *manifattura* are sometimes imprecise. As it appears from a report written in 1811, "Several thousand women spread through Venice, Burano and Chioggia attend to that craft which is said to be in decline." In contrast, however, "Burano lace has a great name since it is worked by needle, a very distinguished type of work which deserved the satisfaction of her majesty, the wife of the viceroy, who deigned to buy some" (Gambier 1981:31).
12. Count Marcello suffered a period of exile after the 1848 uprising against Austria.
13. For an interesting comparison with workers in Friulan silk mills, see Holmes 1989:164 and ff.
14. "Ahi, ahi, m'hai rotto il velo/ m'hai rotto il velo/ Cuore crudele, tu m'hai tradi'!"

References

Accati, L., "Matrimony and Chastity: Symbolic Change and Social Control," *International Journal of Moral and Social Studies*, Vol. 5, No. 1, Spring 1990, pp. 23–38.

Barthes, R., *The Fashion System*, London: Jonathan Cape, 1983 (1967).

Bellavitis, A., N.M. Filippini and M.T. Sega, *Perle e Impiraperle: Un lavoro di Donne a Venezia tra '800 e '900*, Arsenale, 1990.

Bloch, M., *Marxism and Anthropology*, Oxford: Oxford University Press, 1983.

Du Boulay, J., *Portrait of a Greek Mountain Village*, Oxford: Oxford University Press, 1974.

Brooke, M.L., and M. Simeon, *The History of Lace*, London: Stainer and Bell, 1979.

Durkheim, E., and M. Mauss, "De quelques formes primitives de classification,"

Année Sociologique, Vol. 6, 1901.

Campbell, J.K., *Honour, Family and Patronage: A Study of Institutions and Moral Values in a Greek Mountain Community*, Oxford: Oxford University Press, 1964.

Clark, M., *Modern Italy, 1871–1982*, London: Longman, 1986.

Crawley, A.E., *The Mystic Rose: A Study of Primitive Marriage*, London: Macmillan, 1902.

Cuthbert, N., *The Lace Makers' Society. A Study of Trade Unionism in the British Trade Industry. 1760*–1960, London: The Amalgamated Society of Operative Lace Makers and Auxiliary Workers, 1960.

Davanzo Poli, D., ed., *La Scuola dei Merletti di Burano*, Comune di Venezia, 1981.

Davis, J., *People of the Mediterranean: An Essay in Comparative Social Anthropology*, London: Routledge and Kegan Paul, 1977.

Devoto, G., *Dizionario Etimologico*, Firenze, 1962.

Eliade, M., *Le Dieu Lieur*, Paris: Gallimard, 1952.

Fambri, P., *La Contessa Andriana Marcello*, Firenze: Cellini, 1893.

Friedl, E., "The position of women: Appearance and reality," *Anthropological Quarterly*, Vol. 40, 1967, pp. 97–108.

Gambier, M., "Testimonianze sulla lavorazione del Merletto nella Repubblica di Venezia," in *La Scuola dei Merletti di Burano*, Comune di Venezia, 1981.

Herzfeld, M., "Honour and Shame: Problems in the Comparative Analysis of Moral Systems," *Man*, Vol. 15, 1980, pp. 339–351.

Holmes, D.R., *Cultural Disenchantments*, Princeton: Princeton University Press, 1989.

Lienhardt, G., *Divinity and Experience*, Oxford: Oxford University Press, 1961.

Lukacs, G., *History and Class Consciousness*, London: Merlin, 1971 (1968).

de Martino, E., *Sud e Magia*, Milano: Feltrinelli, 1971 (1959).

Marx, Karl, *Das Kapital*, Chicago: University of Chicago Press, 1952 (1867–1894).

Mies, M., *The Lace Makers of Narsapur*, London: Zed Press, 1982.

Mottola-Molfino, A. and M.T. Binaghi Olivari (eds.), *I Pizzi: Moda e Simbolo*, Milano: Electa: 1977.

Neufeld, E., *Ancient Hebrew Marriage Laws*, London, 1944.

di Nola, A., *L'Arco di Rovo*, Torino: Boringhieri, 1983.

Okely, J., "Privileged, Schooled and Finished: Boarding Education for Girls," in S. Ardener (ed.), *Defining Females*, London: Croom Helm, 1978.

Pasqualigo, G., *I Merletti ad Ago o a Punto in Aria di Burano*, Trieste: Pastori, 1887.

Peristiany, J.G., ed., *Honour and Shame, The Values of Mediterranean Society*, London: Widenfeld and Nicolson, 1965.

Pitt-Rivers, J., *The People of the Sierra*, London: Widenfeld and Nicolson, 1954.

Pullan, B., *Rich and Poor in Renaissance Venice: The Social Institutions of a Catholic State, to 1620*, Oxford: Basil Blackwell, 1971.

Reiter, R., ed., *Toward an Anthropology of Women*, New York: Monthly Review Press, 1975.

Rossi, F., *Capitoli della Compagnia Delle Donzelle Periclitanti, 1749:* and *Will of Don Francesco Rossi, 1757, with Codicils, 1760 and 1762*, Archivio I.R.E. Venezia.

Sciama, L., "The Problem of Privacy in Mediterranean Anthropology," in S. Ardener (ed.), *Women and Space: Ground Rules and Social Maps*, London: Croom Helm, 1981.

Sciascia, L., *1912 + 1*, Milano: Adelphi, 1986.

Semi, F., *Gli "Ospizi" di Venezia*, Venezia: Helvetia, 1983.

Simmel, G., quoted in *Current Anthropology*, April 1986, p. 173.

The Soncino Chumash, or Five Books of Moses, London, 1975 (1947).

Van Gennep, A., *The Rites of Passage*, London: Routledge and Kegan Paul, 1977.

Vecellio, C., *Degli Habiti Antichi e Moderni di Diverse Parti del Mondo, Libri Due*, Venezia, 1590.

Vigarello, G., *Lo Sporco e il Pulito*, Venezia: Marsilio Editori, 1987.

Williams, R., *Key Words*, London: Penguin, 1976.

9

Pachamama

The Inka Earth Mother of the Long Sweeping Garment

Penny Dransart

There is an image of Pachamama, the "time/earth mother" of the Inkas[1] and other Andean peoples, walking on earth wrapped in a red dress that sweeps over the sacred ground. Typically, however, she was not represented in human form. Her body was the earth itself. It was not created, for it seems that the earth (her body) always was ever present.

According to widespread beliefs in the sixteenth century concerning the mythical peopling of the Andes in former times, different ethnic groups believed that their ancestors emerged from a specific point of origin in the landscape. At that time the Andean people told the newly arrived European missionaries that their ancestors issued forth from natural features of the landscape or from animals or birds, depending on their own particular point of origin. It is of great interest that when the ancestors left the obscurity of the inner world to enter this world, they arrived fully clothed, wearing the dress which identified the sex and the ethnic origin of the wearer.

Fabric clothes the body and also wraps material objects. The importance of clothing to the various peoples of the Inka Empire has been commented upon since the sixteenth century (Cieza de León 1862 [1550]). More recent interpretations stress that the production of fabrics was one of the most important methods deployed by the Inka Empire (Tawantinsuyu) for organizing society.[2] In fact, a type of cloth, *kumpi*, was one of the most valued political commodities in Inka society. However, my concern here is to examine the intimate association between fabric and the body, in particular, the female body. What is of importance is that the cloth with which the bodies of the women were wrapped (the *aqsu*) was considered to be more than just a garment that protected and adorned the wearer. It formed an outer skin that stood in a metonymic relationship to the self; in other words, it was considered to be an integral part of the person who wore it. The *aqsu* forms an outer surface that simultaneously conceals and reveals an interior. In this work, I will consider how the mother's body (or the pregnant body), wrapped with a sweeping garment, was connected to the rest of the world and how this body brought into being the Inka lineage in a continuous process of becoming. I would like to suggest that fabric is inextricably caught in a web of associations expressed in cosmological and mythical themes that legitimize the power structures of societies in the Andes. For not only were living people clothed, but the progenitors of lineages were dressed, and divinities were perceived as being clad. Here I propose to examine some aspects of the portrayal of autocreative powers (or autogenesis) and mythically sanctioned incest, and the interlinking of these themes with descent, as constituted by lineages of clothed persons. In particular, the main garment typically worn by women in Inka times will be considered.

Inka women wore a dress known as *aqsu*, a large rectangular cloth formed by sewing together two woven loom lengths. This was wrapped around the body and held in place by a firmly woven belt at the waist and was pinned at the shoulders. Over the shoulders, women wore a shawl and noblewomen also wore a headcloth. Inka men wore a headband wound several times around the head, a tunic, and a square mantle; other items of male dress included a bag with a long strap for carrying coca leaves, which was worn over the left shoulder with the bag hanging at the right side, a breech cloth, fringes around the knees, and sandals. Thus a clear difference exists between the feminine *aqsu*, which was a flat piece of cloth, and the main masculine garment, the tunic with sewn side seams. The male garment, in fact, was called *tawa kaqru* (four openings) by the indigenous writer Guaman Poma (1980 [1615]: 60) because of its four openings (for arms, neck, and legs), which is in stark contrast to the large cloth with which women were wrapped.[3]

In the Andean highlands, female and male dress was, and still is in some areas, made from the fleece of llamas and alpacas. These animals also had a mythical origin parallel to that of humans from specific points in the landscape, often from watery places. As the limits of space prevent me from exploring the mythical origins of domesticated animals, I will only quote the words of a Quechua speaker from Pinchimuro in the Department of Cusco, on the subject of the Pachamama, the "time/earth mother" of Andean peoples: "Here beneath the Holy Earth, inside the earth she lives. The earth lives . . . The earth never dies. When we die we disappear into the earth, she is absorbing us. From her, hair grows. That is pasture and that is wool for animals. The animals are nourished with that pasture" (Gow and Gow 1975:154). This is a view that might well be shared by very many Quechua and Aymara peoples today. An early seventeenth-century Aymara-Spanish dictionary hints at conceptual links between fleece and water, for the author lists *havi*, "woollen fleece," which shares the same root with *havira*, "river," and *havitha*, "to flow" (Bertonio 1984 [1612], Bk II:125). Although Zuidema and Urton (1976:67) admit that these meanings might simply be homonyms, they draw our attention to a conjoining of fleece with water in an early seventeenth-century myth which provides a symbolic context for these associations in the form of a celestial llama, which was said to drink water from all sources, and which came down from earth in an abundance (described as a deluge) of fleece (Taylor 1987:425–31). The argument developed by Zuidema and Urton (1976:68) becomes frankly speculative as they proceed to equate the concept of a creational deluge with procreational birth, with its accompanying flow of amniotic fluids, although they again cite Bertonio in support of their interpretation: "*Havitatatha, Llumchitatatha.* To sprinkle water, or flood the earth" (Bertonio 1984, Bk II:125). However, by cross-checking the second word given here by Bertonio, we find that *llumchitha* means "to flood water on the ground to excess," and that the root *llum–* is combined with words that indicate movement, spreading out and the sweeping motion of a long garment (Bertonio 1984, Bk II:208). The long sweeping garment supposed to have been worn by the Pachamama is relevant here, and this article proposes to explore the theme of descent as consisting of lineages of clothed people and, in particular, the metaphorical role of the large cloth made from the fleece of alpacas or llamas with which women wrapped their bodies. Divine birth, procreation, and genealogical links between dead ancestors and the living are interconnected with the wearing of this dress, the *aqsu*.

The Cult of the Ancestors

Andean peoples believed in the multiple origin of humanity from different points of origin, a difficult concept for the Europeans, who claimed to have been descended from the union of one human couple, Adam and Eve. Albornoz discovered that Andean peoples said that they were descended from ancestors who emerged from a natural feature of the landscape, a place that was venerated and known as *wak'a* in both the

Quechua and Aymara languages. Any place or sacred object is known as *wak'a*. Interestingly, this word also means a woven belt in Aymara. Albornoz reported:

> There is, as I said above, the chief class of *huaca* [*wak'a]* which they had before they were subject to the ynga [Inka], which they call *pacariscas*, which means that which gives existence to all created beings. They take different forms and names according to the provinces: some have stones, others springs and rivers, others caves, others animals and birds, and others species of trees and grasses, and with this difference they profess to be created and descended from the aforementioned things, like the Ingas [Inkas] say they left Pacaritambo, which is a cave called Tambo Toco and the Angarae and Soras peoples are descended from a lake called Choclo cocha, and likewise, all the provinces of Pirú. . . . Moreover all the aforementioned *huacas* have services, fields, cattle [camelids] and clothing, and they have their particular mode for sacrifices, and *moyas* which are pasture grounds where the cattle graze, belonging to the aforementioned *huacas*; and they have a great amount of everything (Albornoz 1967 [1568]:20).

When in material form, such as a stone or tree, the *wak'a* possessed its own clothing of precious textiles with which it was dressed during ceremonies held in its honor. Albornoz goes on to explain that if an ethnic group migrated or was forced to relocate under Inka rule, the textiles were carefully carried to the new place of residence. A new *wak'a* stone would be dressed with the precious clothing and would be given the name of the original place of origin in their former lands. In the early seventeenth-century Huarochirí manuscript[4] many instances of the petrification of a hero or heroine were recorded. Gerald Taylor points out that the *wak'a* have a double meaning in that they are the visible and accessible cult objects of a community, and also the metamorphosis of the founder of a lineage (Taylor 1987:145, 195).

Among the eternally snow-clad peaks regarded as the most important holy places in the Andes, Albornoz lists Sulimana (or Surimana), the greatest of such places in the Inka province of Kuntisuyu (this included the Arequipa area of southern Peru). He says its shrine was rebuilt by the Inkas, who allocated herds (probably of llamas and alpacas) as well as officiants to serve the cult of Sulimana (Albornoz 1967:21). We know that the cult was maintained after Christianity was introduced, for in 1671, an old Indian woman was punished for idolatry and confessed to having woven the white robes for the stone image of Surimana (Duviols 1966). The cult of this particular volcano as deity eventually disappears from written records. However, there are archival papers that demonstrate clearly that the persistence of the cult of the ancestors was combined with a refusal to pay taxes to the colonial authorities.[5] Documents record the trial of indigenous leaders from the town of Andagua in the Valley of Ayo, north of Arequipa between 1751 and 1754, for such offenses.

Shrines containing the bodily remains of the ancestors were a more local manifestation of the phenomenon represented by the great regional deities such as Surimana. The mummified ancestors of Andagua were perceived as mediators between the people who live in "this world" and the beings of the inner world, the fertility of which was the source of wealth for the inhabitants of this world. Andagua mummy worship, as described by Salomon, formed a "seamless web of obligations from hearthside level to the outermost limits of self-defined collectivity" (Salomon 1987:159). Every individual of indigenous descent in Andagua recognized a mummy as representing the progenitor of his or her lineage. Salomon assumes that each ancestor shrine was honored by various households, which comprised a unit called "family" in the Andagua papers. In this account, the ancestors were perceived as the true owners of the land, enabling the descendants to claim local rights; each lineage regarded its shrine as a corporate symbol and any aggrandizement of its cult raised the status of its members relative to other lineages (Salomon 1987:160–61). Every Friday night after nightfall, people made clandestine visits to their shrine where they greeted their ancestor with Aymara invocations and dressed it with clothing of "ancient design." The supplicants requested that they be granted favors, such as a profitable caravan journey to La Paz or success in learning to weave. It is interesting that the dress of the mummies is described in some detail; they wore tailored furs, sandals, and multicolored headdresses adorned with garlands of grass.

Mama Huaco: Mother of the Inkas

In the mythical past, Mama Huaco, the mother of the Inkas, crawled from a cave which formed an opening leading from the inner world. In other words, she crawled from the womb of her mother, the Pachamama. It should be remembered that the Pachamama is the "time/earth mother;" she is the ever-present and independent Andean divinity who has her own self-sufficient and creative power to sustain life on this earth. When Mama Huaco emerged in this world from the body of her mother, she was already wrapped in a pink *aqsu*, the dress worn by Inka and other women. Not only was her own birth the result of an autogenerative process, but Mama Huaco in turn gave birth, magically, to a son without the intervention of a man. She then married her son, who was called Manko Qapaq. The children of this union between mother and son became the sibling spouses who were the rulers of the Inka Empire. Brother and sister henceforth had custody over each other's fertility and their descendants came from within the lineage in a self-perpetuating stream.

Many versions of the Inka origin myth have been recorded. The bare outline just presented is my reading of two accounts given by authors of indigenous descent. More characters appear in most of the versions of the myths; in fact, most versions tell of the entrance of four men and four women into this world. These first Inkas crawled out of the cave, which is called *Paqaritampu* ("the house [or] inn of origin") in the myths. These four couples of sibling-spouses are known by different names in the different versions, and they are made to undergo various adventures.[6] Here we may note particularly that they left the cave wearing garments that identified their sex and noble status. Moreover, it is said that the brothers took weapons from out of the cave, and the sisters took cooking vessels.[7]

After the Spanish invasion of the Inka Empire, the chroniclers attempted to write an Inka "history," basing it on the succession of the Inka emperors. Their efforts to reconstruct Inka history were beset by contradictions, since they assumed that the senior legitimate son of the deceased monarch would succeed his father, as was the current practice in Europe. However, Rostworowski (1960) has shown that, theoretically, all the sons of an Inka emperor possessed equal rights and all could aspire to become the next sovereign. The Inkas kept detailed records of the genealogies of their royal houses by means of the *khipu*, a series of cords into which knots were tied, representing information that was interpreted by trained officials, and through formal songs, which were probably different for the various Inka kin groups.

The chroniclers were also wrong in assuming that only one emperor ruled at a given time. The versions of the Inka succession as reconstructed by the Spanish chroniclers are unsatisfactory because they leave out the succession of the women rulers. According to Guaman Poma, the empress (*Quya*) was co-ruler of the empire alongside her spouse (Guaman Poma 1980:101, 128–29). It should be emphasized that, in any case, the emperor gained his status through his marriage to a particular woman. Although the Inka emperors tended to have many wives (whose sons were not illegitimate), the reigning empress was the woman whom the Inka emperor married on the day that he received the royal tassle, the red fringe that was the mark of his new status. Silverblatt suggests that the Inkas structured their universe by parallel hierarchies of gender that ranked gods and categories of mortals in the language of descent: the emperor was son of the Sun and the *Quya* was daughter of the Moon (Silverblatt 1987:41), thus the emperor was ruler of the men, and the *Quya* of women. It is beyond the scope of this article to discuss in detail the different versions of Inka genealogies, but I wish to refer briefly to two pedigrees offered by authors of indigenous descent, Guaman Poma[8] and Santacruz Pachacuti Yamqui.[9] These pedigrees include different types of genealogical knowledge. In the more recent levels, they contain statements about interpersonal relationships, and the marriages and children of historically identifiable persons are recorded. The higher levels of these same two pedigrees are mythological, and they constitute the alleged unions of the primeval ancestors of the Inka people. Both pedigrees end with the former type of genealogical information and begin with the latter. At which point the mythical information yields to statements concerning interpersonal relationships between identifiable people is not clear.

For reasons that are not entirely clear (perhaps not to offend Spanish sensibilities?), both authors felt obliged to find parents for Mama Huaco, the mother from whom the royal Inka lineage sprang. Santacruz Pachacuti Yamqui gives the names of Pachamamaachi[10] and Apo Tambo, this second name meaning "lord [or] lady inn [or] house." These two names constitute a double personification of the sacred cave. It should be noted that the mid-eighteenth-century mummy worshippers of Andagua honored their ancestors in openings into the earth; the ancestors were perceived as the progeny of the earth itself, or in other words, of the Pachamama.

The cave is portrayed by both Guaman Poma (1980:79) and Santacruz Pachacuti (1879:245) as having three exits. While Guaman Poma's drawing is of a naturalistically drawn cave, that of Santacruz Pachacuti is very schematic. He explains that the three openings are "windows," the first was named Tampottoco, the second Marasttoco and the third Suticttoco, belonging respectively to the "uncles," maternal grandparents, and paternal grandparents of the first Inka ruler, Manko Qapaq, who was the son and husband of Mama Huaco. These names are significant. The word *ttoco* (*t'uju* in modern Aymara) means "window" or "niche" in both the Quechua and Aymara languages. Maras, in the Urubamba Valley near Cusco, was the center of the Ayarmaca people, whose ruler Tocay Qapaq was already established by the time Manko Qapaq arrived, according to Guaman Poma (1980:80). Another historical source, collected for the Viceroy Toledo, mentions that the Sausiray people, who lived in what was to become Hurincusco, were said to have come from Sutic Toco (Levillier 1942, Vol II:86,89). Santacruz Pachacuti offers a drawing of a rectangular geometric design[11] flanked on each side by a tree, one of which he says stands for Apo Tambo, and the other for Pachamamaachi.

The pedigree presented by Guaman Poma (1980:86–143) is significantly different from that of Santacruz Pachacuti in the female line, although the same men appear in a similar order. Guaman Poma explains that the full title of the Inka Emperor was *Capac Apo Ynga*, and that of the Empress was *Capac Apo Quya*: "To be king *capac apo ynga*, he has to be so through the legitimate strength of his wife the queen, *capac apo coya*, and he has to be married to his sister or mother" (1980:118). Guaman Poma has been accused of presenting a very idealized Inka genealogy, yet he includes very specific and detailed drawings and descriptions of the clothes these people wore. It suggests that he himself saw the royal Inka mummies and was able to describe the garments in which they were dressed at the time, or that he had access to very detailed information. He himself says he wrote his document with the aid of various *khipu* (Guaman Poma 1980:11).[12]

The founding mother of the pedigree presented by Guaman Poma is Mama Huaco, said to be daughter of the Sun and Moon (Fig. 9.1). She has divine qualities because she gives birth to a son without the intervention of a man, and her son is therefore conceived in the matrilineal line. Guaman Poma, speaking as a Christian, condemns her as an idolator. He describes her as a witch, "*hechisera*," mentioning her ability to converse with stones, mountain peaks, and lakes (Guaman Poma 1980:81,121), but he also describes her beauty, her elegant dress, and her wise government of Cusco (Guaman Poma 1980:121). In modern Aymara communities, the ability to elicit speech from mute objects and from the spirits is a feature of a *yatiri*, a specialist ritual healer. In most communities, *yatiri* are often men, and in other accounts of Mama Huaco's activities, she is described as having warlike and masculine qualities. Betanzos relates an episode in which Mama Huaco, accompanied by her sisters and by Manko Qapaq and Ayar Oche, was walking toward the place where they would found Cusco. They passed a small town called Waylla, where Mama Huaco knocked down a man with *boleadoras* (a weapon used in hunting game), killed him, then removed his heart and lungs, into which she breathed air (Betanzos 1968:13). This is a method of divination used by *yatiri* on animal lungs. Although the Inkas were Quechua speakers, her name may be explained with reference to Bertonio: "*Huaccu*, see *Chachanco*: mannish

Figure 9.1 "The first history of the queens coia. Mama Huaco Coia, reigned in Cuzco" (Guaman Poma 1980 [1615]:120).

woman, she who takes no notice of the cold nor of work and is free speaking, without any kind of shirking" (Bertonio 1984 [1612], Bk II:142).

Mama Huaco and her female descendants are portrayed by Guaman Poma as wearing a long dress; this is, in fact the *aqsu* (the Aymara word for it is *urk"u*). Noblewomen wore the same type of dress as commoners, but the quality and possibly the materials (the use of vicuña fleece was restricted to the Inka rulers) were superior. Nowadays the *aqsu* or *urk"u* is almost invariably of a dark natural color of alpaca or llama fleece (it is still worn in some areas, such as by the Aymara-speaking women of Isluga and Cariquima in northern Chile). The dresses of the empresses described by Guaman Poma are all of dyed colors. Mama Huaco, he says, wore a pink *aqsu*; other colors mentioned for the *aqsu* are scarlet, purple, blue, and green. The *aqsu* worn by Chinbo Urma, daughter of Mama Huaco, is described as being "Maras scarlet" (*encarnado de Maras*; Guaman Poma 1980:123). It is not clear whether this refers to the color of the female garment habitually worn in Maras, or whether Maras was the source of a prized red dye stuff. It should be remembered that Marasttoco was associated with the maternal grandparents of Manko Qapaq, the son and husband of Mama Huaco. It would be appropriate for Mama Huaco and her daughter to be clad in pink and red, since red is the color held by many Andean peoples to be associated with the inner world, from where Mama Huaco emerged. The colors worn by the Inka emperors and the *Quya* seem to constitute a symbolic code, but Guaman Poma does not give any clues as to their significance.

Guaman Poma is insistent that the emperor married one of his full sisters, except for Manco Capac and possibly Ynga Roca, who both married their mother. His pedigree is couched in terms that express Inka ideology in an explicit manner. Creation is portrayed as an act of cosmogonic incest;[13] Mama Huaco emerges from the inner world (Pachamama) wrapped in a pink *aqsu*, she then gives birth to a son without the intervention of a man, and the progeny of the union between mother and son become the sibling spouses who then become the rulers of Tawantinsuyu. Brother and sister henceforth have custody over each other's fertility. Procreation is expressed in a symbolic idiom, and, according to Moore (1964), in this type of descent the offspring come from within the lineage in a self-perpetuating stream. Guaman Poma states this theme twice, for Cuci Chinbo Mama Micay, wearing an *aqsu* "from Cusco" (1980:131) marries her own son and their children become the sibling spouses, rulers of Tawantinsuyu, but from Hanancusco (Mama Huaco was associated in some way with Maras and her children were of Hurincusco).

Guaman Poma's genealogy is both patrilineal and matrilineal, but this bilateral lineage apparently hinges on the person of Cuci Chinbo Mama Micay, who married her son Inga Roca. This is a crucial point for understanding Inka leadership, because it would seem that Guaman Poma has unhinged two lineages (representing the rulers of Hanancusco and Hurincusco respectively) to create a unilineal sequence that would conform to European expectations.[14]

The constant reenactment of cosmogonically inspired incest was a violation of the incest prohibitions undoubtedly observed by the commoners of the Inka Empire. Mother-son incest would have been unthinkable in the local community, where it would be feared that such a violation would wreak havoc of cataclysmic proportions on the whole community. However, the word *mamahuaco* appears as a kinship term for "great grandmother" in Pérez Bocanegra's explanation of kinship terminology in the Quechua language of Cusco in the early seventeenth century (Pérez Bocanegra 1631:609).[15]

Conclusions

A Quechua oration, recorded by Cristobal de Molina, El Cuzqueño, reveres the Pachamama as mother of the Inkas. She is addressed by an honorific name: *Pachamama Suyrumama,* "time/earth mother of the sweeping garment." Pachamama is perceived as wearing a long dress, the hem of which drags over the ground.[16] During harvest rituals observed in 1547 at a time of full moon, a young woman wearing a long dress (which swept out behind and was supported by an older woman "of much authority") and puma skin played the role of Pachamama Suyrumama (Cieza 1862 [1550]:454). A long dress indicated the noble status of the wearer, as is made clear in the drawings of Guaman Poma, since peasant women are depicted wearing shorter dresses.[17]

By way of conclusion, I would like to suggest that clothing for the various peoples of Tawantinsuyu formed a second, culturally defined skin, patterned according to the sex and hierarchical status of the wearer. Clothed bodies became symbols uniting kinship and cosmology in which the distinction between human ancestors and divine persons was blurred, at least by the Inka rulers.

After the Spanish invasion, conditions changed radically. Rolena Adorno suggests that changes in attire indicate that ethnic self-definition changed with the fragmentation of the Empire. As external European values encroached on internal Andean space through colonization, different Andean peoples experienced the reduction of their own internal space to a local province, which was no longer an integral part of Tawantinsuyu (Adorno 1981:62–63). A similar reduction was observed in the case of the mid-eighteenth-century Andagua mummy worship. The textiles that dressed the bodily remains of the ancestors were ancient and traditional (although they also incorporated European-style tailored furs), but the worship took place against the waning influence of the formerly widespread dominance of the powerful deity Surimana.

Dress continued to be a critical marker of gender. In Inka times, the male garment was the *tawa kaqru*, a tunic with four openings, whereas the female garment was a large cloth that wrapped the body, without seamed openings (the *aqsu* or *urk"u*). This long garment, with an all-encompassing border, was an attribute of noblewomen, and also of the Pachamama. Women's dress prompted the creation of particularly potent images. Shortly before the arrival of the Spanish conquerors in Tawantinsuyu, Ataw Wallpa sent rich presents to his half-brother, the Emperor Waskar Inka. In reply, Waskar returned a full set of women's clothing, complete with gold pins, and a mirror and comb, plus gold vessels (Guaman Poma 1980:117; Santacruz Pachacuti Yamqui 1968: 312). These are the items with which the first Inka women entered this world when they left the cave of *Paqaritampu* in the myths. This was an incitement to a bloody ritual battle between the two brothers, who were each accompanied by a hundred thousand men; after three days the captains of Ataw Wallpa claimed victory and Waskar Inka bitterly cursed the gods (Santacruz Pachacuti Yamqui 1968:313–14). In this context, the *aqsu* provided a powerful incitement in provoking the spilling of blood at a time when Ataw Wallpa was forced into an enactment of the role of the warlike aspects of Mama Huaco.[18]

I wish to conclude with one more image provided by the *aqsu*. In the colonial period, the viceroy, Francisco de Toledo, ordered that women should not carry their babies inside the front of their dress, as if in a pouch, next to the skin (Boman 1908:447). This must have been common practice at least in parts of Tawantinsuyu. An interesting episode occurs in Chapter 31 of the Huarochirí manuscript. The *wak'a* Collquiri, who resided in the lake of Yansa, desired Capyama to be his wife. To achieve this end, he turned himself into *callcallo* (this word is not translated; it might derive from an Aru language equivalent to the Aymara *qallu*, which means a young animal – in this case a newly born llama), which the young woman put in her lap – presumably down the front of her dress. The *callcallo* grew in size, weighing down on her stomach and causing her great pain. She "gave birth" to a handsome young man who became her husband. Again, we have the symbolic marriage between mother and son, a fruitful union of two sexes in one body, which stresses the magical aspects of matrilineality that we also observed in the case of Mama Huaco, the founding mother of imperial Cusco. Access to political power and status were granted to the living through one's genealogy, which formed an unbroken thread between the dead ancestors and the living progeny. Clothing provided a rich source of metaphor in expressing these themes.[19]

Notes

1. Andean languages were recorded in written form after the Spanish invasion of 1532. Consequently, various methods exist for writing these languages. I have endeavored to use standardized spellings for Quechua and Aymara words in my text (thus I prefer to use "Inka" instead of "Inca"), but I respect the versions employed by the various authors when citing their texts. The original year of publication is presented in square brackets when an author is quoted for the first time. Subsequent quotes are accompanied only by the year of the edition consulted for this work. All translations into English are by myself.
2. The Inka Empire comprised the provinces of Chinchaysuyu, Antisuyu, Kuntisuyu, and Qullasuyu. John V. Murra has shown that the traditional reciprocity as practiced by individual communities was the model for Inka state revenues; massive textiles exactions (in the form of labor) were complemented by a redistributive policy, which emphasized institutionalized state "generosity" (Murra 1962). More recently, Murra has commented on the storage of clothing in storehouses. He suggests that cloth withdrawn from circulation acquires enhanced value; the possession of cloth grants privilege and power to those who redistribute it (cited by Schneider and Weiner 1986:179).
3. See Posnansky (1958:plates 44ff) for illustrations of Inka style clothing depicted on wooden *keru* cups. Although many of the nations that formed the empire of Tawantinsuyu wore the same type of garments as the Inka people, there were subtle differences, particularly in headgear, which made clothing a marker of ethnic identity. Clothing was, and still is in many Andean communities, a vehicle for visual symbolism that expresses the cultural values of the ethnic group. See Adorno (1981:62–69) for a

discussion of costume and ethnic identity in Inka and immediate post-Conquest times.

4. This document contains the oral traditions of Huarochirí, a province in the Department of Lima, Peru, recorded in Quechua at the beginning of the seventeenth century. The manuscript is untitled, and commences with the words, *runa yndio ñiscap machocuna* . . . ("ancestors of those called Indians"). The edition consulted here is that of Taylor (1987).
5. Frank Salomon has analyzed the events that took place in Andagua in the context of Andean history, in which revolt is seen as an endogenous process; and not just an automatic and instantaneous response evoked by outside pressures (Salomon 1987).
6. Urbano (1981) presents extracts from the different origin myths recorded in the chronicles. In Betanzos ([1551] 1968), Ayar Cache is the husband of Mama Guaco; Ayar Oche of Cura; Ayar Auca of Ragua Ocllo; and Mango Capac of Mama Ocllo. Guaman Poma ([1615?] 1980:84) lists the men as Uana Cauri Ynga; Cuzco Uanca Ynga; Mango Capac Ynga; and Tupa Ayar Cachi Ynga. The women are: Tupa Uaco, *ñusta*; Mama Cora, *ñusta*; Curi Ocllo, *ñusta*; and Ypa Uaco, *ñusta* (*ñusta* is Quechua for "princess"). Santacruz Pachacuti Yamqui ([1613?] 1968:284–87) gives the same names for the men as Betanzos, but he uses a different spelling: Mancocapacynga; Ayarcachi; Ayaruchu; and Ayaraoca. However, he only gives the names of two of the women: Mama Ocllo, whom he says was sister-wife of Mancocapacynga, and Ypamam[a]guaco. Garcilaso, El Inga, ([1609] 1966) says the sister-wife of Mango Capac was Ocllo Huaco. Garcilaso's version appears to conflate Mama Ocllo and Mama Huaco (or Ypa Huaco) of the other versions.
7. According to the myths, two of the brothers, Ayar Awqa and Manko Qapaq, each accompanied by two wives, arrived in Cusco, which was already inhabited by the Allcahuiza people, but where they founded what was to become the imperial center of Tawantinsuyu. Historically, Cusco had a moiety division into Upper and Lower Parts (*Hanan* and *Hurin*, respectively). Since the emperor Manko Qapaq is known to have belonged to Hurincusco, it has been suggested that Ayar Awqa was the founder of the Hanan moiety (Rostworowski 1986:131). Ayar Awqa was a warrior, as his name *awqa* signifies, but he later was transformed into stone. María Rostworowski attributes the role of warmaking to the Hanan Inkas, who made the imperial expansion of the state possible, while Hurin Inkas devoted themselves to priestly and agricultural activities, centered on the Temple of the Sun, which was located in Hurincusco. To the Inkas, war and agricultural fertility were seen as being interdependent.
8. Don Felipe Guaman Poma de Ayala was son of a native ruler of Lucanas in Chinchaysuyu. His father married *ñusta* Curi Ocllo, a younger daughter of the Emperor Inka Tupac Yupanqui. His chronicle was written over a period of thirty years, and he finished it about 1615. The edition consulted here is Guaman Poma (1980).

9. Don Joan de Santacruz Pachacuti Yamqui Salcamaygua was born in Orcosuyu in Qullasuyu, descendant of native rulers of the area. His account of Inka history was completed about 1613. The editions consulted here are Santacruz Pachacuti Yamqui (1879; 1968). Both authors adopted the foreign language and writing of their conquerors, and attempted to create a diachronic narrative of events that would be understood by the Spanish, but that would be based on an intimate knowledge of authentic Andean principles. Salomon (1984) has studied the legacy of these writers of indigenous descent, claiming that there are fundamental contradictions in this approach, since European and Andean principles were, and are, irreconcilable.
10. *Achi* is used here as a suffix attached to the name of Pachamama. As a separate word, it means "great great grandmother" in Cusco Quechua (Pérez Bocanegra 1631:609).
11. The rectangular motifs of this drawing resemble a textile design known as *tuqapu*, which appears on garments worn by the Inka emperors and empresses in the drawings of Guaman Poma (1980) and Morúa [1613]. See Ossio (1985). *Tuqapu* were colored woven designs used for the clothing of the nobility, and Duviols points out that the word is doubly associated with the Emperor Wiraqucha, named after the deity Wiraqucha; he cites the Spanish chronicler Sarmiento, who said that this Emperor was industrious and that he was the inventor of clothing and elaborate works, "called in their language *Viracocha tocapo*" (Duviols 1977:61–62). From the Quechua orations to the deity Wiraqucha recorded by Molina, El Cuzqueño [1571], analyzed by Duviols, it would seem that Wiraqucha was conceived of as a splendidly and richly dressed divinity. It is interesting to note that in the Huarochirí manuscript, the name Wiraqucha has been combined with that of a local god, Cuniraya, who was supplicated and to whom coca leaf offerings were made by master weavers when they had difficult work to do (Taylor 1987:51).
12. The manner in which Guaman Poma presents much of his information and especially the lists of various categories of people would seem to be influenced by the use of the *khipu*, in which information is stored by means of splayed, linear arrangements of knots. His discourse is couched in lineal categories, and in this context it is interesting to compare Jack Goody's discussion of the use of lists in societies with restricted access to literacy, even though the Inkas did not use writing (Goody 1977). The discrepancy between the women in the two pedigrees presented here is interesting. The men may not have had access to what Inka women regarded as their own knowledge, over which the women had control. Guaman Poma describes the *Quri kancha* (temple of the Sun), which was built by Manko Qapaq, in great detail (1980:87, 264–65). It is clear that he had access to information about where men worshipped the Sun. It is equally clear that although he knew that women worshipped the Moon at a place called *Pumap chupan* ("Puma tail"), he had no further access to the details of women's worship

(1980:265). It is probable that Inka women would have been in possession of a more authoritative version of female Inka lineages. Unfortunately, this information is lacking.

13. I use the term cosmogonic incest because I am talking about an Inka cosmogony, or, in other words, the generation of the Inka people, their begetting from an incestuous union between mother and son. This should not be confused with cosmology, which is the theory of the universe as an ordered whole.
14. For a detailed discussion of the Inka genealogies as presented by Guaman Poma and Santacruz Pachacuti Yamqui, see Dransart (unpublished manuscript), where the genealogies are presented in full.
15. According to Pérez Bocanegra (1631:609–10), *apuzqui* is an ancestor in the male line and *payay* is an ancestor in the female line. Inka kinship terminology and marriage have been discussed by Lounsbury (1978) and Zuidema (1980). Both authors interpret Inka descent as being both matrilineal and patrilineal, that is, women transmit to their daughters and men to their sons. However, Zuidema disagrees with Lounsbury's theory of asymmetrical alliance, in which a man marries the great granddaughter of their common great grandparents (this would create lines of bilateral filiation with gaps of three generations). Zuidema argues for a geographically located corporate social unit with an internal structure of masculine and feminine lines of descent, each of which consist of four generations descended from a male progenitor. However, Zuidema's emphasis on the male founder of an *ayllu* ignores the mythically sanctioned importance of the progenitrix who has the autoprocreative power to give birth without the intervention of a man.
16. *Suyru* is listed in the dictionary of Gonçalez Holguín (1952:333). However, the word does not seem to have been understood by Aymara speakers. Bertonio (1984, Bk II:242) lists Pachamama Suyrumama as a title of reverence for this deity, but the Aymara word for a long sweeping garment is *llumi*; Bertonio (1984, Bk II:208) lists *Llumitha*; *Arrastrar el vestido* ("to drag one's garment").
17. I observed an echo of a perceived difference in status among the ethnic Aymara peoples of the north of Chile. In the highlands, the Isluga women greatly esteem the textiles and dress of the people of Chiapa, a community situated in the valleys to the west of Isluga. Although Western dress is now worn in Chiapa, older people in Isluga remember the long garment of the Chiapa women, and they describe it as being unseamed, like the Inka *aqsu*.
18. The preserved corpse of Mama Huaco was thought to bring fertility to the fields; it was processed around the fields of Sausiro where she was said to have planted the first maize. This ceremony was observed in the month of Ayri-guay which, in Molina El Cuzqueño's account, corresponded to April (Molina 1943:66–67). The spilling of blood in a ritual encounter was

to promote the fertility of the earth, the Pachamama herself, from whose body Mama Huaco emerged.

19. I would like to thank Denise Arnold and Alison Spedding for discussing some of the themes expressed in this paper, although I am responsible for the form they take in this essay, along with any errors of interpretation. Finally, I wish to thank Shirley Ardener for her valuable advice in matters of presentation.

References

Adorno, R., "On pictorial language and the typology of culture in a New World chronicle," *Semiotica*, Vol. 36, No. 1/2, 1981, pp. 51–106.

Albornoz, C. de, "La instrucción para descubrir todas las huacas del Pirú y sus camayos y haciendas," *Journal de la Société des Américanistes*, Vol, 56, No. 1, 1967 (1568), pp. 7–39.

Bertonio, L., *Vocabulario de la lengua aymara*, La Paz: MUSEF, 1984 (1612).

Betanzos, J. de, "Suma y narración de los Incas," *Biblioteca de Autores Españoles*, Vol. 209, Madrid: Ediciones Atlas, 1968 (1551), pp. 1–56.

Boman, E., *Antiquités de la région andine de la République argentine et du desert d'Atacama*, Paris: Imprimerie Nationale, 1908.

Cieza de León, P. de "La crónica del Perú (Vol. 2)," *Biblioteca de Autores Españoles*, Vol. 26, Madrid: M. Rivadeneyra, 1862 (1550).

Dransart, P., "Pachamama Suyrumama: a study of dress and genealogy in the Inka Empire," manuscript, n.d.

Duviols, P., "Un procès d'idolâtrie. Arequipa 1671," *Fénix*, Vol. 16, 1966, pp. 198–211.

———, "Los nombres quechuas de Viracocha, supuesto 'Dios Creador' de los evangelizadores," *Allpanchis*, Vol. 10, 1977, pp. 53–63.

Garcilaso de la Vega, El Inga, *Royal Commentaries of the Incas and general history of Peru*, trans. H.V. Livermore, Austin: University of Texas Press, 1966 (1609, 1616).

Goody, J., *The domestication of the savage mind*, Cambridge: University Press, 1977.

Gonçalez Holguín, D., *Vocabulario general de todo el Perú llamada Qquichua o del Inca*, Lima: Instituto de Historia, 1952 (1608).

Gow, D. and R., "La alpaca en el mito y el ritual," *Allpanchis*, Vol. 8, 1975, pp. 141–64.

Guaman Poma de Ayala, F., *El primer nueva corónica y buen gobierno*, eds. J.V. Murra and R. Adorno, Mexico: Siglo Veintiuno, 1980 (1615).

Levillier, R., ed., *Don Francisco de Toledo, supremo organizador del Perú*, 3 vols., Buenos Aires: Espasa Calpe SA, 1942.

Lounsbury, F.G., "Aspects du système de parenté inca," *Annales: Economies, Sociétés et Civilisations*, Vol. 33, No. 5–6, 1978, pp. 991–1005.

Molina, C. de, "El Cuzqueño," "Ritos y fábulos de los Incas," *Los Pequeños Grandes Libros de Historia Americana*, Series 1, Vol. 4, Lima, 1943 (1571).

Moore, S.F., "Descent and filiation," *American Anthropologist*, Vol. 66, 1964, pp. 1308–1320.

Murra, J.V., "Cloth and its functions in the Inca State," *American Anthropologist*, Vol. 64, No. 4, 1962.

Ossio, J.M., *Los retratos de los Incas en la Crónica de Fray Martín de Morúa*, Lima: COFIDE, 1985.

Pérez Bocanegra, J., *Ritual formulario, e institución de curas, para administrar a los naturales de este reyno*, Lima: Geronymo de Contreras, with the Convento de Santo Domingo, 1631.

Posnansky, A., *Tihuanacu. La cuna del hombre americano*, Vol. 3, La Paz: Ministerio de Educación, 1958.

Rostworowski de Diez Canseco, M., "Succession, coöption to kingship, and royal incest among the Inka," *Southwestern Journal of Anthropology*, Vol. 16, 1960, pp. 417–27.

———, *Estructuras andinas del poder*, Lima: Instituto de Estudios Andinos, 1986.

Salomon, F., "Crónica de lo imposible: notas sobre tres historiadores indígenas peruanos," *Chungará*, Vol. 12, 1984, pp. 81–98.

———, "Ancestor cults and resistance to the state in Arequipa, ca. 1748–1754," in S.J. Stern (ed.), *Resistance, rebellion and consciousness in the Andean peasant world, 18th to 20th centuries*, Wisconsin: University Press, 1987, pp. 148–65.

Santacruz Pachacuti Yamqui Salcamaygua, J. de, "Relación de antigüedades deste reyno del Pirú," in Jimenez de la Espada (ed.), *Tres Relaciones de Antigüedades Peruanos*, Madrid, 1879 (1613), pp. 229–328.

———, "Relación de antigüedades deste reyno del Perú," *Biblioteca de Autores Españoles*, Vol. 209, Madrid: Ediciones Atlas, 1968 (1613), pp. 281–319.

Sarmiento de Gamboa, P., "Historia Indica," in R. Levillier, (ed.), Vol. 3, 1942 (1572), pp. 1–159.

Schneider, J., and A.B. Weiner, "Cloth and the organization of human experience," *Current Anthropology*, Vol. 27, 1986, pp. 178–84.

Silverblatt, I., *Moon, Sun, and Witches*, Princeton, New Jersey: Princeton University Press, 1987.

Taylor, G., *Ritos y tradiciones de Huarochirí del siglo XVII*, Lima: Instituto de Estudios Peruanos, 1987.

Urbano, H.O., "Wiraqucha y Ayar," *Héroes y funciones en las sociedades andinas*, Cusco: Centro de Estudios Rurales Andinos "Bartolomé Las Casas," 1981.

Zuidema, R.T., "Lieux sacrés et irrigation: tradition historique, mythes et rituels au Cuzco," *Annales: Economies, Sociétés et Civilisations*, Vol. 33, No. 5–6, 1978, pp. 1037–56.

———, "El sistema de parentesco incaico: una nueva visión teórica," in E. Mayer and R. Bolton (eds.), *Parentesco y matrimonio en los Andes*, Lima: Pontificia Universidad Católica del Perú, 1980.

Zuidema, R.T., and G. Urton, "La constelación de la llama en los Andes peruanos," *Allpanchis*, Vol. 9, 1976, pp. 59–119.

10

Kalabari Dress in Nigeria

Visual Analysis and Gender Implications

Susan O. Michelman and Tonye V. Erekosima

This paper analyzes Kalabari women's and men's dress by utilizing a method of visual analysis (DeLong 1987). Formal design qualities related to dress will be examined within a cultural context to help ascertain the significance and social meaning of dress. Highly developed contrasting forms of Kalabari women's and men's dress help transfer biological differences into socially prescribed gender roles. Additionally, as men and women rise in status, increasingly greater amounts of the body are covered with cloth and adornment.

DeLong (1987) provides a framework of terminology and methods for the systematic observation of dress as it interacts with the body and the surrounding environment. The term apparel-body-construct is used to mean "the visual form presented by the interaction of apparel on the human body, i.e., a construct or concept of a physical object based upon sense data" (DeLong 1987:3). Initially, the whole image is observed: shapes, sizes, texture, color, and all materials on the body, such as hats, jewelry, shoes, hair, cosmetics, or body modification. Next, the whole is subdivided into its parts: the head, trunk, and extremities. Circumstances of viewing include the immediate, adjacent space as well as the broader cultural context.

Ethnographic Orientation to the Kalabari

The Kalabari, a subunit of the Ijo ethnic group, reside in the Rivers state of Nigeria in the former Degema local government area. The Kalabari number about 800,000 to 1,000,000 people. This is a relatively small number as an independent cultural unit compared to Nigerian ethnic groups, such as the Yoruba or Igbo who are estimated to number

20,000,000 each. The Kalabari, however, who live in indigenous towns like Abonnema, Bakana, and Buguma, as well as several other village settlements, present a historical pattern of competitive trade relations with other Ijo subgroups. These include the Bonny, Okrika, and Nembe peoples – with whom they share similar cultural roots, as well as occupancy of the eastern delta of the Nigerian Atlantic coast. In addition, the Kalabari and these other peoples had a complex and independent political system prior to colonization, all of which contributed to defining them as distinctive cultural Ijo subgroups. These all trace their origin to the central delta region in which Ijo communities appear autochthonous.

Kalabari refers not only to the people who share a similar history, but also to a dialect of the northeastern Ijo language (Williamson 1968). Many of its speakers, however, are not necessarily of the same ethnic origin. The Kalabari dialect is one of seven divisions of the Kwa branch of the Niger-Congo language family, and shares cognates with the Benue-Congo branch. This distinction in Ijo linguistics contributes to its difficult classification, and emphasizes the major dialectical cleavage between the eastern Ijo and central-western Ijo groups, as well as within the eastern Ijo dialectical groups. Unlike other eastern Ijo groups, the Kalabari do not normally refer to themselves as Ijo, a term which was originally used by the central and western Ijo groups and has been extended to include the Eastern Ijo by administrators and ethnologists (Williamson 1968:124).

Exploitable resources from the eastern delta environment were limited and its inhabitants relied primarily on occupations of fishing, saltmaking, and trading, along with produce exchanged from the hinterland (Jones 1965:9). Although Kalabari towns and villages were somewhat isolated, these communities have never been self-sufficient. They depend on men's fishing, the exchange of their smoke-dried fish, and the sale of salt made by the women for trade with the people of the hinterland for bulk foodstuffs, tools, clothing, and domestic gear (Jones 1965:9). Environmental and dietary factors contributed to early movement and interchange of the indigenous people and promoted early internal and external trade relationships for valuable foodstuffs and other material goods, including textiles. This occurred even before the sixteenth century, when the first European contacts were made (Alagoa 1972). Transportation was accomplished by canoe and later by motorized boats, although more recently, through land dredging and road construction, roads now connect some areas in the delta. Within towns and villages, people travel on foot or by limited public transportation, such as cars, minibuses, motorbikes, and motorcycles, usually on a single thoroughfare.

Since employment opportunities are limited in small towns such as Buguma or Abonnema, residents often maintain two households; Monday through Friday they live in the neighboring industrial city of Port Harcourt, and return to these islands (which they consider their real home) on the weekend.

Kalabari History

The history of the Kalabari begins around 1000 A.D., by tracing the migration of various ethnic groups who converged on an island in the Niger Delta estuary of the Atlantic Coast, called the Rio Real. This settlement of diverse peoples assumed the name Kalabari, which was the name of the patriarch of one of the major migrant groups (Erekosima 1989:201). They may have initially settled in Owame, a village outside Amafa in the northern fringe of the Niger Delta (Tamuno and Alagoa 1980:1). The next generation moved to a new site, Elem Kalabari (New Calabar, Old Shipping), which was located further south on the estuary of the Rio Real.

The Kalabari themselves claim Elem Kalabari as their main ancestral home. As early as the 1600s, traders referred to Elem Kalabari as a major trade center on the West African Coast (Barbot 1746), important for indigenous people and later for the Portuguese, Dutch, and English until the 1880s (Alagoa 1972:135). Geographical location was advantageous to the Kalabari, as they acted as intermediaries both in the east-west and north-south trade routes (which were well established prior to the introduction of trade with the Europeans in the seventeenth century). Consequently, they grew politically influential and financially prosperous in the trade of slaves and palm oil within the eastern delta (Alagoa 1972)

By the fifteenth century, these groups had organized into a collective community of interacting sections or wards, not a small accomplishment, since local legend refers to earlier cannibalism between groups (Talbot 1932). Elem Kalabari was divided into seven wards (*polo*), that represented an autonomous group of people who had come from various geographic locations. In each ward the people worshiped different deities and practiced customs unique to their traditions (Alagoa 1965:112). Consequently, the town lacked economic and political solidarity against outside forces. In the middle of the eighteenth century, Amachree, a well-respected citizen of the Endeme ward, was acknowledged by the

Kalabari as the recognized founder and king. At that time, the Kalabari recognized Elem Kalabari as their common birthplace and King Amachree as their leader who united and founded a forceful dynastic tradition (Alagoa 1965:112). King Amachree expanded his power, offering protection and encouraging alliances with the established neighboring villages. This way he brought groups who were not originally Kalabari into the new polity of the Kalabari city-state.

Currently, the Kalabari inhabit about thirty communities in both urban and rural settlements in the eastern Niger delta along the Santa Barbara (Owuanga-Toru), San Bartholomeo (Kula-Toru), Sombreiro (Oloto-Toru) and New Calabar (Kalabari-Toru) Rivers (Horton 1970). Today, they recognize the towns of Abonnema, Bakana, and Buguma and Tombia as their major commercial and cultural centers.

Kalabari Kinship

The basic social unit of the Kalabari is the house (*wari*). Originally comprised only of descendants of a given progenitor, the composition of "house" members was altered during the period of European slave trade in the eighteenth century. Rivalry for this trade forced the Kalabari to incorporate thousands of non-Kalabari into their house system. They served as manpower to pull the large boats that a Portuguese adventurer had described in 1499 as capable of "carrying eighty men" (Pereira 1937). They also helped defend the island settlements against plundering by neighboring groups, and several of them were settled in the distant fishing ports that helped feed the crowded Kalabari towns.

These non-Kalabari were adopted as family members. The degree of assimilation of these non-Kalabari was total, including strict adherence to the Kalabari dress hierarchy. Each adoptee's head was shaved upon arrival by his or her putative mother, as another symbol, and this certified that from that moment, the new house member (who had been bought at one of the local slave markets) must be treated to all the rights and privileges as all other natural-born children of the family. Also, the adopted son who proved capable was able to marry the biological daughter of his "father," was financed by his parents to develop an independent economic base of his own as a trader, and was sponsored to start off a subsegment of the family unit as a house chief. He could also rise to leadership over the entire house at the death of the family patriarch (through processes of nomination and voting by its adult members or direct appointment by the patriarch himself while alive). This would be a succession overriding the normal rights of a firstborn son who had not fared well, in which the adopted son then assumed the power of disposing of all properties and affairs of his adoptive father. He managed family affairs, however, with the active participation of every adult and the advice of other elders.

This is a radical break with the traditional African practice, but one which the Kalabari justify by saying that the allegiance of such a stranger to his adoptive family is more secure than that of natural-born sons. This is because the latter also have loyalties to their mothers' family groups. This has been defined as the "expanded" family type of kinship group (Erekosima 1989).

The need to reconstruct society in the face of the prevailing challenge largely induced by the European slave trade was one reason the Kalabari had to reinforce the gender roles of "man" and "woman" as the foundations of the family, which they highlighted by giving a significant place in the communication of these roles to dress.

To maintain their house supremacy within the community and to rival outsiders, groups incorporated non-Kalabari peoples. Therefore, historically, the basis of membership in Kalabari society changed from common descent and kinship to general acceptance of the political and cultural leadership of the new "house" system and of the king (*amanyanabo*). Membership in the wards was enforced through strict practices. For example, various classes of people in the Kalabari community were acculturated through membership in two important age-graded men's and women's associations, called *sekiapu* and *egbele-ereme*.

Currently, many marriages are monogamous, but polygamy is also practiced and socially accepted (Daly 1984), although prior to Christianity, marriages were polygamous. Whether monogamous or polygamous, two forms of marriage are practiced currently: the *iya* and *egwa* bridewealth arrangement (Talbot 1932:437). The residence pattern of an extended as well as expanded family often corresponds with the type of marriage alliance. *Egwa* is the more common form of marriage where a small payment is given to the bride's family, giving the husband conjugal rights. The less frequent and and more prestigious *iya* marriage requires a high payment to the bride's family, usually in the form of gifts of land, or a house for the wife, and cloth (Talbot 1932:438). An *iya* marriage is culturally desirable to women, men, and children, as all parties thereby augment their social status. In the *egwa* marriage, children are designated to the lineage of both the mother and father, while in the *iya*, to that of the father alone. An *egwa* marriage can be changed to an *iya* after marriage, while the reverse does not occur.

As a final note, it is important to consider the ideal or traditional marriage arrangement for the Kalabari in relation to current practices. An *iya* marriage is uncommon in current practice, particularly among new or recently married partners who are establishing families and/or careers. *Egwa* marriages are more common, and are often associated with civil ceremonies as opposed to elaborate traditional practices. The *egwa* marriage, however, is often mixed with a church wedding, which entails most of the *iya* values. Not only is the marriage then regarded as indissoluble, but the children adhere to the male partner's lineage and inheritance pertains to this order.

Kalabari Ideology

The Kalabari belief system is a complex relationship between the person and a hierarchy of the ancestors, village deities, or heroes, and water people or modalities, each governing his or her "own particular range of human and natural concerns" (Horton 1970; Daly, Eicher, Erekosima 1986). They work both in cooperation and conflict with each other, and together provide an explanation of everything that happens in the Kalabari world. Their level of cooperation is much higher, however, and the Kalabari world is a largely optimistic and creative one. At the village level, the community heroes (*oru*) oversee the community and guard its principles of well-being, such as justice, peace, and artistry as a common heritage; within the lineage group, the ancestors (*duen*) influence their descendants in terms of moral conduct and achievement reflecting contributions to the collectivity; and the water spirits (*owu*) control animal and nature forces. Finally, the spirit of personal destiny (*so*) determines the pivotal actions of the individuals in relation to their particular talents or unique conduct, as well as unusual fate or fortune (Erekosima 1973:26). Compared to the community deities and the ancestors, the purported water denizens or nature forces are the most powerful and are more attuned to individual aspirations. Although they have never lived among men, they materialize in the human world today and are symbolized as pythons and rainbows or as masquerades that appear in Kalabari dance dramas.

Although many Kalabari profess to be Christians, their traditional beliefs still pervade their daily and ritual life. They divide their universe into two orders, the bodily or material (*oju*) and the spiritual or nonmaterial (*teme*). *Oju* has counterparts in *teme*, as objects can have a spiritual quality. Also, the Kalabari acknowledge the power of a divine female and male concept represented by *tamuno* and *so*. *Tamuno*, the female principle, governs the form and origin of life; while *so*, the male, rules its process and course.

Kalabari Dress

Kalabari dress has been examined by several authors from different points of view. Erekosima and Eicher have discussed the concept of cultural authentication (Erekosima 1979; Erekosima and Eicher 1981) expressed through Kalabari dress. Through trade, foreign goods – and particularly European cloths – were introduced into the Delta area as early as the sixteenth century (Alagoa 1972:291). The Kalabari incorporated these Western items into their indigenous system of dress and aesthetics, modifying them to make them part of their own ethnic identity. "The availability of clothing and adornment used throughout *iria* is a result of active internal and external trade relationships in the Delta rather than from locally developed technologies. These items usually are not of local manufacture, but are culturally authenticated expressions that are organized into characteristic, recognizable and uniquely Kalabari ensembles" (Daly 1984:97). For example, *pelete bite*, a textile unique to the Kalabari, is produced by extracting threads from imported madras (*injiri*) to form motifs on the textiles. This cloth is worn by both men and women as wrappers, incorporated in the decoration of funeral beds and rooms, and worn on other formal or ceremonial occasions (Erekosima and Eicher 1981; Eicher and Erekosima 1987; Daly, Eicher, and Erekosima 1986).

Dress and adornment are also associated with hierarchy and status among the Kalabari (Daly 1984; Erekosima and Eicher 1981; Erekosima 1989; Michelman 1987). Clothing choices not only represent an aesthetic expression, but also indicate the position of that person within Kalabari society. Status demarcations serve to distinguish between insiders and outsiders, as well as indicating differences between ranks within that social system.

Men and women achieve status separately in Kalabari society: women achieve recognition through the process of *iria* (change in status associated with attaining physical and moral maturation and eventually reproducing), while men ascend through age, economic and political achievement, and personal accomplishments. Each progression, for men and women, is associated with a change in attire that reflects their newly acquired position.

Hierarchy of Kalabari Men's Dress

The four main categories of Kalabari men's status are: 1) *Asawo* or "young men that matter": These are youth of secondary-school age or young workers who carry out duties of community interest like undertaking interments or disciplining public miscreants. This is the lowest category of political importance. 2) *Opu asawo* or "gentlemen of substance": These older adults monitor the affairs of state and are spokesmen for various interests. They also adjudicate among members of the community through the Sekiapu or Ekine Society. 3) *Alabo* or chiefs: These men administer the corporate units that make up the Kalabari expanded family houses, villages, and towns that form the city-state. 4) *Amanyanabo* is the sovereign who rules the Kalabari state and people. There are specific dress forms associated with each of these categories.

The *etibo*[1] is a version of a European shirt that is elongated to the knee, more free flowing, and has the collar removed (Plate 10.1). Worn with a wrapper, it is generally a light, white fabric worn with one stud of gold or silver at the neck. An *etibo* shirt tail is always kept loose over the wrapper and is never tucked in. Sleeves are usually folded to a point between the wrist and elbow. Socks are not worn with shoes and the head is usually bare. This category of dress is associated with *asawo* or "young men that matter."

The *woko*[2], worn more formally than the *etibo*, extends to between the knee and ankle and may be combined with a wrapper or matching trousers, an English hat, and a walking stick. (Plate 10.2) The front of the garment often has some embellishment of ladder or fish-gill design, and accommodates three stud buttonholes and attached chain. The studs would be gold or silver to match the color of the particular *woko*. *Woko* is associated with *opu asawo* or "gentlemen of substance."

Doni is also derived from the basic shirt form, but extends from the shoulders to the feet (Plate 10.3). Made of thick, woolen material (*blan-gidi*) or silk (*loko*) with bright, multicolored compositions or stripes, it has a short, frontal collar with a provision of four stud buttonholes connected by a gold or silver chain. Long sleeves are folded back to expose a bright, white shirt worn underneath with links holding the sleeves together. It is worn with an *injiri* wrapper that barely shows below the long gown, where shoes and socks may be worn if preferred

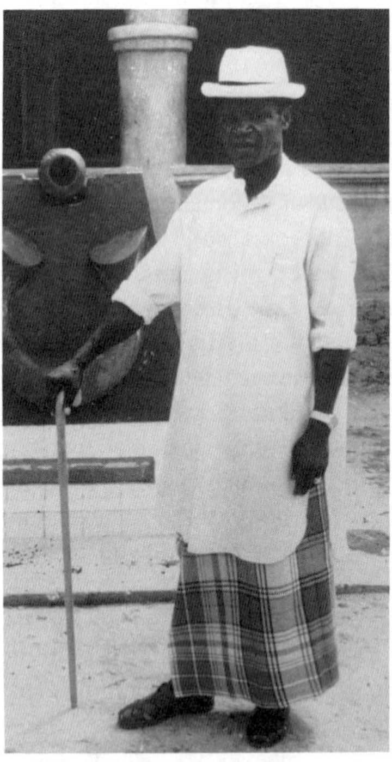

Plate 10.1 Kalabari man dressed in *etibo* that conforms with *asawo* or "young men that matter" category of men's status. (Photographed by Joanne Eicher in Buguma, Nigeria)

Plate 10.2 Kalabari man dressed in *woko* that conforms with *opu asawo* or "gentlemen of substance" category of men's status. (Photographed by Joanne Eicher in Tombia, Nigeria)

to the bare feet. On ceremonial occasions, the *doni* would be worn with the elaborate indigenously developed hat, *ajibulu*, which has multi-colored feathers, tinsel, beads, and mirrors. A variety of other hats may be worn, such as a top hat, or a martial helmet with feathers. Necklaces of leopard's teeth or cowrie shells and corals, gold rings, a fan of feathers, or an elephant tusk in the left hand and a walking stick in the right completes the ensemble.

One other form of men's dress is the *attigra*, which is worn by chiefs (and is associated with the same status as *doni*) but is especially adopted for men's dance displays and other ceremonial occasions. A long, flowing robe, similar to the *doni*, it is made of elaborate fabric, usually velvet embroidered with gold or silver thread. The *ajibulu* is

Plate 10.3 Kalabari men dressed to indicate different status; Western attire, *doni*, or chief's status (two center men), and *woko* (on right) that conforms with *opu asawo* or "gentlemen of substance" category of status. (Photographed by Joanne Eicher in Buguma, Nigeria)

worn on the head, and cane, elephant's tusk, and fan are carried in the hands as with the *doni*. All other adornments correspond with those worn with the *doni*, except more elaborately. For example, it is permissible to wear gold rings on almost all the fingers with the *attigra*.

The *ebu* is the most revered dress among Kalabari men. A long, flowing garment that extends from shoulders to feet, it is usually made of *injiri*. The neck is cut in a "V" and has a flap of material that falls over the shoulders and forms a square-shaped collar that ends just below the scapula, somewhat like a collar on a sailor's suit. This may have been the model for the design, since the sailor was truly a fitting symbol of the foreign trading tycoons. Under the *ebu* a wrapper of *injiri* is always worn and is the same fabric as the upper garment. The dress is simple, with few accompanying adornments. Earlier in Kalabari history, it was normally worn only by the king or a few outstanding chiefs, whereas today it is more widely worn. The importance of the *ebu* is associated with its being made of madras (*injiri*), which is regarded as the cloth most representative of Kalabari culture, the way that a flag symbolizes a people's identity. *Injiri* invariably features in the birth and funeral ceremonies of the Kalabari.

Hierarchy of Kalabari Women's Dress

Traditionally, status distinctions among Kalabari women were recognized through the process of *iria*, or rites of passage that define the forms of appearance representing the five stages of Kalabari womanhood. These five stages correlated with prepuberty, puberty, maturity, marriage, and motherhood. The sequence of these stages depended on external signs of physical maturation and public acknowledgement of these changes (Iyalla 1968; Daly 1984; Akobo 1985). Each stage corresponded to a public display of appearance that correlated with her developing role status within Kalabari society. Because of the expense involved in dressing and adorning the girl, parental ability to pay was also a consideration. For example, during *ikuta de* (bead display) the girl would normally wear three different types of *ikuta* (beads), one for every week. Some parents could dress their daughter with as many as eight types of beads. Therefore, the duration of each ceremonial stage corresponded to the wealth of the parents and its display.

Bite pakiri iwain (translates as "tying half the length of a piece of cloth") marks the start of the Kalabari girl's menses. Up until this time, she had mainly been instructed on social etiquette and domestic responsibilities. Now she was considered physically mature (although not yet socially mature), potentially able to bear children. She wore cloth to cover the pubic region (navel and buttocks were exposed as well as the upper part of her body). Adornment consisted of small, inexpensive, colored glass beads and simple earrings.

Ikuta de was the stage that marked the girl's initial budding breast development. By this time she had been instructed more extensively on matters of intimate feminine hygiene, friendships, and morality. Participation in *ikuta de* indicated both physical and social maturity. The wearing of beads was emphasized in this stage through a formal outing or display, and clothing was considered less important, since it obscured the visibility of the female body and its development. In the era predating European trade, young girls wore no cloth, only waistbeads. Later, they covered their buttocks and breasts with cloth underneath their waistbeads (Daly 1984:56).

Konju Fina ("waist tying stage") demonstrated that a Kalabari female was old enough to tie cloth at the waist, and had attained maturation of her reproductive capabilities. Of equal significance with this physical sign was that of social skills for relating to men. A stream of homilies warned about misadventures in the handling of men, and formulas were shared on how to put them in their places. For instance, a Kalabari woman never declared her full financial worth to a man, even her husband. She always kept a reserve of funds in escrow to draw upon, pending a family emergency, or to meet some immediate needs of her children and herself, or to help her weather unexpected exigencies, like divorce or the death of a spouse. Her developed figure, particularly her breasts and buttocks, allowed her to wear wrappers properly. The Kalabari qualitatively judged this maturity by running the palm of the hand over the buttocks to determine whether they were substantial enough to carry the wrapper (Daly 1984). Short wrappers (a set of one to four) were worn and layered (probably to increase the desired effect of bulk at the midsection), with the most prestigious cloth on the outside. The breasts were entirely covered with a blouse. Many beads of coral worn as bracelets, kneebands, and necklaces adorned the ensemble at the outing ceremony.

Bite sara was the traditional clothing ensemble worn by the adult Kalabari female. (Plate 10.4) Apparel includes a "down" wrapper that is worn to the ankle and a second "up" wrapper that is worn over the down wrapper and extends to the knee. The blouse must conform in costliness to the rest of the wrapper ensemble. Most desirable are imported lace or beaded blouses. Body adornment includes jewelry such as bracelets, rings, necklaces, and earrings made of gold or coral. Head treatment, including hairstyle or head tie are more of personal choice. Sandals or shoes, handkerchiefs, and purses complete the attire.

Iriabo refers to the final stage of traditional Kalabari womanhood, or postpartum practices following childbirth, and is largely a ceremonial phase. (Plate 10.5) Periods of confinement and fattening terminate with the process of "coming out." Complex patterns of clothing, body adornment, movement, and decorum are associated with this practice (Daly 1984).

Analysis of Kalabari Men's and Women's Dress

The following concepts adapted from DeLong (1987) will be used to provide the basis for a visual analysis of Kalabari men's and women's dress (see Table 10.1).

Table 10.1 Visual Priorities of the Apparel/Body/Construct

Closed: A form that is self-contained, with the silhouette acting as a visual boundary.	Open: The apparel-body-construct and the surrounding environment visually interact with each other.
Part: A unit of the whole which has a measure of separation or distinction from the rest of the apparel-body-construct.	Whole: The apparel-body-construct is perceived as a unit.
Planar Separation: Visual distinction between foreground and background on the apparel-body-construct.	Planar Integration: The foreground is integrated with background on the apparel-body construct.
Flat: The apparel-body-construct is perceived initially as a two-dimensional form.	Rounded: The apparel-body-construct is perceived as a three-dimensional form.
Determinate: Surfaces appear definite, sharp, regular and clear-cut. These surfaces usually have little visual texture and have little potential for light and shadow.	Indetermine: Surface appears less definite, blurred, or soft, or with infinite levels of figure-ground ambiguity.
Vertical Orientation: The apparel-body-construct is viewed as columnar.	Horizontal Orientation: Through multiple use of horizontal expressions in body and dress the eye tends to move across the body rather than up and down.

The *doni* (see Plate 10.3), for men, will be compared and contrasted with the *bite sara* (see Plate 10.4), for women, as they are of parallel status for women and men. Initially, the *doni* presents a vertical orientation due to the long, uninterrupted head-to-ankle presentation of one cloth type, specifically, *blangidi* or *loko*. Additionally, the vertical row of buttons and vertical design of fabric on the bodice accentuates a columnar quality. In contrast, the *bite sara*, indicates a horizontal orientation. The use of multiple types of cloth and adornment function to segment and draw the eye across the body. Visually, this tends to

Plate 10.4 Kalabari woman dressed in *bite sara* stage of women's dress, indicating that she is an adult female, married, and probably had a child. (Photographed by Joanne Eicher in Buguma, Nigeria)

Plate 10.5 Kalabari woman attired as an *iriabo* or dress associated with traditional postpartum practices. (Photographed by Susan Michelman in Abonnema, Nigeria)

accentuate the rounded features of the body, particularly the torso.

When examining determinate/indeterminate aspects of the *doni* and *bite sara*, the *doni* is made of one type of fabric, making the surface appear to have less potential for light and shadow. In contrast, the *bite sara* utilizes multiple fabrics of varying texture, pattern, and color, creating infinite levels of figure-ground ambiguity and a softer, more indefinite surface.

The *doni* appears more flat, or two-dimensional, in its presentation while the *bite sara* is perceived as more rounded and three-dimensional. Again, this is probably due to use in the *doni* of a simple, streamlined fabric in a vertical presentation, while the *bite sara* exhibits multiple cloth types wrapped horizontally around the body, accentuating its rounded form, particularly the mid-section. This becomes more pronounced in postpartum *iria*, where the roundness is associated with ample fat on the woman's body.

Planar segregation is more consistently a description of the *doni* while planar integration is exhibited with the *bite sara*. The *doni* is a simpler, less complex shape, showing uniformity of color, while the *bite sara* demonstrates the use of complex shape, color, and line contrasts found in the ensemble of blouse, combination of wrappers, and display of adornment such as the headtie.

The silhouette of the woman is viewed part to whole. Each part of the costume is viewed independently. Sections of the body are segmented by distinct pattern and color differences. The wrappers and blouse are distinguished from each other by pattern and color. The coral necklaces and bracelets segment the body, as contrast is made with her skin color. She appears as multiple segments before she is perceived visually as a whole. Part to whole viewing accentuates the display of horizontal, rounded aspects of the body, particularly the torso. In contrast, the man in the *doni* is visually perceived as a whole before noting individual parts. The *doni* promotes viewing the body in a unified, linear, visual image.

Both men's and women's dress are closed forms that do not interact with the surrounding environment, and both are self-contained. For the woman, the roundness of her head, arms, torso, and cylinder-like shape of the lower half of her body (suggested by use of the wrapper), describe a convex shape that tends to enclose the figure. Headtie, necklace, ring, and bracelet accentuate the tubular nature of the woman's body. The Kalabari man also wears rounded shapes that are created by voluminous fabric, rounded at the shoulder with continuous folds and curves. Dark skin color against a light background also tends to give an impression of separateness from the surrounding environment. While the closed form conveyed by the woman focuses on the rounded visible body, the man's closed form is demonstrated more through display of textiles and adornment than body silhouette.

Significance of Kalabari Men's and Women's Dress

Both Kalabari women and men have prescribed rules of clothing assemblage that have been documented by Daly (1984) and Erekosima (1989). Daly states, "The cloth or wrapper was chosen first and the upper body clothing selected to match or coordinate with the cloth type worn during *iria* in three ways: it should be comparable in costliness to the cloth type worn, contain one or more corresponding colours found in the cloth, and be of similar ornateness" (Daly 1984:50). Men also pay equal attention to detail when considering clothing assembly. Each item, including accessories, has been prescribed according to status. Erekosima writes that "a white cotton shirt is worn as *etibo* . . . with one stud of gold or silver attached to it. The long sleeves are also frequently folded to a point on the arm, half-way between the wrist and elbow. A white handkerchief around the neck gives an added touch of class" (Erekosima 1982:36).

Men's attire demonstrates social and political achievement, particularly among other Kalabari men, and does not emphasize the procreative aspect of social development, as does women's dress. Thus, men's dress emphasizes power and social responsibility, and women's dress draws attention to moral and physical development. An example of dress emphasizing power is shown by the increasingly ornate or elaborate hats that are worn as men progress in status. The *etibo*, or dress of the lowest status level, appears with a simple small-brimmed felt hat or none at all. In the next status level, *woko* is generally worn with an embroidered, round "smoking cap" or with a simple small-brimmed felt or straw hat. The *woko* is worn with a greater variety of hats than *etibo*. The *doni*, which is reserved for the category of a chief, designates that a variety of elaborate hats may be worn, such as the top hat or the imported martial helmet of bygone days, with a plume of white feathers flying from the top. On ceremonial occasions the *doni* would also be worn with the elaborate *ajibulu*, which has multicolored feathers and components of tinsel, as well as brass-bead borders. The *attigra* and the *ebu*, the domain of distinguished chiefs, is worn frequently with the *ajibulu* and top hat, or, in the case of the *amanyanabo*, a crown. This progression implies increased attention to hat size, decoration, expense, and variety.

Kalabari females progressed to full womanhood through wearing distinctive styles of dress with ascending values of complexity that marked physical and social maturity. In a society where sexual looseness was abhorred, discipline was required to avoid early pregnancy, mainly through chastity. An austere cultivation of character was, therefore, the underlying expectation for young women who progressed through the maturation hierarchy to an honorable marriage and eventual childbirth. Through this process, the society avoided unplanned childbirth and desecration of family sanctity, and obviated the economic disaster of unviable parenthood. The *iria* system, therefore, constituted a powerful social regulation mechanism for women and men through the device of incentives symbolizing the multistage forms of dress and associated acts of recognition.

Few men completed the hierarchy by achieving chieftaincy, a rare and competitive event reserved for men in middle age. In contrast, most Kalabari women progressed to *iria* and achieved *bite sara* by age sixteen prior to the introduction of universal primary education (UPE) in modern Nigeria in 1976 (Daly 1984). The women continually replenished society with new participants, while men controlled the activities that served public ends. The extent of the Kalabari woman's role-independence is illustrated by the fact that with *egwa* marriage, all her meals, cooked in the husband's lineage abode, were carried back to her own family's abode to be eaten. Traditionally, this did not end until an *iya* ceremony was performed, even if the marriage had lasted for decades. With the *iya* form of marriage, her husband's family had to provide her with land or a residence that was entirely her own. Then, at her death, her corpse was still returned to her family of birth. The Kalabari have a saying that with *iya*, although a husband obtained permanent conjugal rights over his wife and an inheritance of all her offspring, he did not simultaneously acquire her person.

Conclusions

As men and women rise in status, greater amounts of the body are covered and more cloth and adornment are added. For example, with men, hats increase in usage as well as in complexity of decoration. At the highest levels of men's dress, *ebu* and *attigra*, the entire body was covered except for the face and hands. The functional role of dress has been superseded by social role and cultural identity, as evidenced in the multiple layers of cotton, wool, and velvet material used by the Kalabari in their humid and equatorial environment.

The early age at which Kalabari women fulfill their role may be a result of two factors. One may have been in response to the physical readiness of the female to reproduce by adolescence, and the cultural demands of chastity. Historically, the second may have been the need of society for a rapid population growth to accommodate its manpower needs in the slave trade environment.

The premium placed on the integrity of the social order called forth such dire sanctions as the disgrace of having a woman who died in childbirth be thrown to the vultures, instead of being given the honor of a burial; an ominous threat that stood alongside the systematic and highly visible rewards of the *iria* symbolic system that encouraged conformity.

In conclusion, use of visual analysis (DeLong 1987) to examine formal design qualities of Kalabari women's and men's dress enhances how we see and interpret Kalabari dress. Visual analysis is a methodology that delineates the visual process: observing the whole image, breaking it into visual units in order to study their makeup and interaction, and then putting them back together again. This methodology applies a vocabulary appropriate to understanding the visual effects of apparel on the human body within a cultural context. This visual analysis of Kalabari dress demonstrates that the contrast of male and female prescribed dress hierarchies relates to this people's interpretation of physical maturity and gendered social roles developed within the context of the Kalabari cultural system.

Notes

1. *Etibo* is a Kalabari version of the English words that indicated the original cost of the shirt, eight "bobs" or shillings in British currency (Erekosima 1984:9).
2. *Woko* is an abbreviated form of the Kalabari word *wokorowokoro*, meaning "loose fitting," and is made of a heavier, more expensive fabric than the *etibo*, but never of a bright color or of printed English wool flannel, known as *blangidi* in Kalabari.

References

Akobo, D., "Oral Traditions of Buguma: Iria Ceremony a Case Study," Department of Library Studies, Ibadan: University of Ibadan, May 1985.

Alagoa, E.J., "The Settlement of the Niger Delta: Kuo Oral Traditions," Ph.D. diss., University of Wisconsin, 1965.

Alagoa, E.J., *A History of the Niger Delta*, Ibadan, 1972.

Barbot, J.A., "Description of the Coasts of North and South Guinea," in A. Churchill, ed., *A Collection of Voyages and Travels*, 3d ed., Vol. 5, London: H. Lintot and J. Osborn, 1746.

Daly, M.C., J.B. Eicher, and T.V. Erekosima, "Male and Female Artistry in Kalabari Dress," *African Arts*, May 1986.

Daly, M.C., "Kalabari Female Appearance and the Tradition of *Iria*," Ph.D. diss., University of Minnesota, 1984.

DeLong, M.R., *The Way We Look*, Ames, Iowa: Iowa State University Press, 1987.

Eicher, J.B., and T.V. Erekosima, "Kalabari Funerals: Celebration and Display," *African Arts*, Vol. 21, No. 1, November 1987.

Erekosima, T.V., "The Tartans of Buguma Women: Cultural Authentication," paper presented at African Studies Association, Los Angeles, California, October 1979.

Erekosima, T.V., "The Use of Apparel and Accessories for Expressing Status in Nigerian Societies: The Kalabari Case Studied as an Education Technology," Instructional Resources Centre, Port Harcourt, Nigeria: University of Port Harcourt, 1982.

Erekosima, T.V., "Analysis of a Learning Resource for Political Integration Applicable to Nigerian Secondary School Social Studies: The Case of Kalabari Men's Traditional Dress," Ph.D. diss., Catholic University, 1989.

Erekosima, T.V., and J.B. Eicher, "Kalabari Cut-Thread and Pulled-Thread Cloth," *African Arts*, Vol. 14, No. 2, February 1981, pp. 48–51, 87.

Ereks, T.V., "Categories of the Self: A Philosophical Extrapolation in Cultural Dynamism," *Oduma*, Vol. 1, No. 1, October 1973, pp. 21–27.

Horton, R., "Kalabari Culture and History," *African Notes*, Vol. 2, 1970, pp. 5–7.

Iyalla, B.S., "Womanhood in the Kalabari," *Nigeria Magazine*, Vol. 98, November 1968, pp. 216–24.

Jones, G.I., "Time and Oral Tradition with Special Reference to Eastern Nigeria," *Journal of African History*, Vol. 6, 1965, pp. 153–60.

Michelman, S.O., "Kalabari Female and Male Aesthetics: A Comparative Visual Analysis," M.A. thesis, University of Minnesota, 1987.

Michelman, S.O., "Dress in Kalabari Women's Societies," Ph.D. diss., University of Minnesota, 1992.

Pereira, D.P., *Esmeraldo do Situo Orbis*, London: Hakluyt Society, 1937.

Talbot, P.A., *Tribes of the Niger Delta: Their Religions and Customs*, New York: Barnes and Noble, Inc., 1932.

Tamuno, T.N., and E.J. Alagoa, "King Amachree I of Kalabari," in *Eminent Nigerians of the Rivers State*, Ibadan, Nigeria: Heinemann Educational Books Ltd., 1980.

Williamson, K., "Languages of the Niger Delta," *Nigeria Magazine*, 1968, pp. 124–30

11

Whose Sleeves . . . ?

Gender, Class, and Meaning in Japanese Dress of the Seventeenth Century

Louise Allison Cort

The goal of this paper is to outline the multiple ways in which the *kosode*, the principle outer garment of male and female Japanese costume from the late fifteenth through the nineteenth centuries, represented gender, social status, and cultural values. The T-shaped cut of the *kosode* with its wide body and small sleeves did not differ drastically for men and women, although subtle variations in details and drape are observable and meaningful. Instead, the meaningful "content" of the *kosode* was literally the pattern contained within the unchanging outline.

This discussion focuses on the seventeenth century, a period within which Japanese garments underwent increasing differentiation in the patterns associated with gender, while a multitude of new dyeing techniques gave far greater flexibility to the rendering of pattern. The seventeenth century corresponds to the opening third of the Edo period (1615–1868), when the newly established Tokugawa rulers organized their government around a clearly defined hierarchy of social classes. Carefully regulated custom associated certain patterns with the privileged noble and warrior classes. At the same time, growing prosperity among the lowest-ranking merchant class was expressed in increased lavishness of dress, which the government attempted to control with sumptuary edicts. Abundance of monetary means and abundance of textile techniques strained against countervailing rules, creating a vibrant tension that is manifest in textile patterns.

The diverse evidence for this discussion will be taken from selected surviving garments that can be associated reliably with a specific social class,[1] from illustrated manuals of behavior, and from descriptions in contemporaneous fiction of clothing and practices relating to it. The point of departure is an unusual genre of polychrome screen painting that flourished during the late sixteenth and seventeenth centuries, and took as its subject matter the representation of *kosode* draped over lacquered wooden garment racks or folding screens. The garments are never seen in their entirety, only as abstract shapes representing folded and overlapping robes, juxtaposing a delightful jumble of color and pattern. The necessary custom of airing clothing after wearing evolved into a form of interior display, and the painted screens replicate this practice.

These *trompe-l'oeil* renderings might be taken as "mere decoration" were it not for an illustration in an encyclopedia called *Shin chie no umi* (New ocean of wisdom), first published in 1724, of "Rules for displaying *kosode* on the lacquer rack" (Fig. 11.1). Stating that the display should "reflect the scope of the seasons," the page shows women's garments on the upper bar ordered from right to left in ground colors and patterns associated with spring (tie-dyed "deer-spot" pattern; blue), summer (peonies; red), midsummer (embroidered chrysanthemums; yellow), autumn (chrysanthemums and maple leaves; white), and winter (snowflakes; black) (Tanaka and Tanaka 1970:302). The lower bar holds sashes and changes of garments whose colors and patterns can be chosen "at will." This careful ordering of pattern and color suggests that the arrays of garments depicted in the screens probably conveyed encoded meanings now lost.[2] The genre was known as the *tagasode* or "whose sleeves . . . ?" screen, from the use of that term in classical poetry to evoke an absent woman.[3] That the patterns of overlapping garments could be of sufficient meaning – whatever those meanings were – to become the subject of a genre of painting suggests, moreover, the compelling interest of costume pattern for Japanese of the seventeenth century.

Gender

Let us now consider some aspects of the patterning of the seventeenth-century *kosode* and its range and depth of meanings, beginning with the issue of gender distinctions. In the first quarter of the century, men's and women's garments were not yet clearly differentiated by color, motif, or design (Stinchecum 1984:26,40). Both sexes wore brightly and boldly patterned garments; in genre-painting representations, only details such as hairstyles or swords give a basis for distinction. Nonetheless, contemporaneous costumes for the Nō theater convey in exag-

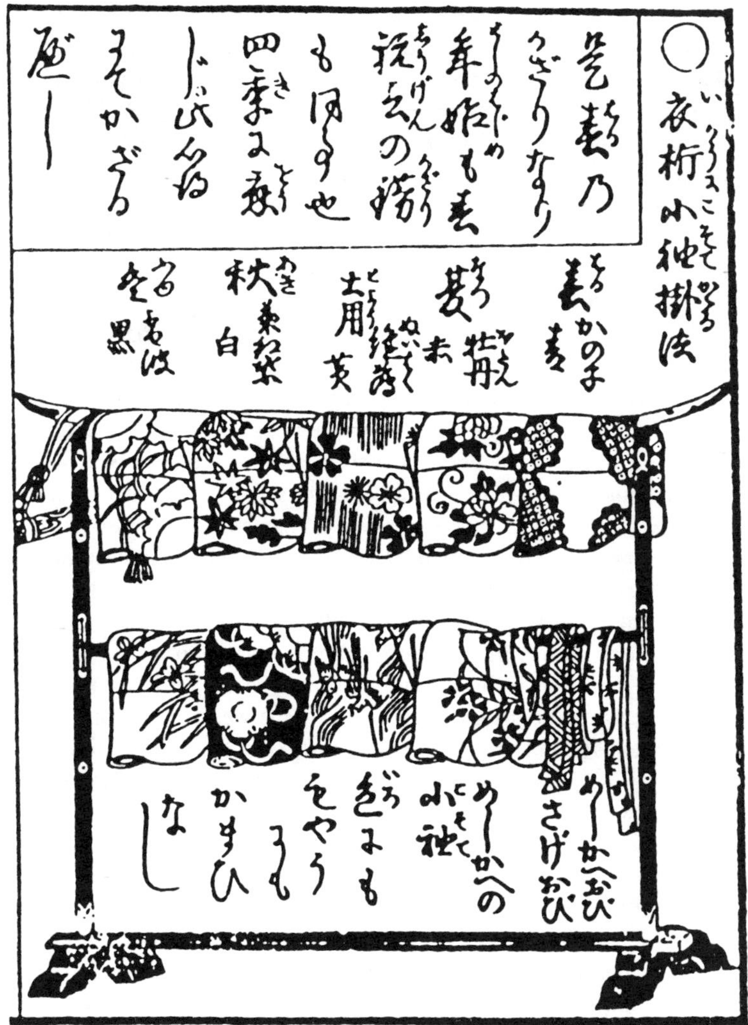

Figure 11.1 "Rules for displaying *kosode* on the lacquer rack," in *Shin chie no umi,* 1724 (Tanaka and Tanaka 1970:302).

gerated form a prevailing association of hardedged geometric patterns or large isolated figures with masculine roles, and softer, smaller pictorial motifs, especially flowers, with feminine roles.[4] In everyday *kosode*, however, gender distinctions became more pronounced through a somewhat different process whereby, by mid-century, large pictorial patterns became associated exclusively with women's robes while men's garments became increasingly subdued, with patterning limited to stripes or small overall geometric figures (Stinchecum 1984:26). Ihara Saikaku's 1686 novel, *The Life of an Amorous Woman*, describes "the appearance that an up-to-date courtesan favours in a man": "his kimono, of which both the outside and the lining are of the same yellow silk, is dyed with fine stripes; over this he wears a short black crested jacket of Habutae[5] silk. His sash is wrought of light yellowish-brown Ryūmon[6], and his short coat is of reddish-brown Hachijō pongee[7], lined at the bottom with the same material" (*Ihara* 1963:145).

The elegant man thus described is a merchant. Warriors wore even more subdued clothing, consisting of a full-length plain-weave silk robe called a *noshime*, dyed in a solid color except for a band of *ikat* patterning around the hips, worn under a sleeveless jacket and full trousers which covered most of the patterned area.[8] The set of jacket and trousers, called *kamishimo*, was tailored from stiff fabric stencil-dyed with fine, over-all repeat patterns ("small figure" or *komon*) of geometric motifs or felicitous plants, animals, or objects. The understated content of such generic patterns was simply "masculinity" or a wish for good fortune. At a distance, however, the small patterns blurred to a monochrome effect; only the conspicuous family crests dyed on the front and back of the jacket stood out to indicate instantly the wearer's affiliation, just as the color and cut of his *kamishimo* showed his rank. Family and rank, not taste in pattern, were of central interest in the increasingly elaborate warrior bureaucracy of the Edo period.

Paintings of genre scenes do show men dressed as merchants or warriors, but the visual interest of male garments clearly paled beside that of women's as the century wore on. Only a few portraits of "Kambun dandies" correspond to the paintings of single flamboyantly dressed "Kambun beauties" of the Kambun era (1661–1673). Printed design books, or *hiinagata-bon*, which began to be published in the same era, focus almost exclusively on women's *kosode*, possibly because the composition of the painted, dyed, and embroidered designs encompassed the entire garment, whereas swatch books were sufficient for the monochrome plain-weaves, woven stripes, and stencil-dyed *komon* patterns for males.

Continuing this identification of "dress" with "female dress," modern museum exhibitions and catalogues offer few seventeenth-century men's garments for consideration.[9] By focusing almost exclusively on women's *kosode* with their large, dramatic patterns, they imply that the understated, almost invisible pattern that became the basis of masculine style is too subtle to be of interest, and so they deprive us of the opportunity of making a balanced comparison. For want of published examples of extant male garments, the discussions of status and content that follow will focus exclusively on female *kosode*, although the contrasting male counterpart should not be forgotten.

Social Status

A hierarchy of status was the core of Tokugawa social organization. Beneath the emperor and court nobility, warriors, farmers, craftsmen, and merchants were ranked in descending order as the four major classes. That dress was an explicit and major expression of status is shown by contemporary books such as *Jinrin Kinmō Zui* (Illustrated enlightenment on human relations, 1690), which describes the dress permitted to warriors and certain merchants and artisans in the course of expounding "the proper conduct [of all] from the most elevated lord to the lowliest peasant" (Tanaka and Tanaka 1969:305).

High status presumed large wardrobes. With status came the responsibility of knowing when and how to wear an array of appropriate dress on everyday and ceremonial occasions and at specified times during the seasons.[10] For example, the summer garment for noble and warrior women was the *katabira*, made from ramie with patterns dyed in the fine paste-resist techniques called *chayazome* (using indigo) and *honzome* (various brown dyes), and accented with embroidery.[11] The precise design of the *katabira* varied according to rank and occasion. On formal occasions, upper-ranking court women wore overall-patterned *katabira* of *honzome*, while middle-ranking women wore similar garments patterned with *chayazome*, and lower-ranking women wore robes patterns on the lower body only.[12] Everyday *katabira* used other forms of dyeing in full or partial motifs drawn in a larger scale.

Poor peasants, at the other end of the social scale, were constrained by rules of the military domains within which they labored to giving minimal attention and outlay to clothing. A 1674 ruling of the Tosa domain restricts peasants to owning "only one hemp garment for summer and one paper garment for winter" (*Toyomasa-kō Ki*, Vol. 14:1674.4.27).[13] A 1670 decree from the same domain forbids "garments inappropriate to farmers and dyed cloth of high price" (*Toyomasa-kō Ki*, Vol. 3:1670.7.17).

Although merchants ranked lowest in status, their professional interaction with warriors and nobles dictated a range of proper modes of dress, while their growing wealth gave access to the most luxurious materials and up-to-date styles for their wives and daughters. The sumptuary edicts on dress issued by the government in 1683 were aimed chiefly at the merchant class when they prohibited women from using gold brocade, heavy embroidery, or overall "fawn spot" tie-dyeing, even though the laws affected noble and warrior women as well (Kirihata 1980:57).[14] The *katabira* worn in summer by women of the merchant class lack the delicate scale and refinement of upper-class garments, but they dazzle with their sweeping patterns, rich textures, and lavish gold embroidery. The full range of social classes of women arrayed in their proper garb is the subject of a 1723 printed book by the Kyoto artist Nishikawa Sukenobu (1670–1751), entitled *Hyakunin jōrō shinasadame* (Determination of the qualities of one hundred women) (Nishikawa 1979:1723). Advances in techniques of woodblock illustration allow more elaborate rendering of detail in dress for women ranging from the empress and court ladies through noble wives, warrior wives, merchant wives of varying rank, artisan's wives, and farm women (Fig. 11.2). (The order follows actual rather than official rank, whereby merchant wives would appear last.) A second volume details the hierarchy of courtesans, moving from the premier entertainment districts of Kyoto, Edo, and Osaka through teahouse maids, bathhouse attendants, and female laborers, ending with snacksellers and fortunetellers who operate on the river bank at night (Fig. 11.3).[15]

A sort of narrative for this illustrated parade of women is provided by the 1686 novel by Ihara Saikaku, *The Life of an Amorous Woman*, which details the path of one woman's life from her birth as the daughter of a courtier father and non-noble mother until her retirement to an ascetic life in a remote thatched hut. In between, she occupies the full range of positions open to a woman of such birth, and the jobs are associated with specific hairstyles and garments. She works as attendant to a noblewoman and to the mistress of a high-ranking warrior before she crosses over (as it were) into Nishikawa Sukenobu's second volume and begins her descent through the complex world of professional prostitution. While a respected courtesan in the Shimabara quarter of Kyoto, she "secures her coiffure with a single hidden paper cord" that is replaced for each use and plucks the stray hairs carefully from the back of her neck (Ihara 1963:137). By the time she has served as a priest's mistress, a teacher of calligraphy and etiquette to young women (one profession open to retired court attendants, but here associated with sexual license), a townsman's parlor maid, and

Figure 11.2 Wife of high-ranking merchant playing kickball, formerly a courtly pastime, in *Hyakunin jōrō shinasadame*, Vol. 1, 1723 (Nishikawa 1979:n.p.).

a hairdresser, and has become a seamstress in a private house in Edo, she ties up her "dishevelled black hair in haste, and, quite heedless of the fact that [her] chignon [is] awry, secure[s] it with an old paper cord" (Ihara 1963:178–79).

This telltale slovenliness is the start of an abrupt downward slide

Figure 11.3 Nighttime snackseller (right) and riverbank prostitute (left), in *Hyakunin jōrō shinasadame*, Vol. 2, 1723 (Nishikawa 1979:n.p.).

in her career: she works as a bedchamber maid, a bathhouse attendant, and a madam in the prostitutes' quarter of Sakai, where she dresses jauntily but cheaply in a "light-mauve apron and a sash of medium width, tied on the left side" (Ihara 1963:192). When she leaves that work, she has "put aside no money for [her] livelihood, and [she is] now constrained to sell [her] last proper clothes" (Ihara 1963:193). Her neighbors are middle-aged riverbank prostitutes who serve dozens of men a night. When she briefly attempts to join their numbers, she contacts an elderly man who delivers a set of garments "especially made for rental . . . . Indeed, everything that [is] needed for this profession [can] be had by rental" (Ihara 1963:202). But her voice is too hoarse to sing the advertising tune, "In Your Nightdress," and she retires to her hermitage to pursue salvation.

This and other tales of Saikaku describe the meanings of clothing as property as well as emblems of status and taste. A father's duty to his daughter involves providing a dowry and a generous trousseau.[16] Garments can be accumulated like wealth, and passed on from mother to daughter: a wealthy merchant's wife plans to give her daughter, an only child, "sixty-five robes which I've never worn" (Befu 1976:34). In an emergency, clothes have value at the pawnshop, because old clothing has a ready market for rental or sale (Fig. 11.4).[17] The replacement, by sumptuary edicts and by evolving taste, of gold brocade and heavily embroidered silk with dyed patterns meant that the very silk had extended value: advertisements for the best dyeing techniques, such as *yūzen*, emphasized their washability, but at the same time professional cleaners knew how to remove the stubbornest dye and return "figured plain-weave silks, figured twill-weave silks, varieties of plain silks, pongee, crepe, or any stuff whatsoever to white cloth" (Gotō 1980:84).

Cultural Values

The most interesting meaning of pattern in seventeenth-century Japanese women's garments, however, goes beyond simple issues of gender, status, or wealth to aspects of cultural values assigned to women, in which all these issues are bound up. Despite Saikaku's scorn for frivolous women who "have all the clothes one would want and are still making arrangements to purchase *kosode* robes of the latest pattern for New Year's" (Befu 1976:34), the patterns of women's garments indicate positive meanings embodied by women. Nonetheless, the conspicuous expression of these positive meanings in costume patterns that contrast increasingly with the nearly invisible patterns on male costume seems to grow in proportion to the degree that women are confined to an all-consuming identity as womanly wife (or as womanly companion in the form of courtesan) (Dore 1984:67). We will consider here two major themes of patterns on women's clothing: auspiciousness and literacy. Both themes appear in patterns across the

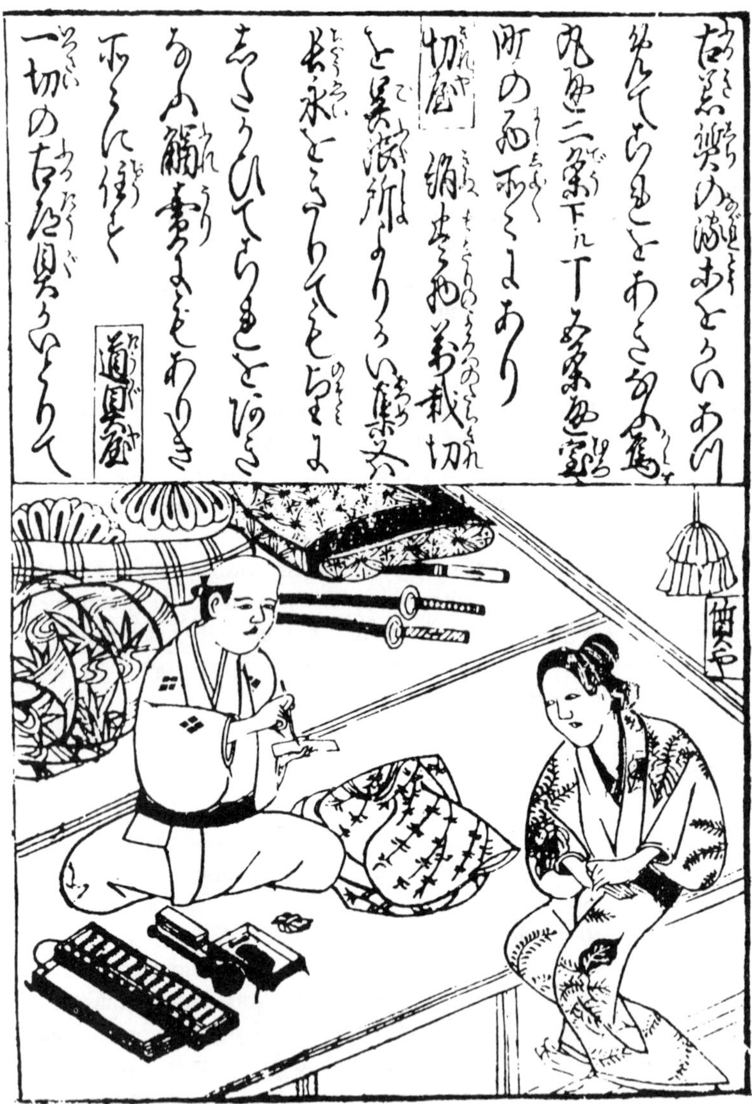

Figure 11.4 Woman pawning *kosode* at pawnshop, in *Jinrin kinmō zui*, 1690 (Tanaka and Tanaka 1969:143).

gamut of noble, warrior, and merchant classes; issues of status are conveyed in the subtle differences in rendering of similar patterns.

Auspicious motifs associated with longevity cover the wedding garments of merchant-class brides, signaling the benefits coming to the groom's household.[18] Auspiciousness is embodied in the motifs embroidered densely on the robes worn by warrior wives over the *kosode*, either draped over the shoulders (*uchikake*) or wrapped around the hips (*koshimaki*), as if the woman moving through her properly managed household spreads auspiciousness in her wake (Stinchecum 1984:No. 49). Auspicious motifs on noble women's garments associate them with the long tradition of the Imperial court (Ishimura et al.:No. 17).

Literacy resulting from a sound classical education is alluded to by patterns on garments of warrior and merchant women alike. Patterns known as "views of the imperial palace" (*goshodoki*) on robes worn by warrior women appear at first glance to be simple landscapes, but objects contained within the landscape provide riddles and clues to connect the scene with classical literature: for example, a bundle of brushwood and a gourd placed under a waterfall suggest the Nō play *Yōrō*, about a filial woodcutter's son who saves his father's life by collecting water from the Yōrō waterfall (Ishimura and Maruyama 1988: No. 48). In similar fashion, embroidered characters either write out or simply hint at Chinese and Japanese classical poetry. On snowflake roundels float two poems from a tenth-century imperial anthology whose meanings convey both winter and auspiciousness (Stinchecum 1984:No. 26). Chinese characters enclosed in medallions representing sake cups compose for the knowledgeable a verse by a ninth-century Chinese poet famed for his poetry and his love of wine (Stinchecum 1984:No. 26). Large single characters worked into the patterns of *kosode* surely made for merchants' wives or courtesans convey auspicious meanings in themselves (*chitose*, "one thousand years") at the same time as they evoke literary associations (Stinchecum 1984:No. 34).

Conclusions

Thus the widespread value placed on literacy for women in the seventeenth century as a means of enhancing moral virtue and refining social graces emerged in the patterns of women's garments (Dore 1984:64–67, 288–90). That the patterns took the form of riddles and allusions agreed with contemporary opinion that women should express their learning indirectly, by their behavior, rather than blatantly:

"when women are learned and clever in their speech it is a sign that civil disturbance is not far off" (Dore 1984:66, quoting Matsudaira Sadanobu (1758–1829)). The presence of written characters in garments associated with courtesans as well as with warrior women implies, moreover, that the same attitude prevailed in the parallel worlds evoked by Nishikawa Sukenobu's two volumes, the world of the legitimate wife and the world of the courtesan.

To a well-informed seventeenth-century Japanese man or woman, the mere glimpse of a patterned robe conveyed multiple answers to the question "Whose sleeves . . . ?" The task for current research on dress is to rediscover those lost answers.

Notes

1. In general, specific association is difficult except when garments have been preserved in the collections of warrior or merchant families.
2. At a minimum, the colors of the five upper garments correspond to the Five Elements and Five Virtues according to Chinese cosmology: blue (wood, humanity); red (fire, politeness); yellow (earth, faith); white (metal, justice); and black (water, wisdom).

   A suggestive example of allusions contained within ostensibly ornamental paintings of single standing women, gorgeously arrayed (known as Kambun beauties because the type developed during the Kambun era, 1661–1673), was presented by Okudaira Shunroku (1989), who demonstrated that the details of one woman's costume pattern alluded to a well-known episode about a faithful wife in the tenth-century literary classic *Tales of Ise*.
3. The screens suggest the lovers not seen – male garments are often included on the racks. But the meanings of the screens do not seem to be solely or even chiefly erotic. This point could be clarified if ownership of a screen of this type could be established, thus associating or disassociating it with a brothel, the only locale where an erotic meaning would be appropriate.
4. Tokugawa 1977 shows a representative array of male and female Nō costumes and their patterns. Gender distinctions are especially clear in the full length garments, which make use of fabrics that are distinguished by technique as well as by pattern: the *karaori* brocades used for female costumes make use of long, lustrous floats in the supplementary weft patterns that are absent from the tightly-woven *atsuita* brocade used for male costumes.
5. *Habutae* silk: thin, soft plain-weave silk fabric woven from untwisted warp and weft threads, with pairs of warp threads passing through a single-reed opening.

6. *Ryūmon*: "dragon pattern," silk figured with dragons and other Chinese animals in either metallic-thread brocade or damask.
7. *Hachijō pongee* or *tsumugi*: fabric of spun silk produced on the island of Hachijō off the coast south of Edo (modern Tokyo).
8. Warrior's garments are illustrated and explained in Tokugawa et al. 1983:126–31; the stencil paste-resist dyeing technique used for *komon* patterns is described in Stinchecum 1984:68. More elaborately patterned fabric was used in the Nō costume, also known as *noshime*, worn by low-ranking warriors, monks, and commoners (Tokugawa et al 1983:No. 127).
9. Among the fifty-six garments in Stinchecum 1984 taken from the Nomura collection now in the National Museum of Japanese History, only one (No. 56) was unquestionably worn by a man. It is an undergarment or *juban* worn under the *kosode* and therefore hidden from public view. The cotton garment is embroidered overall with scenes of Edo and lined with yellow satin. The wearer's concealment of such a lavish garment under a plain outer robe suggests dandyism, but it also complied with nineteenth-century sumptuary laws.
10. Court women's dress was regulated by long-established rules concerning seasonal changes: fourth month first day (4.1) to 5.4 – lined silk *kosode*; 5.5 to 8.30 – ramie *kosode* (*katabira*); 9.1 to 9.8 – lined silk *kosode*; 9.9 to 3.31 – padded *kosode* (Satō 1981:13). A manual of proper dress for a warrior family is illustrated in Tokugawa et al 1983:No. 113.

    One sign of poverty or of falling beneath the proper conduct of one's status was the inability to observe the proper seasonal changes. Thus the heroine of Ihara Saikaku's 1686 novel, *The Life of an Amorous Woman*, describes a great courtesan who has been reduced to begging outside a temple gate: "Wretched indeed was her appearance! One could imagine that in the summer she must wear heavy padded clothes, and that in the winter, when the mountain winds blow fiercely from all directions, she would have nothing to protect her but an unlined summer dress" (Ihara 1963:137).
11. The man's *katabira* was usually plain except for the family crest; an example is shown in Tokugawa et al 1983: No. 238.
12. Warrior women above a certain rank wore silk robes called *koshimaki* over their *katabira* as part of their formal dress. The *koshimaki* was secured at the waist with a sash and folded over the hips like a train. Details of rank extended to the color of silk used to line the neck and sleeve openings of the *katabira*.
13. Mulberry-fiber paper was a major product of the Tosa domain, so paper garments (*kamiko*) were used commonly. Other domains would have allowed layering of bast-fiber garments for winter.
14. The "fawn-spot" (*kanoko*) tie-dyeing technique is described in Stinchecum 1984:220–21. According to the popular image, merchant-class preoccupation with dress varied from city to city: Kyoto merchants knew no bounds

in their expenditures on clothes but scrimped on food, whereas Osaka merchants spent abundantly on good food and only a minimum on clothing. Saikaku writes sarcastically of their stingy satisfaction with cheap provincial cloth in lieu of the fine silks from Kyoto workshops: "For everyday clothes they wear handwoven pongee, which is durable enough to withstand their unhurried movements and yet, while being economical, has an elegant appearance" (Befu 1976:82).

15. The proper separation of women presented in the first and second volumes is suggested by Saikaku's criticism of merchant wives with bad taste regarding appropriate dress: "Now women these days imitate what they see and have taken up the manners and customs of the gay quarters. Ladies who are fortunate enough to be married to drapers are all so made up that they are mistaken for courtesans. Women whose husbands rose from the status of hired clerks are generally spitting images of 'bathhouse harlots'. Wives of tailors and embroiderers who have their shops on the side streets look exactly like 'teahouse harlots'" (Befu 1976:63).
16. "According to the laws on bequeathal . . . . if [a man with a fortune] also has a daughter, she should be provided with a cash dowry of 30 kamme and another 20 kamme for her trousseau, and married off" (Befu 1976:60).
17. "Our story begins on the seventh day autumn, the Tanabata Festival day, when silk clothes – guaranteed never to have been worn before – are piled up seven high, right sleeve over left, to be rented to celebrants" (Ihara 1958:76).
18. For example, *Textile Art* No. 21 (1983:pl. 64), pattern of one thousand cranes rendered in "fawn-spot" tie-dyeing and gold embroidery on a *kosode* made for the daughter of the Mitsui merchant house of Kyoto in 1809. "Night and day for three years his wife diligently performed the many tasks which married life required of her, carefully spinning raw-silk thread by hand, supervising the weaving of cloth by her servant women, looking after her husband's appearance, burning as little fuel as possible for economy's sake, and keeping her expense accounts accurate and up-to-date. In fact, she was just the sort of woman any townsman would want in his home" (Ihara 1956:128).

References

Befu, Ben, *Worldly Mental Calculations: An Annotated Translation of Ihara Saikaku's Seken munezan' yō*, Berkeley: University of California Press, 1976.

Dore, R.P., *Education in Tokugawa Japan*, London and Ann Arbor, Michigan: The Athlone Press and Center for Japanese Studies, 1984.

Gōtō Shōichi, *Nihon senshoku bunken sōran* (Conspectus of texts on Japanese textiles), Kyoto: Tanaka Nao Senryōten, 1980.

Ihara Saikaku, *Five Women Who Loved Love*, trans. W.T. deBary, Rutland, Vermont and Tokyo: Charles Tuttle, 1956.

———, *The Life of an Amorous Woman and Other Writings*, ed. and trans. Ivan Morris, Norfolk, Connecticut: New Directions, 1963.

Ishimura Hayao and Maruyama Nobuhiko, *Robes of Elegance*, Raleigh, North Carolina: North Carolina Museum of Art, 1988.

Kirihata Ken, "Yūzen-zome no utsukushisa" ("The beauty of Yūzen dyeing"), *Senshoku no bi* (*Textile Art*), No. 3, Kyoto, 1980, pp. 53–60.

Nishikawa Sukenobu, *Hyakunin jōrō shinasadame* (*Determination of the qualities of one hundred women*), Kinsei Nihon fūzoku ehon shūsei, Vol. 1, Kyoto: Rinsen Shōten, 1979 (1723).

Okudaira Shunroku, "Painting, Literature and the Theatrical Arts in Edo Genre Painting: Images of the *Beauty on the Veranda*," papers from the *International Conference on Japanese Art History: The State of the Field,* Berkeley: University of California at Berkeley, 1989, pp. 25–27.

Satō Yasuko, "Chayatsuji to natsu ishō" ("Chayatsuji dyeing and summer costumes"), *Senshoku no bi (Textile Art)*, No. 12, 1981, pp. 65–72.

Stinchecum, Amanda Mayer, *Kosode: 16th-19th Century Textiles from the Nomura Collection*, New York and Tokyo: Japan Society and Kodansha International, 1984.

Tanaka Chitako and Tanaka Hatsuo, eds., *Kaseigaku bunken shūsei zoku hen* (*Collected documents on home economics, supplement*), Edo Vols. 3, 9, Tokyo: Watanabe Shōten, 1969, 1970.

Tokugawa Yoshinobu, with Ōkochi Sadao, *The Tokugawa Collection: Nō Robes and Masks*, New York: Japan Society, 1977.

———, *et al., The Shogun Age Exhibition*, Tokyo: The Shogun Age Executive Committee, 1983.

Toyomasa-ko Ki (*Annals of Lord Toyomasa*), Yamauchi Homotsukan, Kochi City: Kochi Prefecture.

12

The Significance of Dress for the Orthodox Hindu Woman

Julia Leslie

This paper is an excursion into the religious ideology of orthodox Hinduism as it relates to the proper dress for women. My evidence is drawn from the massive body of literature produced by *dharmaśāstra*, Sanskrit religious law.[1] The term *dharmaśāstra* denotes texts that purport to describe the principles of cosmic law (*dharma*) as they are enacted at the level of the individual in his daily life (*svadharma*) or hers (*strīdharma*). The earliest example of such a text (the *Gautamadharmasūtra*) was composed between 600 and 400 B.C., the latest around the middle of the nineteenth century. The primary purpose of these texts is a concern not for legal procedure ("law" in the European sense) but for "righteousness" (*dharma*). This notion of religious law is thus more akin to traditional Islamic or Judaic law. *Dharmaśāstra* is the teaching or science of what is right.

My starting point is a little-known text within this tradition: a digest of rulings entitled the *Strīdharmapaddhati*, or *Guide to the Religious Status and Duties of Women*.[2] This long and complex manual was compiled in Sanskrit between 1720 and 1750 by a court pandit named Tryambaka, minister to the Maratha kings of Thanjavur in southern India.[3] Tryambaka's stated aim (and, no doubt, his royal commission) was to summarize the views of Sanskrit religious law relating to women – a tradition already over a thousand years old in his day – for the purpose of instructing his eighteenth-century audience. But he was not writing solely for his own time; nor was he describing a bygone age. The set of norms for women presented in the *Strīdharmapaddhati* was intended as eternally valid for the orthodox Hindu. Indeed, while these rulings may not hold for all Hindu women in India today, a surprising number of them are still praised or adhered to in traditional areas even now.[4]

Like much of Sanskrit religious law, the *Strīdharmapaddhati* presents a bizarre mixture of reality and utopia. Aspects of the real world may be detected beneath the prohibitions. For prohibitions inevitably indicate two things: both what actions merit disapproval or condemnation, and – simultaneously, and more interestingly – what is actually being done. Clearly, if women were not "misbehaving," there would be no need for prohibitions. Thus, prohibitions regarding the nakedness of the upper female body during the day (1989:91) evidently suggest a tendency on the part of at least some women to wear no blouse, a tendency sufficiently pronounced for the ruling to be deemed necessary. Similarly, we may infer from the prohibition on wearing heavy earrings during lovemaking (1989:241) some persistence in doing this despite the apparent dangers and discomforts resulting from the practice.

Injunctions, on the other hand, betray the ideals of utopia. Examples abound. The good wife should always wake before her husband (1989:52). In the last part of the night, she should sift, pound and prepare the grain for the coming day (1989:58–59).[5] She should clean the house thoroughly before the first rays of the sun can touch it (1989:59). She should always attend upon her husband herself instead of delegating such duties to servants (1989:64–65). Apart from traders and so on, she should converse with no man other than her husband (1989:170 ff.). She should serve her husband without regard for her life, accepting even his sale of her (1989: 305–308). In effect, the good wife should think only of her husband, worshipping him as her god.

This notion of the husband as deity is not intended merely as a figure of speech; for many women, it is a sociological reality.[6] For Tryambaka repeatedly stresses that the duties of the wife are in fact the signs of her chosen religious path, that of devotion to her husband. This devotion is described in two ways: serving and obeying him as her teacher (*guru*); and worshipping him as her god. The second requirement receives the greater stress. Numerous quotations either liken the husband to a god, or describe him directly as the wife's only or highest god. Thus, whether he is good or bad, the husband is the good wife's "supreme deity" (1989:274). There is "no deity like him . . . through his grace all desires are fulfilled" (1989:281). The good woman "always regards her husband as her god" (1989:282). When she eats the remains of the meals she has served him, she should receive it reverently as the sanctified food of her god (1989:221–27). Instead of seeking the blessings of other gods by making pilgrimages or worshipping in temples, she should drink the "foot water" of her own husband (1989:137).[7] After her husband's death, she may worship the god Visnu, but only if she keeps the image of her husband in her mind, worshipping him in the guise of the god, bringing him to mind by means of a portrait or a clay model (1989:300). For the husband is "the supreme god among gods," whose law she must fulfill without question (1989:308), even if what he asks her to do is normally considered wrong (1989:309–312).

Let us now narrow our focus to Tryambaka's rulings on dress. One of the most interesting major sections of the *Strīdharmapaddhati* describes in detail the daily practice of the good Hindu wife (*strīnām āhnikam;* 1989:44 ff.). Everything that she should do – from the moment she wakes in the morning to the moment she sleeps at night – is discussed from the point of view of the "sacred norms" of religious law. This large body of rules is further subdivided into four: those pertaining to the period before dawn; those concerning the rituals performed at dawn; those relating to the daytime; and those associated with the evening. The predawn rulings include a variety of household tasks and detailed instructions on the wife's daily ablutions and appearance.

If we look at Tryambaka's rulings on how the good wife should dress herself every morning (1989:88–101), we find a gender dimension that accurately reflects the religious roles of men and women. The following discussion falls into four parts: first, a brief preliminary exploration of the implications of nakedness for women; second, an examination of the rulings on dress for women that take the form of prohibitions; third, a consideration of those that take the form of positive injunctions; and fourth, a more detailed look at the forehead mark or *tilaka* worn by married women.

The Nakedness of Women

A woman's life is traditionally divided into four stages: childhood (*bālya*; that is, until she begins to menstruate); unmarried girlhood (*kaumāra*; the three years or, according to some, the three months following puberty, during which time a husband must be found); youth (*yauvana*; a woman's childbearing years); and old age (*sthavira*; the years when she is beyond childbearing).[8] The early textual discussions of when a girl should be given in marriage are detailed, the central question being whether the ideal bride is an adolescent girl or a prepubertal one. A term that crops up repeatedly in these discussions is *nagnikā*, meaning "a naked girl." A *nagnikā* is a girl who has not yet begun to menstruate and who is therefore young enough to run around without any clothes. Once she begins to menstruate, she covers her body "out of embarrassment in the presence of men." She is called "a naked one," a child, as long as she needs no upper garment to cover her breasts and as long as she does not menstruate. When nakedness carries such powerful sexual associations, it is hardly surprising that a married woman, even when bathing, is not permitted to be naked (1989:83–84).

Prohibitions on Women's Dress

For the purposes of this paper, I have reduced the rulings on dress for women into two main groups: those that tend to be couched in the form of prohibitions, and those that tend to take the form of injunctions. First, let us look at what the good wife should *not* do.

The following quotation is greatly emphasized by Tryambaka. The greater part of it appears three times at different points in his treatise. In his view, therefore, these are the most important modifying rules relating to the dress of women. The quotation is also to be found in a variety of other *dharmaśāstra* texts, always attributed to Saṅkha. Tryambaka (or Sankha) tells us that "a woman should not show her navel. She should wear garments that extend to her ankles. She should not expose her breasts. She should not go outside without an upper garment" (1989:91). This passage constitutes the primary advice given by Tryambaka on the correct appearance of the good Hindu wife.

If we compare this passage with the rulings on dress usually given for men, we find a significant difference in tone and intention. On some points, there are no parallels. Men are often enjoined to put on "clean white clothes" (1989:88). Elsewhere, we are told that the brahmin (*brāhmaṇa*) should wear white, the warrior class (*kṣatriya*) red, the merchant class (*vaiśya*) yellow, and the serving (or *śūdra*) class dark blue or dirty clothes (1989:89). But there are no recommendations regarding the colors that a woman should or should not wear. The only exception is the widow who should not wear dyed cloth (1989:299).

Another significant difference between the rulings on dress for women and those for men is that only the latter refer to the sacred thread, the sign of initiation into Vedic education. We are told, for example, that the male householder should always wear both an upper and a lower garment; but, if he is poor, he need only wear the sacred thread on his upper body (1989:89). For a number of reasons, however, women have long been excluded both from the ritual of Vedic initiation and, consequently, from the body of sacred literature and knowledge to which initiation is the key.[9] We should therefore not be surprised that Tryambaka's rulings for women make no mention of the sacred thread.

A closer parallel between the rules on dress for men and those described by Tryambaka for women is to be found in the instructions on how a man should wear his *dhoti.* This is the length of white cloth worn about the loins by men of the higher castes in northern India. The end is passed between the legs and tucked in at the waist so that the material hangs down to either knee. Textual instructions agree that it should be tucked in at three points: near the navel, on the left side, and at the back. A brahmin who does this incorrectly is held to be a low-class *śūdra.*

A comparison of these rulings with the ones quoted above for women demonstrates that both the purpose and the emphasis of the two sets of rules are quite different. A man is required to fold and tuck his garment in the right way for otherworldly or "unseen" (*adṛṣṭa*) reasons.[10] No mention is made of which parts of his body the cloth is meant to conceal. The rules for women, on the other hand, give no guidance on how one should fold, wind, and tuck the sari. This is especially surprising in view of the fact that there are a number of ways of wearing this garment. In Maharashtra, for example, and presumably in the Maratha kingdom of Thanjavur where Tryambaka was writing, the *sakaccha* style was held to be a mark of the upper classes, the *vikaccha* of the lower classes. According to the former style, part of the sari is passed between the legs and tucked up behind at the waist; the other end passes over the left shoulder to hang down from the right. According to the latter style, the sari is worn wrapped about the legs without any part of it tucked up behind.[11] In Tryambaka's treatise, however, the rules concerning a woman's dress merely stipulate which parts of her anatomy she may not reveal: her breasts, her navel, and her legs down to the ankle. This is obviously another kind of ruling altogether.

Several points may be made here. For example, the prohibition on showing the ankles can only apply to women who are not expected to work out of doors. As anyone who has been to India will know, women working in the fields or in coastal fishing villages wear their saris hoisted well above their ankles so as not to impede their work. In this context, Tryambaka's ruling is a mark of social class as well as decorum.

The ruling that a woman should not expose her breasts is more complex. Certainly, the literature of *dharmaśāstra* agrees on this point:

the breasts should be covered, either by a bodice or by the sari, or by an additional "upper garment." But then how may we account for the many examples of barebreasted women in the sculptures and paintings of southern and central India? We need to disentangle several related questions here. First, what is the role of the artist in Indian society? What artistic conventions apply in the portrayal of Indian women or goddesses in sculpture and painting? According to the realistic convention, for example, figures may be shown wearing the dress of the period and place in which the artist is working. According to the supernatural convention, mythological figures may be depicted according to the religious tradition espoused by the artist. Thus the ornaments, headdress, and garments worn by a sculptured goddess will probably reflect the customs of the period, while the sacred thread presumably reflects the religious tradition. But to which convention does her naked upper body belong? Second, what is the relationship between the artist and the specialist in religious law? Third, what was the effect of foreign, primarily Muslim, influence on the conventions of dress for women?

These questions are too complex to tackle here.[12] Let me say only that Tryambaka was presumably a product of his time. In order to understand how he might have interpreted his "eternally valid" rulings on the appearance of women in terms of the dress of women in his day, we may therefore look to contemporary evidence. One such example is a collection of illustrations entitled *Drawings of the Costumes of the Southern Peninsula of India by a Native of Tanjore*, compiled by a Reverend Christian David in 1815. This portfolio of paintings depicts a man and woman in each of several categories. Women of high status wear bodices. Women of middle status wear no bodices, but cover their breasts with the loose end of the sari (often worn in the *sakaccha* style). Women of low status leave their breasts uncovered. Tryambaka is surely making a similar point.

One last prohibition is that neither women nor men should wear damaged or contaminated cloth. The rulings usually take the form of a requirement to wear *anupahata* ("undamaged") or, more commonly, *ahata* ("unbeaten") cloth (1989:90). The term *ahata* (from the root *han*, meaning "to strike, injure or kill") is glossed by commentators, and translated by scholars, in a variety of ways depending on the context. For example, since clothes are "beaten" (often with a stick) in the Indian washing process, *ahata* may mean "unbeaten" in the sense of "unwashed." In one context, a prohibition against wearing "unbeaten" cloth is a prohibition against wearing dirty clothes.[13] In another context, the requirement to wear "unbeaten" cloth is a requirement to wear cloth that is perfect. This, in turn, may be interpreted to mean either brand new cloth that has never been "beaten" or washed,[14] or cloth that, although "beaten" or washed a little, is still new, with its fringes intact, and therefore ritually pure. When Tryambaka applies the term to the daily dress of all orthodox Hindu women, he presumably intends the less rigid definition of the two. The good wife should wear garments that are in perfect condition, perfectly clean, and therefore ritually pure.

The term *ahata* may have another meaning, too. For the requirement to wear "undamaged" cloth may in some contexts be a requirement to wear cloth that has never been cut or stitched; that is, the full woven length[15] of the sari or *dhoti*, as opposed to the cut cloth of the bodice, skirt, or shirt. On these grounds, even today, men may not enter the inner sanctum of a temple while wearing a shirt. Similarly, women wearing a stitched blouse or bodice beneath their saris were barred from entry into some south Indian temples even fifty or sixty years ago.[16] These rulings may represent a veiled allusion to the "thread" of lineage (*kulatantu, saṃtanārtham*) which should never be cut. For it is commonly agreed that "women were created to have children" and men "to continue their line," their joint responsibility as a married couple being to continue the "thread" of progeny (as is stated in *Manusmṛti* .96). In support of this interpretation, we may note Tryambaka's ruling that the menstruating woman should neither spin thread nor plait or cut rope; if she does, her unborn child will be impotent, which is to say that the "thread" of progeny will be cut (1989:285).

Positive Injunctions on Women's Dress

The second group of rulings relating to a woman's appearance or dress consists of those that tend to be given in the form of injunctions, telling us what the good wife *should* do and wear. A prime example, quoted by Tryambaka and others, is attributed to Vasiṣṭha:

> The short bodice [*kañcukī*], the marriage necklace [*kanthasūtram*], a pair of earrings, collyrium, glass bangles, anointing with turmeric [*haridrā*], and putting the sectarian mark [*pundraka*] on the forehead, arranging the hair, wearing ornaments on one's feet and nose, betel and so on – all these are declared to be the marks of women who have been blessed with good fortune [*punyayositām*]. If a woman wears glass ornaments at wrist and throat, her behaviour is meritorious, and her cooking is said to be pure. If she does

> not wear glass ornaments at wrist and throat, she is understood to be a widow [in this life] and [she will also become a widow] in life after life (1989:100).

The last sentence provides the clue we are looking for. Another passage, taken from the *Skandapurāna*, makes it clear:

> The devoted wife [*pativratā*] who wishes her husband to live long should not neglect these things: turmeric [*haridrā*, put between the eyebrows and used as an unguent]; collyrium [for the eyes]; *kunkuma* [saffron or a reddish paste, for the forehead mark]; *sindūra* [saffron or a red powder, to mark the parting of the hair]; the short-sleeved bodice [*kūrpāsaka*]; betel [to make the lips red and the breath sweet]; the auspicious ornament [of marriage, *mangalyābharanam*]; and the adorning of ears, hands and carefully styled hair [with ornaments, flowers, and so on] (1989:96).

All these things form a necessary part of the wife's appearance.

More to the point, each item carries a significance beyond the simple appearance of the woman concerned. It tells us about her relationship with her husband. Is he around, for example, or off on a journey? Is she accessible to him sexually, or is she menstruating and therefore out of bounds? Most significant of all, is he alive or dead? Each of these items indicates that the woman's husband is not absent, that she is sexually available to him, and (most important of all) that he is alive. I shall take each item in turn.

Turmeric (*haridrā*) is the yellow substance with which the images of deities are smeared. It is believed to be a mark of good fortune capable of offering protection and warding off demons. It is also one of the signs that a woman is once more sexually available to her husband after her menstrual period. On the fourth day of menstruation, as Tryambaka explains, the wife should take her ritual bath, think only of her husband, and make herself beautiful. That evening, she should make sexual advances (*upasarpati*) to him. The following quotation describes the signs of her availability:

> Anointed with unguents of ground turmeric [*haridrā*] and saffron [*kuṅkuma*], wearing bright garments, thinking of her husband's 'lotus foot,'[17] gazing at her own toes [her eyes down], not looking at other men, thinking only of her husband, thinking of him as light itself, always [keeping herself] pure [by taking care not to touch anything polluting], beautifully dressed and ornamented and anointed with perfume, and in good spirits, she should go to bed (1989:287).

During her menstrual period, on the other hand, she should not massage her body with any ointment or oil; if she does, we are told, her child will be born with a skin disease (1989:285). Like so many prohibitions relating to the menstruating women (see also below), this callous threat levelled at the unborn child is evidently intended to prevent women from making themselves attractive to their husbands at such a time. Hence, too, the added prohibition against lovemaking during the crucial first three days of the menstrual period: if a woman does so, her child will be deemed untouchable or cursed. Perfumed ointments are also forbidden to the woman whose husband is away (1989:291), and to the widow (1989:299).

Collyrium, or lamp-black, is obtained by inverting a small earthenware dish over a sooty flame. Applied to the inner eyelid, it serves to outline the eyes and to exaggerate their length (Plate 12.1).[18] Since it makes a woman attractive, collyrium is prohibited to the menstruating woman, the woman whose husband is away, and the widow. Tryambaka adds that the woman who uses collyrium during her menstrual period will give birth to a child who is blind in one or both eyes (1989:285).

Saffron was used originally for both the forehead mark (*tilaka*) and for the red line in the hair parting (*sindūra*). Nowadays, a less expensive red powder or paste is used. The *tilaka* is usually a round dot in the center of the forehead, although this may vary according to family or caste tradition. The women of Vai in Maharashtra, for example, prefer

Plate 12.1 Woman holding mirror and applying collyrium to her eyes. *Bhāgavatapurāṇa, rāsakrīḍa* section (chapters 29–33 of the tenth canto); palm-leaf manuscript; Sanskrit text in Oriya script. Orissa, early eighteenth century. British Library: OR. 11689, folio 3r (detail).

a horizontal red line. The red line in the hair parting (*sindūra*) is more commonly associated with north Indian women and is rarely found in Tamilnadu today.[19] Both *tilaka* and *sindūra* indicate that a woman is married and that her husband is alive. That this custom goes back a long way is indicated by an inscription at Khajuraho dated 953 A.D. Describing a battle in which many of the enemy were killed, the inscription notes that their wives were thereby deprived of the use of *sindūra*.

The short-sleeved bodice (*kañcukī, kūrpāsaka*) is worn under the sari by married women but traditionally not by the widow. As I have discussed above, the significance of the woman's bodice or blouse depends on the context. On ritual occasions, for example, the wearing of stitched cloth is problematic. For daily wear, a context in which notions of decorum and secular status are more important, the blouse is recommended. In the bedroom, however, it is inappropriate. According to Tryambaka, the woman who makes love with her husband while wearing a bodice will certainly be a widow within three years, possibly sooner (1989:241). It seems that a woman's naked breasts are associated more often with sexual intimacy than with fashion or custom.

Betel (*tāmbūla*) is taken both as an aid to the digestion, especially after meals (1989:231–32), and as a means of cleansing the mouth and freshening the breath. The context of sexual intimacy is relevant here too. For example, the detailed preparations of the bedchamber before the husband and wife come together for sexual intercourse specify a cozy candle-lit room, complete with containers for such things as sandalwood paste, perfumed ointments, and betel (1989:238). Not surprisingly, any attempts to make oneself attractive by sweetening the breath – whether by the use of betel or even by cleaning one's teeth – are prohibited to the woman whose husband is absent, out of bounds, or dead. If a menstruating woman cleans her teeth, we are told, her child will be born with discolored teeth. If she takes a bath, her yet unborn child will die by drowning.

Ornaments and flowers in the hair also make a woman attractive, so they, too, are forbidden to the woman whose husband is (for one reason or another) out of reach. The woman whose husband is away should not adorn herself in any way (1989:291). If the menstruating woman combs her hair, her child will be bald. Complicated hairstyles are also prohibited to the widow, either because her head is shaved, or her hair close-cropped, or, alternatively, because she must wear it in a simple bun (1989:303–4). The widow who binds her hair on top of her head is said to cause her husband to be bound in the other world (1989:299).

The marriage necklace (*mangalasūtra, mangalyābharanam, kantha-sūtram*), the "auspicious thread" on which (usually) black or gold beads are strung, is fastened around the neck of the bride by the groom during the marriage ceremony. Mantras are recited to ensure the wife's fidelity to her husband, and the goddess Gaurī bestows good fortune (*saubhāgya*) on the bride. The term *saubhāgya* is not used here in a general sense: it denotes specifically the good fortune of the married woman whose husband is alive. The prefix *sau*, with which the married woman is addressed, stands for *saubhāgyavatī*, "she who is fortunate by virtue of her marriage." Like the auspicious mark on her forehead and the red line in the hair, the marriage necklace is an indispensable sign of the married woman whose husband is alive. As long as he lives, they must be worn.

Glass bangles, a late development,[20] are another such sign. As soon as a woman hears of her husband's death, she breaks her bangles.[21] The ritual purity of cooking is important for a number of reasons: for eating itself; for the ritual of eating (traditionally learned by heart and followed to the letter by young initiates); and for the ritual of offering food to the deity before every meal. Both the upper-caste Hindu and his god may only accept food cooked by an individual who is deemed pure; hence the refusal of the orthodox brahmin to eat in a public restaurant; hence too the importance of brahmin cooks at temples and religious institutions. But the cooking of a high-caste married woman whose husband is living is always deemed auspicious and pure. If she is menstruating, her touch will pollute the fire, so she may not cook (1989:284). In the case of the widow, if she shaves her head (as, for example, in Maharashtra), her cooking is held to be pure; if she does not, it is unacceptable. We may now interpret Tryambaka's statement regarding glass ornaments and the wife's right to cook. To say that a woman wears glass bangles and a glass necklace is another way of saying that her husband is alive. His continued survival is in turn proof of her virtue and purity (as his death is the mark of blame). Since she is virtuous, auspicious and pure, her cooking, too, is pure.

Nose- and toe-rings[22] seem to be another late development, probably the result of Muslim influence.[23] For Tryambaka, as for many other later writers on *dharmaśāsra*, the nose-ring is also an indispensable sign of *saubhāgya*, the good fortune of the woman whose husband is alive.

The Auspicious Forehead Mark

The forehead mark or *tilaka* is commemorated in a famous image taken from the Sanskrit epic, the *Rāmāyaṇa*. Tryambaka uses this image to good effect both in his commentary on the epic (the *Dharmākūtā*) and in the *Strīdharmapaddhati*. The passage (more or less identical in both works) begins by quoting *Rāmāyaṇa* 3.8:

> "When the sun resolutely remains in the direction frequented by Death [the south], then the northern direction like a woman without her *tilaka* does not shine."
>
> The lady, in the form of the northern direction, whose husband – husband of the directions, jewel of the day [the sun] – has gone to the south [has died], is described as not wearing the *tilaka*.
>
> Therefore the lack of *tilaka* and so on [all the items described above] is the defining mark of the widow. Correspondingly, wearing the *tilaka* and so on is the defining mark of the woman whose husband is alive. (1989:98–99)

The image is drawn from the division of the year into two parts. When the ecliptic tends toward the north, days become longer, nights shorter, and the sun appears to "live" in the north. But when the ecliptic tends toward the south, days become shorter and nights longer, the sun appears to "live" in the south, and leaves the northern sky dark. At such times, it is said that the northern direction, bereft of the sun's rays, does not "shine." Similarly, this famous image tells us, a wife whose husband has died is bereft of the *tilaka* mark that radiates her good fortune; and so she, too, no longer shines.

To put these rulings into perspective, we need to consider the equivalent rulings for men. In text after text, we find elaborate rules laid down for the marks to be made on a man's forehead after his morning bath. Whether called *tilaka* or *pundra* (*ka*), these are sectarian marks intended to indicate the religious persuasion of the wearer. A vertical mark of one or more lines indicates the follower of Viṣṇu. These may be made with earth taken from a selection of sacred spots, such as the top of a mountain or the bank of a sacred river, or, alternatively, with earth after one's bath. Three horizontal lines indicate the follower of Śiva. These should be made with sacred ash. The circular *tilaka* is made with sandalwood paste after making obeisance to the gods in the ritual of image worship (*devapūjā*). There are rulings on how this mark should be made (with which fingers, for example), what it should look like, and on which twelve parts of the body it should be placed (on the forehead, chest, throat, arms, and so on). There are even rulings on the size and shape of the *tilaka* (or *pundra*) according to a man's class (*varna*): the size and shape of a bamboo leaf for a brahmin, a fish for a warrior, even smaller for a merchant, and a half-moon for a śūdra.

The rulings for women explain none of this. In Tryambaka's treatise, for example, there is a brief reference to the sectarian mark (*pundraka*, see above), but that is all. The remaining references to the *tilaka* bear no relation to either Viṣṇu or Śiva. The mark is made with neither sacred earth, sacred ash, nor sandalwood paste, but with saffron, the sign of a woman's marital happiness (*saubhāgya*). For the *tilaka* is the visible symbol of a woman's religious allegiance, as distinct from that of men. It declares first that her husband is her deity; and second that he is still alive to receive her daily service and worship. As we have seen, the bulk of the rulings on a woman's appearance carry the same message: her husband lives; all religious devotion must be directed to him alone.

A man without his sectarian mark is a man without a god. A woman without her *tilaka* is one whose god is dead.

Conclusions

The rules on dress classify the individual in religious terms. The sacred thread signals the twice-born male, one who has taken initiation into Vedic ritual followed by long years of religious education and service to his teacher. When, as a grown man, he leaves his teacher to marry and become a householder, the colors of his garments and the way they are worn display his class (*varna*). The symbols carefully marked out on his forehead each morning indicate his sectarian allegiance. These are the signs of the religious status of the high-caste Hindu male. They constitute his reward for merit accumulated in past lives, and they establish his innate virtue and purity.

The rules on dress for a woman classify her in religious terms too, but in a remarkably different way. First, there is the evident fact that she has been born as a woman, a fact widely agreed to be itself a demerit earned in a previous life. Tryambaka himself discusses this point at length.[24] But all the rulings on dress for women imply compensatory merits. For the entire appearance of the high-caste married woman – from the flowers in her hair to the rings on her toes–carry the same loud message: her husband, her personal deity in the home, is alive. She celebrates in her own person the survival of her god. That survival, and her pious celebration of it, stand as proof of her religious virtue. They constitute her ritual purity. They establish her authority in the home.

Notes

1. All foreign terms in this paper are given in Sanskrit, the precursor of the modern languages of northern and western India. Because of the importance of Sanskrit as a sacred language, the language of the sacred texts of early Hinduism, even later texts composed in Sanskrit carry a weight of religious authority that is absent from works in the vernacular.
2. An analysis and partial translation of this manual is presented in *The Perfect Wife* (Leslie 1989). Unless otherwise stated, all page references are to Leslie 1989.
3. For further information on the origins of the Maratha Rajas of Thanjavur, and their political and intellectual background, see Leslie 1989:13–19.
4. Hence my use of the present tense in much of the following discussion. Tryambaka may have been writing in the eighteenth century, using source material dating back a thousand years, but the rulings he gives (and others just like them) are still deemed authoritative in much of India today. The text is historical, the message eternally valid.
5. In fact, the sounds of this tedious process of cleaning, grinding, and pounding may still be heard throughout village India in the dark early hours of morning.
6. For ethnographic evidence to this effect, see Doranne Jacobson's description of the life and ideals of a high-caste brahmin woman in Madhya Pradesh (1978).
7. Maharashtrian women followed this custom only fifty years ago. Village women in Nepal still do so (see Bennett 1938:174–75).
8. See Thieme 1971; see also Leslie 1989:86–88.
9. For the historical background to this exclusion, and the effects deriving from it, see Leslie 1989:34–39. Like most other writers on *dharmaśāstra*, Tryambaka proclaims that the ceremony and institution of marriage have taken the place of the woman's initiation. He quotes the much-revered *Manusmrti*: "For women, the marriage ritual is held to be the equivalent of initiation, serving one's husband that of residing in the teacher's house, and household duties that of the worship of the sacrificial fire" (*Manusmrti* 2.69; see Leslie 1989:35). The fact that women are still not entitled to wear the sacred thread, however, indicates that the female form of initiation is not deemed truly equal to the male.

10. In the context of *dharmaśāstra,* rulings based on practical considerations relating to this world are said to have a visible or "seen" basis. Those for which no such "this-worldly" considerations are evident are held to have a more compelling invisible or "unseen" basis, such as the acquisition of merit that will take effect only in the next life. A third type combines both "seen" and "unseen" considerations.
11. See Altekar 1978:289–91; Plates IV, V, VII.
12. For a preliminary investigation of some of these questions, see Leslie 1989:92–95.
13. When performing rituals, for example, a man should wear cloth that he has washed himself, not cloth that has been washed by a washerman, and certainly never cloth that is "unwashed" (*ahata*), and therefore dirty.
14. According to one commentator, only brand new cloth "straight from the loom" should be worn on ritual occasions by the sacrificer and his wife, or for auspicious rituals such as the marriage ceremony.
15. The commentator's gloss, "straight from the loom," may be taken in this way too.
16. This issue gains an added significance in the context of rulings relating to whether or not a woman should wear a bodice during the day (see above).
17. The epithet is *padipādābjam*, indicating the reverence appropriate to one's teacher or god.
18. According to Jan Meulenbeld, two different substances are used: one for medicinal purposes, the other for cosmetic effect (1974:438).
19. See Fuller and Logan 1985:90.
20. See Altekar 1978:298.
21. See, for example, Wood 1980:172; Jameson 1976:251.
22. Saskia Kersenboom-Story discusses the significance of the toe-ring in the context of the *devadāsī* tradition of hereditary dancers. As she explains, the toe-rings of the married woman mark the auspiciousness of her married state: on the death of her husband, they will be removed. In contrast, the toe-rings of the traditional dancer (and hence the auspiciousness of her married status) will never be removed: for her divine husband will never die (1987:xv,xx note 2).
23. See Altekar 1978:301 ff.; Kane 1962–1977, Vol. II, Part I:537.
24. For details of Tryambaka's arguments relating to the inherent sinfulness of women, and yet their innate virtue and good fortune as women, see Leslie 1986 and 1989:246–72.

References

Altekar, A.S., *The Position of Women in Hindu Civilization from Prehistoric Times to the Present Day*, Delhi: Motilal Banarsidass, 1978 (1938).

Bennett, Lynn, *Dangerous Wives and Sacred Sisters: Social and Symbolic Roles of High-Caste Women in Nepal*, New York: Columbia University Press, 1983.

David, Rev. Christian, *Drawings of the Costumes of the Southern Peninsula of India by a Native of Tanjore. Explanation of the Several Figures, their Cast, Language etc. by the Revd. Christian David*, 1815. Colombo: [Volume of original paintings held in the iconographic department of the Wellcome Institute for the History of Medicine.]

Fuller, C. J., and P. Logan, "The Navarātri festival in Madurai," *Bulletin of the School of Oriental and African Studies*, Vol. 48, Part 1, London, 1985.

Jacobson, Doranne, "The Chaste Wife," in Sylvia Vatuk (ed.), *American Studies in the Anthropology of India*, Delhi, 1978.

Jameson, A.S., "*Gangāguru*: The Public and Private Life of a Brāhman Community of North India," D. Phil. thesis, Oxford University, 1976.

Kane, P.V., *History of Dharmaśāstra (Ancient and Mediaeval Religious and Civil Law in India)*, 2d. ed., 5 Vols., Pune: Bhandarkar Oriental Research Institute, 1962–1977.

Kersenboom-Story, Saskia C., *Nityasumangalī: Devadasi Tradition in South India*, Delhi: Motilal Banarsidass, 1987.

Leslie, I. Julia, "*Strīsvabhāvā*: The Inherent Nature of Women," in N.J. Allen, R.F. Gombrich, T. Raychaudhuri, and G. Rizvi (eds.), *Oxford University Papers on India, Vol. 1, Part 1*, Delhi: Oxford University Press, 1986.

———, *The Perfect Wife: The Orthodox Hindu Woman according to the Strīdharmapaddhati of Tryambakayajvan*, Oxford University South Asian Studies Series, Delhi: Oxford University Press, 1989.

Manusmrti, Sanskrit text with seven commentaries, ed. V.N. Mandlik, Bombay, 1886.

Meulenbeld, J., *The Mādhavanidāna and its Chief Commentary: Chapters 1–10, Introduction, Translation and Notes*, Leiden: Brill, 1974.

Rāmāyaṇa, Sanskrit text, ed. G.H. Bhatt *et al*, 7 Vols., Baroda, 1960–1975.

Strīdharmapaddhati, see Leslie 1989.

Thieme, Paul, "Jungfrauengatte," in *Kleine Schriften*, Part 2, Wiesbaden: Franz Steiner Verlag, 1970.

Wood, Heather, *Third-Class Ticket*, London: Routledge and Kegan Paul, 1980.

13

Continuity and Change in Hindu Women's Dress

O. P. Joshi

Hindu women's dress in India has been influenced by the socioreligious attitudes and values prevalent in the society. The process of change or the continuation of certain styles and design factors in dress is the result of continuation or change in social attitudes and religious beliefs. In explaining these factors, the prescriptions and restrictions involved in the wearing and adoption of new fashions should also be considered. The way in which women's dress has been influenced by the innovations of dress materials and prevalent designs and the social values that concern covering and revealing the body will be described here.[1]

The dress of Hindu men and women is primarily governed by concepts of purity and pollution, which are the important governing principles of Hindu society. It is believed that the dress, its style, color, and material, and the way the garment is worn – either hiding or showing parts of the body – is regulated by basic principles and customs. The prevailing fashions of the day and new dress material have a limited influence. For example, an important ideological distinction is made between a stitched garment and an unstitched garment.[2] The European-style dress, tailored and sewn together, is a stitched garment, while the untailored cloth that is folded to be worn as a sari is unstitched. The unstitched garment is regarded as more pure. Many educated and Western-oriented women wear the modern stitched dress at school or college or while working in the office, but there is a strong feeling that only the traditional sari, a long length of unstitched cloth, is the correct attire to be worn on all social occasions of importance, such as marriages, festivals, ceremonies, and pilgrimages. In north India, men also wear a long unstitched white cloth called a *dhoti*, which wraps them from the waist down to the legs. The unstitched garment worn by men in south India is called a *lungi*; it is a much shorter version. Furthermore, at death the deceased person, male or female, is always dressed for the funeral in a seamless garment.

In addition, a Hindu woman's dress may include body decorations such as tattoos, decorations made from henna, cosmetics, ornaments, and footwear (Joshi 1976; 1983). All these aspects present an integrated system of ornament regulated by place, occasion, age, and status, as well as values that reflect the social hierarchy.

Purity and Pollution

Hindu lifestyle is governed by ancient religious beliefs and traditions.[3] Hinduism combines individual philosophy with popular forms in which social and congregational participation are expressed in a variety of ways. The Hindu religious system has developed a belief system in which purity, ideas of the sacred, and pollution are critical. The concept of purity has been applied to every aspect of material and nonmaterial culture. Human beings, animals, objects, dress, food, places and times – indeed, everything in existence – are divided according to the principles of the pure and the polluted. This belief system sometimes has scriptural sanction; distinctions are often made on the basis of conventional knowledge transmitted from generation to generation. Religious activities are prescribed for the purification of man's faculties and nature. The worship of different gods, visiting temples, bathing, praying, singing devotional songs, sacrificing according to scriptures, taking part in sacraments, rituals, pilgrimages, meditating, and observing ordained duties are just some of the activities considered to be pure, and these activities help make a person, or a place where they occur, pure and sacred.[4]

The correct dress to be worn whilst observing religious activities and social behavior is prescribed by ancient law givers (as shown in texts from c. 100 B.C. to c. 300 A.D.) as well as by local tradition. In *Homo Hierarchicus,* Dumont recalls the opinion of Harita that external purity is of three kinds: 1) *kula*: bearing on the family; 2) *artha*: objects of everyday use; and 3) *sarira*: of the body (1970:87). The human body is polluted by various voluntary or involuntary acts as well as by bodily secretions and excretions. The purity of dress is governed by these pollutions. For example, clothes worn after the daily bath are purer than those worn at the time of secretions or excretions. There are many situations which make a person vulnerable to impurity. All rituals signify

Figure 13.1 Fon bearer (statue from Bodhgaya, 100–50 B.C.). *A ntariya* is almost ankle-length, of fine cotton, with left end gathered and tucked in at left of waist; the right end is drawn between the legs and tucked in at the back in *kachcha* style. (*All illustrations drawn by Mr. Reva Shanker, artist from Nathdwara, Rajasthan.*)

Figure 13.2 Princess (Ajanta Cave XVI, 600 A.D.). Stitched *choli* of a cream color with floral design and short sleeves. The skirt is in Lehnga style, worn short and of a darker color than the *choli*. In this period there is a marked preference for the stitched garment, and there are many forms of cut-and-sewn garments.

moments of transition. Such instances occur while a ritual is supervised and participated in, or they may affect a brahmin after his bath, a bride and bridegroom in their ritualistic dresses, or a person eating. To guard against the danger of impurity in such situations, the right dress, style, material, and color have to be selected.

Two important differentiations are made in the observation of the principles of purity and pollution with regard to dress among Hindus. In the first, domestic life, the daily observances, and the rites of passage (such as birth or marriage) are based on the *gṛhyasūtras* composed in the fifth century B.C. (See Altekar 1959). The information regarding correct attire to wear at home and for domestic activities is transmitted to female members of the family by their elders. Second, all other social and religious occasions each have different requirements for selecting the correct dress, but the basic rules are kept in mind: silk and woollens are permanently pure, the unstitched dress being more pure than the stitched or tailored garment. A black dress should be avoided on occasions considered vulnerable, such as marriage or birth. Menstruation restricts a woman in her choice of dress, as does a death in the family or among close relatives. A woman who has given birth to a child remains polluted for a few weeks until she takes a ritual bath for purification. After this bath she is permitted to wear the color yellow or bright-colored dresses.

While supervising a ritual a priest wears an unstitched dress.[5] Having taken a bath, he wears the white cotton *dhoti* or a silken loin cloth. At this point he and his dress are highly vulnerable to pollution. The human body itself is the polluting factor. Some fabrics are less pollutable while others are easily polluted. Silk can be purified simply by sprinkling a few drops of purifying water on it, while a polluted cotton garment must be washed in water for purification. The dress of a bride and bridegroom should be of bright colors. Generally the fabric used for their dresses has bright metal threads with cotton or silk. Gold and silver threads are preferred. These dresses are protected from pollution by touch or other polluting acts, as the metal is a purifying agent.

There are places, persons, statuses, activities, food, dresses, colors, and many other things that are considered difficult to purify or that are considered to be permanently polluted. Some of these are regarded as polluted due to contact, touch, activity, or the use to which they are put, and can be purified by purification rites and the observation of rituals. Dumont states that "objects are not polluted simply by contact but by the use to which they are put . . . thus nowadays a new garment or vessel can be received from anybody, and it remains pure because they are new. It is believed that a man's own bed, garments, wife, child and waterpot are pure for him but are impure for others" (1970:50). Purity is also hierarchical; thus, gold is purer than silver, silver purer than bronze. Bronze vessels are considered to be purer than copper, copper purer than iron. Silk is purer than cotton. The wearing of a particular type of dress is influenced by the caste of a person. Caste status is given by birth and people generally marry within their caste groups. The major caste groups are: brahmins, who are the priestly caste and highest in the caste hierarchy; *kṣatriya*, the warrior and ruling caste; *vaiśya*, the trading caste; then the agricultural and serving castes such as potters, carpenters, and agriculturalists; and last, the *sūdra*, formerly known as untouchables.[6] Traditionally a person's caste is visually identified by his or her dress. Women of all castes may wear the sari but the selection of style, floral designs, and choice of ornaments is influenced by the caste of the wearer. In rural areas people recognize the caste of a male by his head gear and a woman's caste by her dress.

Social and Cultural Context of Women's Dress in India

Women's dress in India must be understood in its social and cultural context, which has a long history. This history can be traced to the ancient period, through descriptions of clothes in the epics, dharmaśāstras, and other ancient manuscripts, as well as through study of sculptures and paintings of historical periods. An examination of women's dress of the "ancient past" helps elucidate those values which still influence contemporary dress today.

Interestingly, there are no specific separate words for male and female attire in Vedic literature (1200 B.C. to 600 B.C.). Two garments are alluded to: *vāsaḥ antaram* (undergarment), and *paridhānam* (upper garment). These were the two main items of dress for both men and women, both were unstitched, long lengths of cloth with possibilities of improvisation in wear. A waistband was used on the lower garment, from which the later *ghaghara* (skirt) may have evolved. Rich people and kings wore a gorgeous *drapi* (mantle) on ceremonial occasions, and there are descriptions of *uśnīṣa* (headdresses), which were in vogue for queens and the wealthy; these looked something like a *pagri* (turban).

In the ancient period, the art of weaving was "well-developed, and it is fairly certain that the sari was a long piece, about five or six yards in length" (Altekar 1959:280). It is probable that women of the period used the sari to cover both the upper and lower parts of the body, as is still done today all over India.

In the epics, descriptions of women's dress show that the sari continued to dominate, and there is no reference to stitched garments. At home, women used to wear just one piece of cloth to cover both the lower and upper parts of the body, including the bosom and shoulders, but when going out of the home and on ceremonial occasions, an additional upper garment was worn. Draupadi protested when Dushasan dragged her to the gambling hall of the court because she was wearing only one garment, as she had been at home and was menstruating.[7]

Early sculptures confirm that two garments were worn in public, while at home the sari alone was sufficient because part of it could be used to cover the upper parts of the body (Cunningham 1879). Dharmaśāstra writers stress that women should be dressed so that their navel should never become visible, and legs should be covered down to the ankles (*Sankhasmṛiti*). But Indian sculpture depicts the sari as generally covering the body below the navel, and women depicted as nude and semi-nude are portrayed in early temple and cave sculptures. It has been suggested that the early tradition of showing the dress on these sculptures was by plastering or coloring which was not permanent and has been lost (Altekar 1959:284). Another explanation for women appearing without covering their bust properly in the sculpture and paintings of southern and central India suggests them to be the artistic convention of the time, while some believe that this was a tradition in Dravidian culture.

In the eleventh century, with the increasing inflow of invaders and migrant groups to India and with a probable increase in trade, a change occurred in the garments worn. For example, the *kañcukī* (bodice) and *dukul* or *dupatta* (scarf to cover head and shoulders) were introduced. Traditionally, the dress also included ornaments and body decorations with colors, henna, and tattooing. Although the sari continued to play a very important role in the dress of Hindu women, by the later Vedic and early Epic periods, a number of new garments were mentioned and clothes became more colorful, richly dyed, and decorated. The wealthy wore dresses embroidered and ornamented with jewels. An all-purpose strip of cloth, the *dupatta* (scarf or shawl), was used as headcovering, and at this time stitched fashion garments for women appeared: the *caṇḍātaka* (petticoat), and the *śāmulyam* (undershirt) (see *Katyayanaśrautasūtra*). But the preference for unstitched clothing continued, with the basic dress still consisting of two lengths of cloth. Thus, over many centuries the dress of Hindu women retained basic characteristics, although various new forms appeared and were integrated into the main elements of the dress. Today it combines three pieces: petticoat, blouse, and sari. These three articles of dress are improvised on the basis of new values and fashions. Certain prescriptions and proscriptions are observed when this form of dress is worn on different occasions and at different times, by women of different castes and social status.[8]

Historically, the Hindu woman's dress has evolved from contacts with other cultures, sometimes under the influence of immigrating craftsmen. Spinning and weaving machines, mechanized printing and new chemicals from the West have most recently influenced the availability of dress materials. However, this has still not altered the traditional values that favor the women's saris and other garments that

Figure 13.3 Dress popular among rural women consisting of a *ghaghara* (skirt), *odhani* (upper garment), and *kanchali* (bodice). Most of the middle- and lower-caste women prefer this dress while working in agriculture and other activities.

Figure 13.4 Urban dress, consisting of sari, blouse, and petticoat. The dress is a symbol of sophistication, education, and higher class. The class is distinguished by the quality of the dress material.

retain their traditional appearance. The sari has continued to remain the preferred and most important item of dress for many Indian women, even in these modern times when a variety of garments are available and fashion designers are creating new styles. The designers, printing mills, and manufacturers of garments and dress keep the values and the context of the wearer in mind while manufacturing these dresses.

Fashion

In India, "fashion," both as a word and as a concept, denotes a deviation from the norms of dress, and in the feminine context, generally means the adoption of alien dress and the wearing of Western dress in the masculine context. For that reason, a Hindu woman's dress changes within the limits of sari, blouse, and petticoat. The way the sari is draped and secured and the way the petticoat is worn have changed from time to time. Ideally, both the petticoat and sari should cover the navel, but in the context of urban life a change in fashion occasionally reveals the navel, against traditional norms, and in the face of criticism.[9] Another change in style has increased the length of the sari from four meters to eight or nine meters. This change has been accepted as a symbol of high culture. The *pallu* (the floating end of the sari) has moved from the right shoulder to the left shoulder. It can be worn very long – down to the heels; or mid-length – down to the thighs; or short – covering only the shoulders. As a symbol of fashion, the *pallu* is not used as a veil or to cover the head, but in a variety of other styles. The long sari and gorgeous dress material have become a status symbol in society.[10] Styles in blouses change frequently; sometimes the lower line of the blouse reaches only to just beneath the breasts, sometimes it extends down to the navel or lower, covering the waistline of the petticoat. In an urban context, sleeveless and low-cut blouses are regarded as high society fashion. Different styles in footwear have been adopted without much comment except that high-heeled sandals are criticized for being too Western or impractical for the majority of Indian women.

Since independence in 1947, women's dress in India has become more colorful, bright, and expensive, and the demand for foreign-made fabrics from Japan and elsewhere to be used in saris is expanding. Latest (1990) designs include flowers and ornamental modern abstract designs. Surat, the biggest center of manufacture for saris, caters to a demand for new designs and fulfills popular requirements; for example, specific designs are mass-produced and named after heroines and Indian films.[11]

Variations of Dress

The customs of an individual's class prescribe the style and dress to be worn, as well as the material, colors, and ornaments, although there are regional variations. Among the three higher castes of central India, the brahmins, Rajputs (kṣatriya), and the Baniaś (*vaiśya*), the *odhani* or sari, plus the blouse and petticoat are the prescribed female dress. The warrior caste of Rajputs still require their women to observe *purdah*, as *purdah* became the symbol of aristocracy after Muslim traditions in the eleventh century; their women wear long blouses which cover them from the neck down over the navel and stomach. Generally among higher castes women wear an *odhani* on religious and traditional ritual occasions. The sari is popular among urban women. Among the higher classes and castes the sari is longer and the blouse changes according to fashion.

Women living in rural areas in Central India prefer to wear the *ghaghara* (long gathered skirt), the *kanchali* blouse (bodice of colored cloth with buttons up the front), and *lugadi* or *odhani* (short sari that covers the back and head). These are the traditional and folk forms of petticoats, blouse, and sari. The *odhani* covers the head and hangs down the front and back of the wearer. The *ghaghara* varies in design and style from region to region; its printed designs are associated with different communities. Women from agricultural and working castes tuck the two upper corners of the *odhani* in the front of the skirt. The right corner of the *odhani* is tucked round the waist in order to keep the arms free for work and the portion covering the head is easily maneuverable and can be lowered quickly over the face when a man approaches.

Agricultural castes have a definite preference for colors that are particular to them. In Rajasthan the *ghaghara* (skirt) is generally of dark shades such as deep green or dark blue and the *odhani* is commonly red, yellow, or another bright color. The ornaments are representative of certain social groups.[12] The higher the caste and status group, the lighter in weight will be the dress and ornament. Finer fabrics and ornaments made of gold are preferred and are considered to express high status within a caste group.

Women of Punjab, and Muslims more generally, wear the *salwar* (trousers that tightly fit around the lower part of the leg) and *kameez* (sleeved or half-sleeved shirts that reach down to the knees). Variations of this style of dress have been adopted by the younger generation as fashionable wear all over the country. Secondary-school and college girls prefer *salwar* and *kurta* (Indian long shirt), stitched and tight-fitting dress. However, male or unisex clothing such as jeans, slacks, and shirts have not generally found favor even among educated married women. They feel that their dress represents their gender and therefore unisex clothes have not been adopted, although unmarried or college girls may wear unisex, tailored garments. Once they achieve the status of married women, they wear the traditional sari.[13]

Men in rural areas wear the *dhoti sakaccha*-style (by passing a part of it between the legs and tucking it up behind the waist). *Dhotis* are usually worn while performing rituals. *Dhotis* are invariably of thin

Figure 13.5 Women's dress of the middle classes. Generally worn at home and in small towns.

Figure 13.6 Young girl in *salwar* and *kurta*, a fully cut-and-sewn dress. Popular and preferred by unmarried women, schoolgirls, and college women.

white material and lack the lavish decorative border and designs characteristic of the women's sari. The *dhoti* is shorter in length compared to the women's sari and is worn to cover the body from waist to legs.

Dress and Gifts

Dress is the most important item in the exchange of gifts. Married Hindu women expect to receive gifts from parents, from elder brothers and their wives, from their own husband and his parents as well as elder members of his family, and also from the family into which their daughters marry. Daughters and younger women also expect gifts from their relatives. Indeed the most important gift for women is a garment, and any gift without items of dress is incomplete. A female child starts receiving gifts as soon as she is born. For the newborn girl and her mother, her mother's brother and his wife are expected to bring one or several garments on the occasion of the first ritual bath given to mother and daughter. Other relatives of higher status and position also present garments. As a girl is not a preferred offspring, these gifts are relatively simple. More elaborate and expensive gifts are made on the occasion of her marriage. Her parents may give her many garments: three, seven, eleven (uneven numbers are auspicious numbers), or more. The bridegroom's family makes presentations of various dresses and ornaments. When the bride goes to her husband's house for the first time, she wears a dress presented by her husband's parents. In Hindu India it is the women who receive and give gifts in the form of cloth and garments, while male members may make presentations in the form of cash. Exchanging gifts of dress from one family to another is reciprocal. Whenever a daughter visits her parents after her marriage, she expects to be given an item of dress. On all important social and ritual occasions in a woman's husband's family, the woman's parents and brothers are expected to bring dresses for their daughter or sister. When parents-in-law return from a pilgrimage, the daughter and her in-laws receive garments from them. The gifts should follow certain conventions in color and design; any deviation is criticized and not accepted. The widowed mother-in-law will receive a simple garment, usually white or light in color with only a basic border, as is appropriate for a widow. By contrast, a married woman whose husband is alive will get an expensive dress.[14]

Dresses are prepared and bought by the parents of a daughter in anticipation of her marriage. The bride is provided her wedding attire by the bridegroom and his parents, while her minimum future wardrobe comes from her parents. Concerning cloth in connection with death, on the twelfth day after the death of a married woman a piece of cloth (*kapda*) is distributed to each female relative and other participating women by the parents or brothers of the deceased woman. This gift of cloth at death is supposed to consolidate ties among the living. The transfer of dress and cloth on the occasion of birth, marriage, death, and rituals of initiation and curing confirms and intensifies social relations. The presentation of dress is a symbol of honoring the receiver. Payment in dress is preferred for servants and artisans, such as midwife, hairdresser, potter, and priest. Nowadays a politician would present scarves to people, hoping to win the favor of the electorate.

On the occasion of a marriage feast, guests, relatives, and family members of the bride and groom wear their best dresses and ornaments.

A woman in particular represents the status of her family, so she must wear the best she owns. Apart from widows, women choose brightly colored traditional dresses for the occasion. Ornaments are an important part of the ensemble; among higher castes the weight of gold ornaments is a major sign of status. Lower castes wear silver ornaments, and again, the weight displayed is of importance. Nowadays wrist watches have become part of an Indian woman's ornaments and also a status symbol. The overall dress and color in such gatherings is reaffirmed on each occasion, while slight changes in style are first evaluated by other women. If these innovations are considered to be within permissible standards, they may spread quickly.

Women's Dress, the Media, and the Discipline of Tradition

From watching Indian films, values concerning dress become readily apparent. Cinema in India generally portrays women according to the prevailing mores of Indian society, with a strong preference for traditional dress, emphasizing the importance of "traditional" values and ways of life. Heroines, deities, and normal women all wear saris and traditional dress. The "vamps" or "fast" girls wear jeans, shorts, short frocks, and Western hairstyles.

Folk stories, narratives, and folk songs also reinforce the same traditional values as represented by women's dress. Deviation from the norm is held up to ridicule and criticism, thus leading to a fear or dislike of innovation.

Modern technology such as machine weaving and sewing has not changed the traditional style of dress; indeed, it has helped in creating a universal value system in Hindu India, and indirectly, dress may have been an inhibiting factor in changes in the lifestyle and role of women. To better understand the attitude of women regarding the discipline of dress, twenty-nine women in the city of Jaipur were interviewed. Though the sample was very small it represented all the strata of the city. Interviewees expressed the opinion that their mode of dress establishes a discipline upon them. According to these women, wearing the traditional dress emphasizes the expected position of women at home; their activities and jobs are restricted in this context. The sari encourages them to neither walk quickly nor run, but to move with dignity; it enhances the view Indian society has regarding women.

But the sari is also considered to be practical. By covering her face as part of *purdah*, a woman can conceal herself from public view. By covering her head and sometimes veiling her face she is able to express her respect for her elders. The sari or *odhani* (short sari) is also useful when breast-feeding; mothers can cover the child while they are breast-feeding at home or in public; therefore, the sari can bestow privacy when needed. The sari is also a ritual dress, and no *puja* (worship) is complete without the traditional sari or *odhani*.

It is felt that the unstitched sari has an aesthetic value and creates a certain atmosphere, adding to the status and dignity of the wearer. It makes a graceful silhouette as part of the sari floats behind like a queen's train, and the wearer may express feelings of satisfaction and status from wearing the graceful garment.

Marital status has the greatest impact on the colors and materials of the dress, but age is also an important factor. As she advances in years the colors chosen are more sober. Dress is also related to work. The workplace outside is secular while home is believed to be sacred. Working women choose sober dresses for the occasion, whether in the office or on a farm. However, female office workers have more freedom of choice in matters of dress than manual workers. On death, a woman is covered with a dress provided by her original family, according to her marital status. A married woman will be covered in her marriage dress or a colored dress decorated with metallic strips. A widow after death is dressed in a simple, sober dress. Western dress has been adopted for children and in girls' schools as uniform, but Western dress has not entered into the domain of the married woman. It still indicates a juvenile or vampish status generally considered to be inferior and negative, not a status to be assumed by a respectable married woman.

Conclusions

The written and unwritten rules and socioreligious attitudes govern the style, material, and fashion of Hindu women's dress. The rules and attitudes are passed from mother to daughter and mother-in-law to daughter-in-law, and are supported and reinforced through folk idioms, discipline of tradition, and the media. The principle of purity and pollution is one of the important governing factors in the selection of the dress material, style, color, and fashion of the dress among Hindu women. In the Vedic ages (1200–600 B.C.) marriage was regarded as a social and religious duty and necessity. According to the Avesta, oblation offered to gods or ancestors by a maiden or bachelor are unacceptable to them (Altekar 1978:31). A Vedic passage declares that a

Figure 13.7 *Sakacch* sari, popular in Maharashtra and adjacent areas.

Figure 13.8 Dress preferred by women of Rajput caste.

person who is unmarried is unholy (Taittiríyabráhmana, eighth century B.C.). Here the term unmarried denotes all those who are maiden, separated, widowed, and not living with their ritually married spouses. For a Hindu woman to remain in uninterrupted married life until her death is a most cherished wish even today. For this aim, Hindu women observe many fasts (one of the respondents interviewed observes 104 fast days in a year) and organize feasts and donations every year. While observing fasts and feasts and other rituals, Hindu women use the prescribed dress. The dress has been influenced by wider contacts, innovations, the introduction of new technology and dress material, urbanization, education, and new means of transportation, but the changes have remained restricted within the framework of ritually pure and auspicious "prescribed dress," that is, sari, blouse, and petticoat. Fashions and innovations in dress are permitted to women only while they are maidens. One of the folk songs popular in North India narrates the request of the daughter to allow her to play and dress according to her wish. She says:

Only four days to play, O mother, only four days to play!
After four days, O mother, your son-in-law will take me away.

The unmarried girls who await marriage, the ritual of purification, have the freedom of being fashionable and adopting new dresses while they are studying in schools and colleges and are aware that marriage will restrict their freedom of dress. It is a popular saying that "the burden of maintaining Hindu religion is on women's shoulders." This belief restricts the freedom of Hindu women and provides freedom to men. Men have complete freedom in accepting new forms of dress and in ignoring religious prescriptions. The women earn and accumulate *punya*, merits in spiritual form, and men spend these merits. Men earn money and material merits, and women spend them for earning spiritual merits.[15] Thus the wheels of spiritual and material merits move the cart of the Hindu family in this *kaliyuga*, the machine age.

Notes

1. Data for this paper have come from interviews with twenty-nine women in Jaipur in 1989 who represented all strata of the city, as well as from many years of observing women's dress in India. In addition, as a practicing Hindu, I am interpreting custom from my knowledge of the belief system.
2. In the Indian context the concept of "stitched and unstitched" is a better explanation than "cut and uncut." Sometimes a sari is cut in length according to the choice of size, that is, four, five, or nine meters from a long cloth, but it is not regarded as a stitched dress. In India, "cut-and-stitched dress" denotes tailored and sewn garments, while only "cut" does not explain the sewn garments.
3. The chronology of the periods referred to in this paper is given here to explain the time periods.

1200–900 B.C.	Early Vedic period	
900–600 B.C.	Later Vedic period	Ancient Period
1000 B.C.	*Rāmāyaṇa* and *Mahābhārata*	Epic Period
800 B.C.	*Brāhmaṇas* and *Upaniṣads*	Upanisadic.
500 B.C.	*Dharmasūtras*	
400 A.D.	(Maurya, Ashoka, Shaka, and Gupta Empires)	Sūtra period

750–1175 A.D.	Travellers and Records	Medieval period
1200–1525 A.D.	Court Records	Period of invasion and plunder
1525–1765 A.D.	Court Records	Mughal period
1756–1947 A.D.	Research and Survey	British period

4. Only a brief mention of dress for festivals will be made here, as this topic is worthy of a paper in itself. I shall refer to them in Indian English. The annual calendar of festivals in Hindu India is very long. *Deepavali*, the Festival of Light; *Holi*, the Festival of Colors; *Raksha Bandhan*, the Charm-Tying Festival; and *Pooja* or *Deshehra*, Festival of Worshipping Power, are the main Indian festivals among a whole chain of others. There are also many festivals particularly for women, like *Gangaur*, where young girls worship the deity and request a good husband, or *Teej*, which is the festival of spring and flowers, celebrated by processions. There are also important fasts during the year. These feasts and fasts provide opportunities for women to wear and receive presents of beautiful clothes and socialize young girls into the intricacies of dress and its etiquette. The values of society and of the girls' particular caste or subcaste are reinforced on these occasions. Dress emphasizes kinship and religious relations and can create social tensions and other problems among relatives if norms of dress are not observed. Religious beliefs and taboos surrounding dress and style have significant influence in selection; color, styles, and motif distinguish ordinary dress from ceremonial dress.
5. Altekar (1959:295) says that "society, however, had a general prejudice against stitched clothes, and women were for a long time reluctant to take to jackets, blouses and frocks. We find only dancing girls adopting the new fashion in dress in the beginning. Dancing girls, maid-servants and women of low rank have been depicted wearing jacket and blouses in paintings of Ajanta caves [fifth century A.D.] and sculptures of Bhārhut and Sārnāth [second century A.D.]."
6. There is a popular saying: "Eat according to your liking and wear according to the liking of others," but the word "others" denotes the caste and community fellows in India.
7. The *Māhābhārata*, attributed to Vyāsa, is the world's longest known epic. It describes the war between the five Pandavas (sons of Pandu), and their cousins the Kauravas, the hundred sons of their uncle Dhritarastra. The battle, which lasted eighteen days, was fought between the cousins for the throne. Krishna, an incarnation of Vishnu, was on the side of the Pandavas. The five Pandava brothers married the beautiful princess Draupadi of the Panchal kingdom. The Kauravas were jealous of the Pandavas as they could not win Draupadi in a contest later on another occasion. Draupadi laughed at the ignorance of Duryodhan, the eldest Kaurava brother, when he visited

the new palace of Pandavas, and that was one of the causes of the battle. Pandavas lost the kingdom and Draupadi in the game of the dice, and Duryodhan declared that Draupadi was now his maid-servant, and sent his younger brother Dushasan to bring her to the court. Dushasan brought her against her will and started pulling at her sari to disrobe her. She cried for help to Krishna, who extended her sari endlessly. In the war, the Pandavas were victorious. The epic reinforces the social value of the sari. Draupadi's sari became a legend. She is known as pure and the model for Hindu women. It is sung in folk songs: "Krishna, the honor of Draupadi to save extends the sari endlessly."

The *Mahābhārata* was serialized on Indian television for nearly two years (1988–1990) in ninety-six episodes. It was one of the most popular serials in the country. People avoided travel and meetings at the time of serial days. People could see the dresses of the characters; males have not adopted them as they were outdated, but the styles and saris worn by female characters became popular. The sari used by Draupadi, the princess of the Panchal kingdom, is currently (1990) popular among women and the sari is known as *Panchali* Sari, marketed by various manufacturers.

8. Among the higher classes (caste groups) of the southern states of India, particularly in Maharashtra, the sari was worn *sakaccha* fashion, passing a part of it between the legs and tucking it up behind the waist. In other parts of the country the sari was popularly worn *vikaccha* fashion – without any portion being tucked up behind, and in recent years this mode has become the norm among the elite in Maharashtra as well.
9. Among the rich, educated, and fashionable class, the navel-showing sari has become popular particularly while observing rituals and participating in feasts and parties. The style of the sari is known as *nabhidarshani* sari (navel-showing sari).
10. The prescribed dress for air hostesses in India is the traditional sari. The sari also has influenced fashion in the neighboring countries of Sri Lanka, Pakistan, Bangladesh, and Nepal.
11. The saris and styles used by popular heroines in films are named after the films, such as Dil Ki Pyas, Pakija, and Hare Kach Ki Churiya.
12. Rta Kapur Chisti and Amba Sanyal have written a book entitled *Saris of India*, based on surveys done in Madhya Pradesh. They observe, "The sari is woven three to four standard sizes in a given area, wherever a traditional market still survives. These lengths and widths are woven for specific age groups of girls and women, though the clients often ask the weaver for varying lengths and widths. . . . Today we find the design vocabulary of the sari coming through as a series of coded messages, handed down from generation to generation."
13. Male transvestites known as *hijras* wear women's dress and adopt the latest fashions and designs but restrict themselves to sari, petticoat, and short blouse.

14. There are a large number of folk songs popular in India expressing the demand of the gift of a sari from husband, parents, and brother:
    1. O Sajan, bring me a sari, in rainbow colors.
    2. O Dear, I am waiting for your arrival;
       You promised me a sari in gift.
    3. Teej is arriving, my parents will send me a Laharia Sari.
15. One of the old residents of Bhimlat village of Gujarat, from where large numbers of men go to work in foreign countries, said: "We men folk go to foreign countries to earn money and do hard work and women folk back home spend the money for performing rituals."

References

Alkazi, R., *Ancient Indian Costume*, Delhi: Art Heritage Books, 1983.

Altekar, A.S., *The Position of Women in Hindu Civilization*, Delhi: Motilal Banarasidas, 1959.

Chishti Kapur, R. and A. Sanyal, *Saris of India*, Delhi: Wiley Eastern Ltd. and Amr Vastra Kosh, 1989.

Cunningham, D., *The Stupa of Bharhut*, London, 1879.

Dar, S.N., *Costumes of India and Pakistan*, Bombay: D.B. Taraporevala Sons and Co., 1969.

Dumont, L., *Homo Hierarchicus: The Caste System and Its Implications*, Chicago: University of Chicago Press, 1970.

Ghurye, G.S., *Indian Costumes*, Bombay: Popular Prakashan, 1951.

Joshi, O.P., "Tattooing and Tattooers: A Socio-Cultural Analysis," *International Committee on Urgent Anthropological and Ethnological Research*, No. 18, Vienna, 1976.

———, "Human body Decoration: An Approach Towards Its Methodology," *Eleventh International Congress of Anthropological and Ethnological Sciences*, Vancouver and Quebec City, 1983.

Kane, P.V., *History of Dharmaśāstra*, 5 Vols., Poona: Bhandarkar Oriental Research Institute, 1958.

Roach, M.E., and J.B. Eicher, eds., *Dress Adornment and the Social Order*, New York: Wiley, 1972.

14

Dressing for Dinner in the Bush

Rituals of Self-Definition and British Imperial Authority

Helen Callaway

In *Return to Laughter*, the novel written by American anthropologist Laura Bohannan (under the pseudonym of Elenore Smith Bowen) about fieldwork among the Tiv of Nigeria in the late 1940s, the narrator recounted her first night in the bush. After her bath, she found that her British-trained servants had set out her clothes for dinner – her mosquito boots and her most backless evening dress. Surprised, she decided that her first evening as an anthropologist in the field deserved a celebration, and she donned formal dress for the occasion. While eating her dinner in what she thought was lone splendor, she spotted a slit in the thatch and realized that, in the lamp light, she was fully displayed to the curious local inhabitants. She reflected, "Impervious to the stares of natives, generations of Empire-building Englishmen have sat on boxes in jungles eating their custard and tinned gooseberries in full evening dress. An American like myself can only feel that somehow she's been tricked into going on a picnic in high heels" (Bowen 1954:15).

She did not repeat the ritual of dressing for dinner until months later. This came on Thanksgiving, a specifically American holiday, following a distressing experience of the death in childbirth of her Tiv friend after the elders had refused the anthropologist's plea to get medical help and instead hurled fierce accusations of witchcraft at each other. Feeling deeply confused and depressed, she resolved never again to forget her identity. She had changed her mind: "The English were quite right. One had to dress for dinner. One needed a symbol, some external sign, to assist daily remembrance of what one was" (1954:207). By putting on formal evening dress for a special dinner, she intended to seal herself off from the Tiv community. Yet this passage, with its ironic undertones, cannot be taken in an unambiguous way. She realized that such artificial means of regaining her identity were alien to her, a sign that she was no longer herself.

Discipline and Dominance

Since the Second World War, at least, the British colonial officer dressing for dinner in the middle of the jungle has been a familiar butt of cartoonists and comedians. This image of stiff formality and aloofness remains one of the pervasive stereotypes of the British Empire. Why would a district officer after a long, hot day "dealing with the natives" have his bath, and then, particularly if dining alone, endure the tropical heat in a dinner jacket and tie? Who was his audience? What was the purpose of this ritual?

This seemingly incongruous image serves as the starting point for an investigation of the symbolism of dress in the exercise of imperial domination. At the height of its expansion, around the turn of the twentieth century, the British Empire ruled a quarter of the world's land surface and nearly a quarter of its inhabitants. The individual officer dressing for dinner alone can be seen as one end of a spectrum culminating in the elaborate attire worn for the grand ceremonies of empire, which represented power and authority in a bravura of color and style. Dress became a visual marker for distinctions of race, gender, and social rank.

Records show that dressing for dinner was standard among the ruling elites throughout the era of the British Empire, in its most isolated outposts as well as its social centers, for parties or when dining alone. A *sahib* tells about this custom: "If you dined out pre-1914 anywhere in India privately, it was a tailcoat, a boiled shirt and a white waistcoat, with a stiff collar and a white tie. Long after they gave this up in England we continued to do it in India" (Allen 1976:112). Even a lone tea planter in upper Assam followed this social rule, putting on a dinner jacket as a way of retaining his self-respect. He told his servants, "Now this is a dinner party and every night is a dinner party and you will serve my dinner as though there are other people at the dinner table" (Allen 1976:99).

The wife of a colonial officer in Nigeria during the first decade of this century wrote in her memoirs, "If for some reason our dogcart was out of action, bath-towels were flung over saddles and we rode to dinner parties, I in a long low-necked dress, my husband in white mess jacket and the French-grey cummerbund of Northern Nigeria" (Leith-Ross 1983:48). A woman education officer sent forty years later to a remote area of Nigeria recounted that "in an evening in the bush I always wore a long dress to keep up my morale" (Dinnick-Parr as quoted in Allen 1980:155). She remembered occasions when the development officer would join her for dinner – "he in a dinner suit and I in an evening dress" – and afterward they would walk along the bush path talking. The local inhabitants gathered to see them, wondering "why we were all dressed up and covered ourselves when it was so frightfully hot."

Depending on the position of the observer within the colonial hierarchy, the ritual of dressing for dinner held different values. Opposing views of this social convention were presented by two British wives in Northern Nigeria during the early years before the first World War. The first commentary comes from Sylvia Leith-Ross, a remarkable woman who arrived in 1907 as the bride of a colonial officer. A year later her husband died of blackwater fever, and in her shipboard journal returning to England she noted that, of their original party of five who had gone out thirteen months earlier, she was the only one left. Over the next sixty years, Leith-Ross returned many times to Nigeria – as an education officer, anthropologist, and (during the Second World War) as a member of the intelligence service.

Her memoirs tell of an episode in 1913 when she was being poled up the Benue River in a steel canoe, accompanied on the first part of the journey by a colonial officer in his own canoe. A problem had arisen:

> We had always dressed for dinner. This was a rule that could not be broken, either at home or abroad, at sea or on shore, in the Arctic Circle or on the Equator. But alas, there was very little space indeed in our steel canoes. A compromise was necessary. . . . One evening Armar would change his bush shirt and I would change my khaki skirt; the next, I would change my white blouse and Armar would change his khaki breeches. Between the two of us, we had obeyed our code and had upheld our own and our country's dignity (Leith-Ross 1983:69).

She explained, "When you are alone, among thousands of unknown, unpredictable people, dazed by unaccustomed sights and sounds, bemused by strange ways of life and thought, you need to remember who you are, where you come from, what your standards are. A material discipline represents – and aids – a moral discipline" (1983:69). In the system of ideas of this society, the discipline of dress was linked directly to the discipline of a moral code. She noted details of dress in a photograph taken in 1907: "The men wear helmets and are coated and trousered, collared and tied. . . . The four women present sit in a group apart, in summery but long-skirted, high-necked, long-sleeved dresses, elaborate hats tilted at a becoming angle" (1983:55–56). Correctness of attire characterizes this portrait from the high noon of empire.

As a staunch supporter of British rule, Leith-Ross connected attention to proper dress with the courage and fortitude required for the task of governing alien peoples: "Ridiculous as it may seem to find moral significance in a casual group photograph, one begins to understand how it was that such a handful of men could dominate the land" (1983: 56). In this single image of what was considered to be appropriate dress, she condensed various levels of the colonial vision: personal and national dignity, self-discipline linked with an altruistic moral code, the fortitude required for imperial rule, and a few British men dominating a vast territory.

Despite the sharpness of her observations, Leith-Ross did not discern the hidden assumptions behind this social convention. The lone officer dressing for dinner in the jungle could identify himself with his countrymen, but also, as Wilkinson pointed out (1970:134), the individual's self-assurance was even more bolstered when the etiquette represented that of a traditionally superior class – in this case, the gentry. Many of those who entered the British Colonial Service were not of the upper social strata, but from the middling ranks – the sons of clergymen and schoolmasters. By joining the Service and taking part in its rituals, they could fulfill their aspirations for higher social status, some of them eventually being awarded knighthoods. Interpreted in this wider context, "dressing for dinner" becomes the visible sign of "innate superiority" in the elite social tradition transmitted through the public schools, the military academies, and the ancient universities. Even those officers who had not experienced this privileged background quickly assimilated its unwritten rules and conformed to its code.

The second view comes from outside the Colonial Service during the same period. Mrs. Horace Tremlett related her experience in Northern Nigeria in 1914 as the wife of an engineer for a tin-mining company, a social position deemed inferior. The title of her book, *With the Tin Gods*, appears innocent, an apparent reference to the tin explorers, but it turns out to be a highly charged anti-imperialist pun. She told of the antagonism existing in government circles toward the mining enterprise. While acknowledging that some uneducated miners ignorant of native customs stirred up a great deal of trouble, she added with gentle sarcasm that government officials feared that the prestige of the white man was in danger of being lowered by the arrival of common poeple who did not own dress suits. She commented, "For they are very punctilious in Nigeria on the question of dress clothes" (1915:264). The officer, she explained, "clings so desperately in Nigeria to his dress suit, not because he wishes to look nice, but because he knows he is expected to live up to certain traditions, and because he likes to feel that he is a gentleman – especially if he has any doubt on the subject" (1915:165). In her view, colonial officers in Nigeria were not exactly examples of high moral standards; she hinted at their affairs with African women. Her conclusion was trenchant: "The white man there is king as he is nowhere else in the world; and a most diverting spectable he is, playing little tin god to his black subjects" (1915:238). In the range of colonial literature, this view is unusually subversive.

Superior Persons

Even as late as 1940, Lord Lloyd, then Secretary of State for the Colonies, told a group of young officers about to take up their first appointments: "You are not going to have a soft job. You will indeed have plenty of hard work and not too many of the comforts of life, and quite possibly no lack of danger, but I know you would not have it otherwise. . . . In what other task can you have so much power so early? You can at the age of twenty-five be the father of your people: you can drive the road, bridge the river, and water the desert; you can be the arm of justice and the hand of mercy to millions" (Jeffries 1949:19). These echoes of Kipling were, of course, main themes in the ideology of power, paternalism, and service (service to the British Crown).

Known in India as the "heaven born," officers of the Colonial Service were specially selected for their leadership qualities, ideally developed (though not always in practice) through education in favored public schools, such as Eton, Rugby, or Harrow. This was followed by training in a military academy or by university education in Oxford and Cambridge. This male ruling group saw itself and was seen by the British establishment to have "natural" or innate superiority. In this system of ideas, social hierarchy was legitimated by various "scientific" theories. The anthropology of the late nineteenth century, for example, set out the range of racial groups on an evolutionary scale, at the top of which stood Victorian British society. Again, upper-class men were considered superior by birth to working-class ones, according to arguments based on inherited genetic qualities. In relation to women, men were defined as superior on physiological and medical grounds, which, in turn, provided reasons for limiting women's intellectual and social development. (The sisters of these men gained their education at home until well into the twentieth century.)

The concept of the "gentleman" was pervasive, encapsulating a cluster of meanings: social superiority in the right to bear arms and in the identification with the landed gentry, and moral superiority derived from the code of chivalry. By the late Victorian period, public schools had incorporated this concept into every aspect of school life, from organized games as the means for creating team spirit, to the custom of fagging (older boys ordering younger boys to do menial chores) as a way of training leaders and loyal followers within a hierarchical system. In his biography of Dr. Arnold of Rugby, Lytton Strachey stated that teachers and prophets have strange histories after their lifetimes: "The earnest enthusiast who strove to make his pupils Christian gentlemen . . . has proved to be the founder of the worship of athletics and the worship of good form. Upon those two poles our public schools have turned for so long that we have almost come to believe that such is their essential nature, and that an English public school-boy who wears the wrong clothes and takes no interest in football is a contradiction in terms" (1948:187–88). The schoolboy retained the heightened values of correctness of dress far longer than his declensions of Latin verbs. His education included both compulsory uniforms and compulsory games, encouraging military virtues and the obligations of empire. From the uniforms of schools and military academies, young men graduated to those glorifying imperial rule.

Uniforms and the Man

In her essay, *Three Guineas*, first published in 1938 and written against the threat of growing fascism in Europe, Virginia Woolf took up the subject of what women can do to prevent war. Writing with controlled anger and charged sensibility, Woolf presented a glittering satire on the world of male institutions. As a key symbol in her portrait of male competitiveness and hierarchy, she described the splendor of the clothes worn by professional men in their public capacity:

> Now you dress in violet; a jewelled crucifix swings on your breast; now your shoulders are covered with lace; now furred with ermine; now slung

> with many linked chains set with precious stones. Now you wear wigs on your heads; rows of graduated curls descend to your necks. . . . Sometimes gowns cover your legs; sometimes gaiters. Tabards embroidered with lions and unicorns swing from your shoulders; metal objects cut in star shapes or in circles glitter and twinkle upon your breasts. Ribbons of all colors – blue, purple, crimson – cross from shoulder to shoulder. After the comparative simplicity of your dress at home, the splendour of your public attire is dazzling (1986:23).

She noted that not only are whole groups of men dressed alike summer and winter, but every button, rosette, and stripe has its symbolic meaning and its specific rules regulating its use. Even stranger than these clothes, she went on, are the ceremonies men perform together, always in step, always in the uniform proper to the man and the occasion. The explanation for such decorative garments she found in their advertisement of the social, professional, or intellectual standing of the wearer. These costumes with their symbolic traditions draped the male in mantles of social prestige.

Yet men seemed blind to the remarkable nature of these clothes. In a revealing footnote, she quoted the words of a male judge summing up a case: "Women cannot be expected to renounce an essential feature of femininity or to abandon one of nature's solaces for a constant and insuperable physical handicap. Dress, after all, is one of the chief methods of women's self-expression. . . . In matters of dress women often remain children to the end" (1986:170). Woolf added that the judge himself was wearing a scarlet robe, an ermine cape, and a vast wig of artificial curls, but he seemed unaware of his own elaborate attire. To point up her theme of the absurdity of such venerable traditions, the book's illustrations show unflattering photographs of male decrepitude in professional dress: an ancient general bedecked in medals and ribbons, an elderly archbishop with a richly embroidered cassock, a rotund judge in elegant robes and wig, and gowned male academics in pompous ceremonial procession.

How does this disquisition on professional dress relate to her theme, the prevention of war? For her, the connection was obvious: the finest clothes are those worn by soldiers. These uniforms impress the beholder with the majesty of military office and induce young men to join the service. How a military uniform strengthens a man's image of masculinity has been analyzed: "It gives him a head-dress which exaggerates his height; it puts a stripe on his trousers to exaggerate his apparent length of leg; it gives him epaulettes to exaggerate the width of his shoulders" (Laver 1969:73).

Woolf's vivid analysis of male institutions with their decorations, public honors, patriotic rhetoric, uniforms, and war-making provides an excellent foundation for exploring the symbolism of dress in the exercise of British imperial power. The colorful and ostentatious costumes served to constitute and maintain hierarchies of race, gender, and social rank. While men gained their splendor and glory through their impressive uniforms and professional dress, women were forbidden to wear such clothes, as Woolf pointed out (1986:25). Yet, as shown later, some enterprising women manipulated modes of dress to exercise power in their own ways.

The Theater of Empire

Imperial domination has been seen mainly in terms of standing armies, superior military technology and organization, economic exploitation, and cunning political strategies of divide and rule. In recent years, however, another dimension of the exercise of power has come into focus – that of spectacles, rituals, and mass ceremonies – not only displaying the authority of British rule but subtly incorporating the indigenous princes, emirs, or chiefs as subordinates into a descending hierarchy that brought all the people into the encircling embrace of the British Empire (Cohn 1983; Ranger 1983).

Anthropological analysis reveals how the practice of imperial rule developed into a total cultural mode including not only these special ceremonies, but patterns of order and discipline regulating minute details of everyday existence for the rulers, and extending with far-reaching effects into the lives of their subjects (Callaway 1987:55–82). Power and rank were rendered visible in material forms and social processes. Townships were laid out with majestic government buildings, splendid ceremonial thoroughfares named after British sovereigns, and exclusive residential areas insuring social separation of the rulers from the ruled, as well as hierarchy within the ruling group. The Warrant of Precedence governed precise details of formal behavior both in the official interaction of administrators with native rulers and in the everyday social life of the dominant group itself. In this choreography of empire, the display of dress in all its forms carried a heavy weight of symbolic meanings.

Certain rules were deliberately demeaning. Because the wearing of shoes by Indians in the presence of the British was seen as an attempt to establish relations of equality, Indians were required to remove their shoes or sandals when entering into what the British defined as their space – their offices or homes. At the same time, the British always wore shoes in Indian spaces, including mosques and temples. As an exception, those Indians who habitually wore European clothes in public were allowed to wear shoes for such occasions as receptions and balls (Cohn 1983:176–77).

Elaborate dress became a significant means of asserting authority. Before the young Curzon set out on his exploration of the India's northwest frontier, he prepared for his visit to the Amir of Afghanistan by calling at a supplier of theatrical costumes in London where, for a modest sum, he hired "a cluster of gorgeous stars of foreign orders, mostly from the smaller States of Eastern Europe. To these he added an enormous pair of gold epaulettes in a case the size of a hat-box" (Rose 1969:268). On his journey he gathered a "glittering pair of patent leather Wellington top boots" and "a gigantic curved sword with ivory hilt and engraved scabbard," plus a cocked hat and a handsome pair of spurs. In this spuriously acquired uniform, he considered himself appropriately dressed for his audience with the Amir. Later, as Viceroy of India, Lord Curzon proved himself gifted in producing imperial spectacle of a scale and grandeur never before reached.

Interestingly, these great ceremonies developed in Victorian India to establish and maintain British authority were justified on the basis of the assumption that Indians had a special susceptibility for parades and show (Cohn 1983:188). This theater of empire reached its culmination during Lord Curzon's rule with the series of special events in January 1903 to celebrate King Edward VII's coronation. British India soon dubbed it "the Curzonation," knowing who would be in the durbar's center spotlight (Fowler 1987:280). The Viceroy planned this series of ceremonies and festivities in great detail – some seventy-seven pages in print. Lady Curzon, meanwhile, designed her own range of exquisite gowns to represent the feminine side of this confident masculine authority.

The first event on 29 December 1902 was the State Entry into Delhi with a procession of gaily painted elephants, drugged to keep them docile in the crowds. On the biggest elephant of all, an ancient slow-moving giant, was the silver-gilt howdah of the Viceroy and Lady Curzon. The next great ceremony came on 1 January, the durbar itself, with a multitude of twenty-six thousand people gathered in the middle of the day for the proclamation declaring King Edward VII King of England and Emperor of India. Five days later, after numerous festivities – sports matches, receptions, garden parties, special dinners, balls, fireworks – came the climax of the Delhi durbar. The State Ball was held in the Moghul Palace, where the Viceroy and the Vicereine made their grand entrance to the strains of the national anthem, he in white satin knee breeches, she in her famous peacock dress, with four thousand guests parting to line their route through the length of the ballroom to the marble podium. Lady Curzon's gown was "made of cloth-of-gold, embroidered by Delhi's superb craftsmen, with metal threads and real emeralds in a pattern of peacock feathers so that the cloth beneath had virtually disappeared" (Fowler 1987:290). Her own resplendent creation, she posed in it for photographs and a large oil portrait, which became, after her premature death attributed to over-exertion carrying out imperial duties, the identifying image of this American heiress who played her star role as Vicereine of India.

For these gala events, some eighty distinguished British guests arrived on the SS *Arabia*, among them the Duke and Duchess of Marlborough, the Duke and Duchess of Portland, Lord and Lady Derby, Lord and Lady Crewe, and other members of Curzon's set. They brought with them no less than forty-seven tons of dresses and uniforms (Fowler 1987:283).

It should be noted that in mobilizing the Indian nationalist movement, Gandhi subverted this symbolic authority by calling for Indians not only to return all honors and emblems granted to them by the imperial government, but also to dress in simple homespun peasant dress instead of the Western clothes or "native" costumes decreed by the imperial rulers (Cohn 1983:209). The paradox of dress symbolism was exposed in the drama of nationalism: if the British dressed up in splendid uniforms to establish and maintain authority over the Indians, the nationalists dressed down to grasp back the power that had been wrested from them.

These imperial ceremonies, reaching their height in scale and magnificence in Curzon's India, were transferred complete with dazzling military parades and brilliant uniforms to the far reaches of the empire in Africa and the Pacific. The governor of a colony held unique power, combining the roles of personal representative of the Crown, prime minister, head of the civil service, and leader of the colony's social life. His dress uniform was suitably impressive: "He was entitled to wear either a white uniform with white and red plumes in his colonial helmet or, in cooler climates, a dark blue uniform with a cocked hat and white plumes. Gold and silver gorgets, epaulettes, buttons, and frogging and an elaborately decorated sword completed the uniform" (Kirk-Greene 1978:228–29).

Special ceremonies marked the arrivals and departures of governors to and from their colonies. The triumphant entry of Sir Bernard Bourdillon to the Nigerian scene in 1935 has been described:

> On the morning of his arrival we all went down to the Customs wharf, the men in white uniforms and the ladies superb in their best. . . . The Regiment mounted one of its immaculate guards of honour and the band played on a flank. The invited guests sat uncomfortably in their finery on hard chairs, carefully arranged in the order in which they had to be presented. The guns (brought specially from Zaria) fired their slow salute from across the water. . . . Then the tall figure of Sir Bernard came down the companion way in his blue uniform and plumes, with his dazzling wife (Niven 1982:148).

There were numerous lesser ceremonies as well, requiring uniforms which defined position and rank. Sir Rex Niven recounted the occasion of a Governor's return from leave: "This was quite a show, with guards of honour, and booming guns and waving bunting. . . . It was the first time I wore the very undistinguished khaki uniform prescribed for us juniors, complete with our war medals; we did not qualify for the full white civil service uniform, with its obliterating 'Wolseley' helmet, until we had completed seven years service" (1982:14). It should be noted that the full dress uniform also included a sword – if obsolete as a weapon, a potent symbol of masculinity.

In a colony the official residence of the Governor, known as "Government House," was the center of imperial display, as shown in this glimpse of Lagos in 1921: "When Clifford gave parties or balls at Government House, all the men had to wear full evening dress, with starched shirts and collars, white waistcoats and tails. . . . I remember one ball at which the staircase was lined on each hand by soldiers wearing scarlet and gold zouaves and fezzes while the Governor received at the top" (Niven 1982:21).

If the prescribed dress of the male colonial officers was characterized by pomp and plumage enhancing masculinity, that of their wives was marked by propriety and femininity. The gender division in dress was strongly marked: men wore designated uniforms and robes (even the dinner jacket might be considered such), while women were able to exercise more choice in colors, textiles, and design, as long as they kept to models appropriate for the occasion. The biographer of Lady Curzon noted that she took immense pains preparing her magnificent wardrobe for India with the guiding thought, "She must be ultra-feminine when the men were ultra-masculine" (Nicolson 1977:138). In an unusual case, Lieutenant Governor Palmer of Northern Nigeria sympathized with the sensibilities of Muslim rulers by ordering European women to wear veils for public occasions (Heussler 1968:134).

Wardrobes for the Tropics

In Delhi and Bombay, Lagos and Nairobi, the servants of empire gave even greater attention to dress than their social equivalents back at home. Not only did they self-consciously maintain their identity and prestige, as has been shown in their daily routines of dressing for dinner and their grand ceremonies, but even in small outposts they turned everyday social life into a competitive whirl. London and Paris dictated women's fashions, despite the contrasts in climate, with only a few modifications to meet the threat of the sun and the onslaught of mosquitoes. All too often the assigned quarters in an isolated post seemed a mismatch of social expectations and setting. Airing clothing during the rainy season in Nigeria, Elinor Russell commented, "It always looked incongruous seeing a dinner jacket or evening dresses hanging outside a mud hut in the middle of Africa" (1978:90).

In most cases, a personal wardrobe sufficient for the entire tour had to be acquired. In 1902, Lady Lugard took with her to Northern Nigeria forty-six trunks and cases besides her trousseau, including household items for the new Government House at Zungeru (Perham 1960:75). Women embarking for the tropics gained advice on their wardrobes from relatives and friends or from books such as Mrs. Lyttleton's *How to Pack, How to Dress, How to Keep Well on a Winter Tour of India (for Ladies)* (1892) and Constance Larymore's chapter on "What to Wear" in *A Resident's Wife in Nigeria* (1911).

A photograph of Larymore in Nigeria shows her in an Edwardian floor-length gown of a heavy material, with long sleeves and high neck. It is daunting to think of wearing this in tropical heat with the necessary petticoats and underclothes. Admonishing that leaving off corsets for the sake of coolness was a huge mistake, Larymore allowed no compromise on the necessity of taking at least six pairs: "*Always* wear corsets, even for a *tête-à-tête* home dinner on the warmest evenings; there is something about their absence almost as demoralizing as hair in curling-pins" (1911:288).

In West Africa, mosquito boots were essential. Larymore suggested for ordinary use a pair of black canvas gaiters, buttoned and reaching to the knee: under a long evening dress, these gave protection against the ravaging bites of mosquitoes. Even such a utilitarian item was subject to changing fashions and local customs. Hats for protection from the sun were considered a necessity for both women and men, with stern warnings on the danger of even a few rays of sunlight touching a bare head. While trekking in Northern Nigeria in 1924, Violet Cragg noted, "Our present hut is large, but not sunproof, so that we have to wear hats all the time, even in the bath!" (Cragg n.d.:9). While women, as well as men, were required at all times to protect their heads from the perceived harmful rays of the sun, they were not, however, ex-pected to wear the spine pads essential to men's outfits before the first World War (Kirk-Greene 1955:108–11).

Two types of hats, the double *terai* and the sun helmet, were described by Berry. The first was "side brimmed, of heavy felt and literally one hat over another" (1941:135). In the early morning when the sun was low, she pulled them apart and wore the inside hat, but in the midday sun, even the double *terai* was not adequate. This required the pith sun helmet, with the ventilation holes in the crown carefully covered. Women found ways to make these attractive, as Berry noted, "I frankly lifted an idea from the chic wife of a tin-mine manager; several lengths of chiffon in bright colours; I pinned on over the crown the one best suited to the costume of the day; tan, white, stop-red, or kelly green, leaving a yard or two to float, Lady of Shalott fashion, out behind" (1941:136).

Although few women chalked up the three thousand miles that Constance Larymore rode on horseback during her first tour in Northern Nigeria in 1902, riding habits were essential for most parts of the empire. The question of the "astride" position arose in the early years of this century, for which Larymore advised an ordinary bicycling skirt or else "full bloomers worn with shooting boots and puttees and a rather long-skirted coat" (1911:283).

Unconventional Women and the Messages of Dress

As a visual code, modes of dress carried multivalent meanings within the wider cultural system of imperial authority and privilege. Most women conformed to appropriate feminine dress, but some donned unconventional attire to travel in areas otherwise inaccessible to them, or, in a few instances, to protest against imperial rule itself. Although independent Victorian women travellers took on daring adventures and identified with male achievements, they usually dressed in the prescribed manner.

Mary Kingsley, for example, made her way through the tropical forests of Central Africa in the same long, heavy black skirt and long-sleeved, high-necked blouse that she wore in London and Cambridge. She denied ever wearing trousers, although a shipboard friend divulged that she had brought with her a pair belonging to her brother and changed into them for wading across a river or crossing a swamp (Frank 1986:62). While guarding her feminine appearance, disclaiming any male prerogatives, Kingsley was able to free herself from gender restrictions during her travels in Africa.

Gertrude Bell, during her extensive travels in the Middle East as a historian and archeologist before the first World War, always dressed in clothes appropriate for an Englishwoman. Riding out from Jerusalem into the desert in 1900, she was introduced for the first time to a "masculine" saddle; she reassured her father, "You mustn't think that I haven't got a most elegant and decent divided skirt" (Winstone 1978:63). After she and her brother had attended the Delhi durbar in 1903, they travelled around India, she in a sun helmet, a cotton gown, and a fur coat – a combination she found suitable for the variations in the Indian climate (Winstone 1978:85).

Reporting on the empire as colonial editor for the *The Times* of London during the 1890s, Flora Shaw dressed in dark Victorian gowns, whether touring the mining district in Queensland, Australia, where she "went down three mines, crawled duly on hands and knees down unfinished shafts, looked on while the width of reefs was measured" (Bell 1947:133) or making midnight visits to the gambling saloons of Dawson City to assess the miners' lives in the Canadian Klondike (1947:209). When she married Sir Frederick (later Lord) Lugard, however, she discarded the dark clothes she had considered appropriate for her professional work to wear white gowns in her new identity as the wife of a leading administrator in Africa (1947:250).

Supporting the empire in their various ways, these women claimed the privileges accorded to Europeans on their travels in foreign lands. Because of imperial constructions of racial difference, they were able to gain the status assumed by white males (Birkett 1989). Yet at the same time, they endorsed conventional Victorian gender roles and actively resisted women's suffrage, Gertrude Bell becoming a founding member of the Anti-Suffrage League (Winstone 1978:110) and Lady Lugard joining later. Perceiving themselves as exceptional women, they were able in this way to live the contradiction between their attention to feminine appearance and their pursuit of masculine achievements.

On occasion, women dressed in "native garb" for particular objectives. Adela Nicolson, who published poetry under the name of "Laurence Hope," disguised herself in 1890 as a Pathan boy in order to follow her husband on an expedition through the rugged, lawless country on the frontier between India and Afghanistan (MacMillan 1988: 206–07). Alexandra David-Neel similarly transformed her appearance to that of an oriental woman in order to make the pilgrimage to the holy city of Lhasa, closed to foreigners (Birkett 1989:119).

Of greater significance, because they were perceived as dangerous by the rulers, were those who dressed in local clothing out of sympathy with the people. Amy Carmichael, who worked as a missionary in South India for over fifty years, was criticized for damaging British prestige when she began wearing Indian dress (MacMillan 1988:212). Just before the turn of the century, Sister Nivedita (née Margaret Noble) came to Calcutta, where she studied Bengali and was initiated into a Hindu religious order. Becoming friends with many leading nationalists, she sided with those advocating the most radical measures of protest and was called by her own countrymen a traitor (MacMillan 1988:118). The admiral's daughter, Madeleine Slade, rejected the Raj to become a devoted disciple of Gandhi; on her voyage to India, she dramatically burned all her fashionable Paris clothes to dress in Indian outfits (MacMillan 1988:117)

But these protests were isolated individual cases. In the history of the British Empire, the symbolism of dress served simultaneously to heighten masculinity by contrast with feminine modes, thereby reinforcing the asymmetry of gender roles, and to maintain social exclusiveness by indicating distinctions of position and rank. The uniforms and prescribed clothing brilliantly enhanced the imperial spectacle and the dominant power this represented.

References

Allen, C., *Plain Tales from the Raj*, London: Macdonald Futura, 1976.
Allen, C., *Tales from the Dark Continent*, London: Macdonald Futura, 1980.
Bell, E.M., *Flora Shaw (Lady Lugard DBE)*, London: Constable, 1947.
Berry, E., *Mad Dogs and Englishmen*, London: Michael Joseph, 1941.
Birkett, D., *Spinsters Abroad*, Oxford: Basil Blackwell, 1989.
Bowen, E.S., *Return to Laughter*, London: Victor Gollancz, 1954.

Callaway, H., *Gender, Culture and Empire*, London: Macmillan, 1987.

Cohn, B.S., "Representing Authority in Victorian India," in E. Hobsbawm and T. Ranger (eds.), *The Invention of Tradition*, Cambridge: Cambridge University Press, 1983.

Cragg, V., "Violet in Nigeria, by herself and Margaret Kerrich," manuscript, Rhodes House, Oxford.

Fowler, M., *Below the Peacock Fan*, Ontario: Penguin Books, Canada, 1987.

Frank, K., *A Voyager Out*, Boston: Houghton Mifflin, 1986.

Heussler, R., *The British in Northern Nigeria*, London: Oxford University Press, 1968.

Jeffries, C., *Partners for Progress: The Men and Women in the Colonial Service*, London: George C. Harrap, 1949.

Kirk-Greene, A.H.M., "Those were the Days," *Corona*, Vol. 7, No. 3, 1955, pp. 108–11.

Kirk-Greene, A.H.M., "On Governorship and Governors in British Africa," in L.H. Gann and P. Duignan (eds.), *The Rulers of British Africa*, 1870–1914, London: Croom Helm, 1978.

Larymore, C., *A Resident's Wife in Nigeria*, 2d ed., London: George Routledge, 1911 (1908).

Laver, J., *Modesty in Dress, an Inquiry into the Fundamentals of Fashion*, London: Heinemann, 1969.

Leith-Ross, S., *Stepping Stones. Memoirs of Colonial Nigeria, 1907–1960*, London: Peter Owen, 1983.

Lyttleton, K.S., *How to Pack, How to Dress, How to Keep Well on a Winter Tour of India (for Ladies)*, London: E. Stanford, 1892.

MacMillan, M., *Women of the Raj*, London: Thames and Hudson, 1988.

Nicolson, N., *Mary Curzon*, London: Weidenfeld and Nicolson, 1977.

Niven, R., *Nigerian Kaleidoscope*, London: C. Hurst, 1982.

Perham, M., *Lugard. The Years of Authority*, London: Collins, 1960.

Ranger, T., "The Invention of Tradition in Colonial Africa," in E. Hobsbawm and T. Ranger (eds.), *The Invention of Tradition*, Cambridge: Cambridge University Press, 1983.

Rose, K., *Superior Person: A Portrait of Curzon and his Circle in Late Victorian England*, London: Weidenfeld and Nicolson, 1969.

Russell, E., *Bush Life in Nigeria*, privately published, 1978.

Strachey, L., *Eminent Victorians*, Middlesex: Penguin Books, 1948 (1918).

Tremlett, H.M., *With the Tin Gods*, London: Bodley Head, 1915.

Wilkinson, R.H., "The Gentleman Ideal and the Maintenance of a Political Elite," in P.W. Musgrave (ed.) *Sociology, History and Education*, London: Methuen, 1970.

Winstone, H.V.E., *Gertrude Bell*, London: Jonathan Cape, 1978.

Woolf, V., *Three Guineas*, London: The Hogarth Press, 1986 (1938).

15

Clothes Encounters of the Gynecological Kind

Medical Mandates and Maternity Modes in the USA, 1850–1990

Rebecca Bailey

> Pregnancy ceremonies, like those of childbirth, include a great many rites – sympathetic or contagious, direct or indirect, dynamistic or animistic – whose purpose is to facilitate delivery and to protect mother and child – against evil forces which may be impersonal or personified. These have been studied repeatedly.
>
> — A. Van Gennep, *Rites of Passage*

In the United States, from the mid-1800s onward, the public and private roles of pregnant women have been restricted. This restriction has been sought out voluntarily in hope of keeping the evil forces of the unknown at bay; evil forces that could harm the unborn child or bring pain to the mother. To have a perfect, healthy baby and to avoid suffering in childbirth are elemental desires shared by women from the beginning of time. Until the 1850s it was considered a natural and somewhat unavoidable life process that babies would be born, that birthing would be unpleasant for the mother, that the baby and mother would live or die, and that a female midwife would attend mother and child. A poem by Mary Neal, published in 1854, was an attempt to enlighten men about this onerous aspect of the Woman's Sphere.

My Experience in Babies, Sir!
Oh, you, light-hearted, beauteous maid
Whose greatest care's to curl and braid,
Far from life's lesson have you strayed,
If you ne'er think of babies!

For this alone was woman made,
After her sovereign lord's obeyed,
To nurse and tend the babies.
And Man, thou noblest work of God!
Thou, who canst never see the load
Thy wife sustains through life's rough road,
With thee and with her babies,
Go kneel upon thy mother's grave
And think – that every life she gave
Made her Death's victim or Life's slave;
Then love your wife – and babies!
— Mary Neal, "My Experience in Babies, Sir!"

Male Physicians Discover Pregnancy, Circa 1850

However, man's ignorance of such matters was about to change. In the middle of the nineteenth century, male medical doctors began to perceive management of pregnancy and delivery as a new medical problem, rather than an inevitable life process. Newly defined, pregnancy and delivery could then be solved through the application of Education and Science. Naturally, midwives, who possessed knowledge of neither, were then inferior to the physician, who had both at his command. But what the doctor actually knew, and what he said he knew, and even what he believed he knew, were radically different matters. In terms of pregnancy ceremonies, what is unusual in the case of the United States is the insistence that all physician-directed practices – past and present – have had a sound scientific basis, and the denial that some might more truthfully be classified as rites of protection, with all the magical connotations of that phrase. To have admitted anything else would have left the doctors with few patients. The implicit irony is that most rites of protection were only developed and enshrined by the doctors after magic and ignorance had allegedly been banished by vanquishing the midwives. The legitimacy physicians claimed to dispense advice was based on simple logic:

1. Doctors cure medical problems.
2. People with medical problems are sick.
3. Pregnancy is a medical problem.
4. Therefore, women who are pregnant are sick and doctors can cure them.

Henceforth, medical advice for safe and proper behavior for gravida (pregnancy) was given for every aspect of a woman's life, including what to eat, what to do, and even how to dress. What had been such a short time before an area of total ignorance for men, abruptly became one in which they had preeminence and total authority. The women's voices had been muted and those of society's dominant group, men, had replaced them in this quintessentially feminine process. However, women had so much invested, so much at stake – life itself – that they were willing to be placed in situations that rendered them powerless, even to the point of believing that participation in "medical treatment at once useless, torturing to the mind and involving great liability to immoralities" (Beecher and Stowe 1869:163) was a necessity.

The concept of muted voices in a society where the dominant group has free expression and control is discussed by Ardener (1975:vii–xxiii). While the dominant group acts on its perception of reality, that perception must in fact be flawed when appied to all of society, since the muted group and dominant group do not experience the same reality (Ardener 1975:vii–xxiii). This idea is particularly apropos here as men, who have never experienced childbearing and childbirth (unless certain supermarket tabloids are to be believed), suddenly became experts, and women's voices were silenced. The thorough muting reflects, at least initially, the tremendous faith middle-class Victorian American women had in the power of higher education; a new opportunity for them. Their appreciation for the wonders of "modern science" was no less than that of men of the day. These shared cultural values led them to male physicians. But, once there, they had to commit themselves to a physical examination by an unknown male, the gravest sort of impropriety. Firm belief in the physician's medical credentials allowed women to reconcile this behavior. A midwife, while respectable, was ignorant because she had no schooling. A doctor was preferable because he was learned. He knew more than any woman could. Therefore, an examination was not a personal violation, but done for the good of the woman and her baby. To question the doctor's pronouncements would, however, place this accommodation at risk. If the doctor was not always right – indeed, infallible – because of his book-learned knowledge, a woman might wonder why she was there, unclothed, instead of with a midwife. Thus, the more a patient doubted her doctor's judgment, the more the sexual intimacy of the situation would become intolerable and indefensible in terms of propriety. So, at mid-century, Victorian women muted their voices, hoping that men, science, and education would succor them in childbirth in a way that women and nature had been unable to do through time.

Once they were placed in control of pregnancy by women, doctors proceeded to make sure the situation did not change. Their safest avenue was to say "no." If they didn't know whether a patient might be harmed by an activity, better to forbid it and keep the evil forces at bay rather than risk their patient's injury. Dress for pregnancy became a very telling marker of whether pregnant women were allowed to participate fully in society. The commercial availability of specialized garments, such as swimwear, indicated a pervasive societal view – the view of the dominant, male group – that such an activity was acceptable during pregnancy. Although the activities allowed pregnant women by doctors, and subsequently, the availability of clothing appropriate for such activities, has steadily diversified throughout the twentieth century, this has always occurred years after being adopted by fashionably attired nonpregnant women. Change has virtually always come through gradual acceptance of the activity as benign by the dominant group, and through isolated acts of rebellion by the suppressed, rather than through scientific inquiry. Yet, in still another ironic turn, maternity clothing might never have existed if Victorian medical doctors had not simultaneously condemned tight-fitting clothing (the socially correct garments of the day), while urging pregnant patients out of doors for exercise (socially incorrect behavior), a clear example of the dominant group's less-than-perfect perception of reality for the women in their care. Obviously, attitudes and dress had to change to resolve this conflict as well as many others inherent in the original forging of the relationship between doctor and patient. As women became better educated and more independent, there would be less willing suspension of disbelief for "scientific" directives based on cultural fictions.

Medical Mandates

In this paper antecedents that shaped both medical thinking and the style of maternity wear during the middle of the nineteenth century will be examined to understand the origins of the roles of both doctor and patient, and their reflection in fashion. Then, the evolution of advice and the appearance of specific garments will be traced to the 1980s, when there will once again be some women in the United States who will, while pregnant, wear what they please and do what they please based on their own good judgment – and go to midwives employed by doctors. Information was gathered primarily from popular periodicals and well-known books of the time (Bailey 1981).

As 1850 began, the medical profession was exclusively male. Dr. Elizabeth Blackwell was the one exception. She had received her degree the previous year. The professional interest in women's health care was slight in the early 1800s partly because the perception was that not much could be done. Circa 1852, male physician Dr. Marion Sims became the first American to specialize solely in the treatment of women. Many influential women thought midwives as a group both negligent and ignorant, and male practitioners a gross impropriety. They lobbied for female practitioners. Yet, at the same time, most medical schools refused to admit women. Reasons for refusal were primarily based on cultural values. The impossibility of women studying a frank subject like medicine in the presence of men was cited by both sexes. The Female Medical College of Philadelphia was incorporated in 1849; other medical schools operated exclusively for women shortly thereafter. Separate institutions partially solved the problem of proprieties, but the absence of women capable of teaching medicine left the dilemma of the male professor. Thus, rigid rules of social conduct hampered both the male doctor's quest for basic knowledge of reproduction and female physiology, and the potential female doctor's entry into the profession itself. When J. B. White, a Buffalo, New York, physician, conducted an obstetrics class in 1850 in which a live birth was observed by his students, there was outraged protest from his colleagues and from the public. In other branches of medicine, observation had been accepted on medical training practice from the beginning of the seventeenth century (Skene 1900:476). As a consequence, by 1876 all branches of medicine, except gynecology, were taught through clinical teaching. With a dearth of healthy bodies for study, the male doctor's knowledge of the range of normality, the initial stages of disease, and that basic female function, pregnancy, was slight. Female doctors remained a negligible minority until late in the twentieth century.

Even the process of reproduction was a mystery to the Victorian doctor. Theories abounded, some quite ancient, but still held in high regard. One concept common to most thinking was that the microscopic human being was fully intact somewhere, waiting to be summoned into existence. Noted scientists argued about whether it reposed in the ovum, existed as a spermatic animalcule, or had been scattered in undetectable, microscopic form about the universe directly by the hand of God. The oldest theory, that of Hippocrates, the father of Greek medicine, actually came closest to the truth. He proposed, circa 400 B.C., that the future human comes into existence with "the union of two life-giving fluids, each a sort of extract of the body of the parent" (Owen 1859:35). Menstruation and fertility were also topics for conjecture, speculation, and confusion. Physicians cautiously did not attempt to predict the condition of pregnancy until they could see or hear the fetus move.

Given the doctor's rather rudimentary medical knowledge in 1850 and for several decades thereafter, there appears little reason why women would choose them over "ignorant" midwives. But that is to overlook the appeal of their academic credentials and the promise made by doctors that midwives could not counter – the guarantee of a less painful labor. The successful use of ether to lessen pain in childbirth in 1847 gave doctors something that could entice women away from midwives and toward their practices. By 1872, authority to make pronouncements like this one, by George H. Napheys, was well entrenched: "We shall therefore point out those laws which cannot be infringed with impunity, and indicate the diet, exercise, dress and, in general, the conduct most favorable to the mother and child during this critical period, in which the wife occupies, as it were an intermediate state between health and sickness" (Napheys 1872:173). The patients of male practitioners were progressive women who could overcome a Victorian sense of the relationship's impropriety. They were generally well educated and from the middle to upper classes. And this was their undoing. For, in their doctors' minds, the very women who came to them as patients were the least able to bear children successfully. Prevalent at the time was the belief that to overuse any single portion of the body would not only exhaust that portion in time, but would lead to the deterioration of the body as a whole. Dr. Edward Hammond Clarke's *Sex in Education*, published in 1874, is frequently given credit for applying this general rule specifically to education for women. To educate women was to unsex them. Dr. Ely Van de Warker, President of the American Gynecological Society (1900–1901), published*Women's Unfitness for Higher Education* in 1903, and stated: "It is the educated young mothers that show the sad havoc made by maternity; the class that has developed the cerebral faculties at the expense of this supreme hour of a woman's life. It is among this class that we find the failure of physiological function that results in sterility, in anemia, in neurasthenia and hysteria" (Van de Warker 1903:95). Thus, to accept the care of her physician was tacit acknowledgment of illness. An exemption from normal social responsibilities is an important aspect of the sick role. A doctor serves as the legitimizing agent, making avoidance of duties not only a right, but an obligation of the patient (Parsons 1953: 436–37). From the mid-nineteenth century onward, proper roles, activities, and morality for women in the United States were evolving. However, with the investiture of pregnancy as a sick role, socially and medically acceptable actions for pregnant women changed relatively little.

Maternity Modes

Enforcement and acceptance of the sick role during pregnancy was a regressive tendency, reinforcing a submissive role for women. This becomes more obvious as the scope of things women may do with propriety broadens during the twentieth century. With new activities came many new kinds of clothing, especially specific clothing for each new coed leisure pursuit. Stated another way, one could tell what was becoming popular for young women by reading what pregnant women were told they must not do.

As soon as prenatal care was firmly established as a proper arena for medical guidance and intervention, an abundance of advice on behavior materialized. A summary of the conduct proposed by Dr. George Napheys in 1869 (Napheys 1872:173) suggests that walking is the best exercise. Running and carrying heavy weights should both be avoided. At the end of pregnancy, the woman should not stand or kneel for long periods, "nor sing in either of these postures." Journeys should not be taken while pregnant (train travel was considered especially risky, as the rolling of the train might lead to premature labor). (The first transcontinental rail line was completed 10 May 1869.) Napheys firmly opposed dancing; no waltzes for his patients. As for personal hygiene, "those who have not been accustomed to bathing should not begin this practice during pregnancy."

Some twenty years later, another doctor, John M. Keating, wrote a very influential book on pregnancy entitled *Maternity, Infancy and Childhood* (1891). Dr. Keating, whose advice differs marginally from Dr. Napheys, opens with the usual claim that pregnancy is not a disease. He then urges an enema at least once a week after the fourth month. With the lilting strains of Strauss still playing in the background, Keating thought dancing should be avoided. There had been many sewing machines successfully patented by 1891, enabling women to have far more extensive and diverse wardrobes. According to Keating, no pregnant woman should operate one. Bathing costumes for the seaside were chic when Keating wrote. Swimming was forbidden. His argument against these activities, all recent vogues for young women, is an ingenious one aimed at class consciousness and snobbery. It also reinforces the sick role pact between doctor and patient: "And yet a good strong healthy woman may work over a washtub doing the hardest kind of laboring work until her term is up. The answer to this is that if the young mother who reads this book is as strong as this woman who has been brought up to hardships, she probably could do the same thing. [Instead, he urges] a brisk walk, especially in the evening before retiring; it will enable her to get a good night's rest, and at the same time she will feel a certain amount of freedom in going out at this hour without the restraints of wearing close-fitting clothes" (Keating 1891:28-29). Keating was very opposed to tight-lacing during pregnancy. Like other physicians, he felt it could cause either miscarriage or fetal deformity. The fashion silhouette moved closer and closer to the body from the mid-1850s to the late 1880s. Not only dresses and suits, but outerwear as well hugged the body to reveal Lillian Russell curves made possible by skillful engineering. This left pregnant women with nothing to wear but the cover of darkness (see Plates 15.1–15.3).

G. Stanley Hall developed the first questionnaire to examine the relationship between clothing and the development of the sense of self in 1889. He found that being well dressed made his subjects feel more sociable. Being poorly dressed made them feel unsociable and self-conscious (Hall 1897–98:351–95).[1]

There was no public sanction of appropriate maternity dress outside of a private dwelling during daylight until 1911, when the *New York Herald* agreed to run an advertisement for the previously unmentionable goods of the Lane Bryant Company. The ad text read as follows: "It is no longer the fashion nor the practice for expectant mothers to stay in seclusion. Doctors, nurses, and psychologists agree that at this time a woman should think and live as normally as possible. To do this she must go about among other people, she must look like other people. Lane Bryant has originated maternity apparel in which the expectant mother may feel as other women feel because she looks as other women look" (Mahoney 1950:99–100). The Lane Bryant shop was mobbed by excited pregnant women; not a single street-wear garment was left on the rack. By the close of the day, the entire inventory has been sold (Plate 15.4). Meanwhile, Dr. Homer Oliphant authored a maternity care book in 1909 that was still going through editions in 1923. He extended the ban on the sewing machine (an indoor sport), and added tennis to the list of activities to be avoided (Oliphant 1909: 7–29). Although a rather ancient game, tennis had become recently popular for young women.

In the same vein, Dr. Samuel Meaker's book outlawed virtually all travel except in case of emergency, said no pregnant woman should

Plate 15.1 Assorted wraps, November 1843. From *Godey's Lady's Book*, vol. XXVII, November, 1843, Fashion plate. (Photograph, the North Carolina Department of Cultural Resources)

"Fig. 1. The cloak . . . fitting the figure closely to below the waist in the back . . .; the front is straight."

"Fig. 2. Basque bodice fitting very tightly . . ." (p. 372.)

Plate 15.2 Walking costumes for ladies, April, 1882. From *Godey's Lady's Book*, vol. CIV, April, 1882, p. 305, figs. 1, 2. (Photograph, North Carolina Department of Cultural Resources)

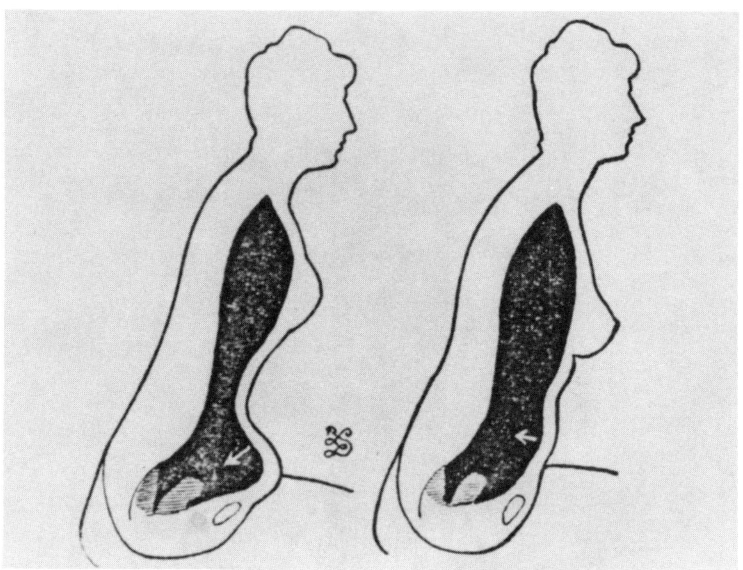

Plate 15.3 How corsets cause prolapses. From Helen Ecob, *The Well-Dressed Woman*, New York, Fowler and Wells Co., 1892), p. 9, fig. 9. (Photograph, Jack Bailey)

drive a car, and found tennis, golf, and dancing, by now the Charleston, all "inadvisable" (Meaker 1927:76–78). One periodical mentioned maternity evening gowns and sportswear after World War I, but published no specifics (Mooney 1926:581–82). No illustrations of these were discovered in the course of this research. The advice regarding clothing by Dr. Samuel Meaker to expectant mothers in 1927 is typical, and more succinct than most: "Wear clothing that is simple and warm, and loose enough so that there is no constriction around any part of the body. During the fourth month, get a special maternity corset" (Meaker 1927:98). This is good, down-home advice, but surely did nothing to lift the spirits.

The passage of the Social Security Act in 1935 brought prenatal care to a larger number of women, most of whom would not have been attended by a private physician. Thirty-eight states set up prenatal clinics as part of their maternal and child health-care programs (Gerdes 1939:1029–33). The increasing number of popular journal articles that focused on prenatal health care may have been in response to this national recognition of its importance.

Plate 15.4 Lane Bryant's Tea Gown, 1903, the first dress designed and advertised, by word-of-mouth, as a maternity garment. (Redrawn from an illustration, The Lane Bryant Company).

An article published midway through 1939 was devoted exclusively to exercises for pregnant women (Sweeney 1939:795–98). What should be worn? It's impossible to say. The illustration shows a drawing of a "pin-up girl" in halter top and culottes briskly exercising on a mat; certainly fashionable, but hardly pregnant. In keeping with the more healthy perception of the pregnant condition, some sports made it off the "no" list by the early 1940s. Golf, dancing, and gardening became acceptable (France 1942:44–45), along with "mild swimming" (Porter 1944:17). If World War II hadn't made it a necessity to have competent and healthy women taking care of things at home, this shift in perception of pregnancy from sickness to near wellness, as shown by exercise recommendations, might have taken longer.

A 1939 *Vogue* (*Vogue* 1939, Vol. 93:78–80) shows several new directions in maternity dressing. Six of the eight garments shown have "sheltering" jackets for "invaluable deception." One of the "sheltered" garments is a swimsuit. It has a raised waistline, full skirt, and below-the-knee-length coat; a marginally updated turn-of-the-century rig. Regular swimsuits by this time could be quite brief and revealing. This maternity suit looks like what was being shown for the stout or older woman. A 1942 *Vogue* article (*Vogue* 1942, Vol. 99:60–61) illustrates an innovative "country-comfortable" slack suit. It is recommended for around the house. Swimsuits are mentioned as being really glamorous, although none is shown (Plates 15.5 and 15.6).

Life magazine featured a lovely and pregnant Lauren Bacall in 1948. The article noted that Bacall "even ventured successfully into shorts," demure Bermudas, and published a picture to prove it. In the world of regular fashion, shorts had been popular since the early 1930s (Stuart 1934:20). The Page Boy Company added shorts to their line in 1949. Maternity shorts had long, full, just-above-the-knee styling; sort of non-elasticized turn-of-the-century gym bloomers. Shorts for the nonpregnant, however, were on their way to becoming extremely short (Anonymous, *Life*, Vol 41, 1956:49–F). However, this marks the first time that all types of clothing were available as ready-to-wear for

Plate 15.5 One of the first maternity swimsuits, 1939. (Redrawn from an illustration in Anonymous, "For Mothers of Tomorrow," *Vogue*, vol. 93, June 15, 1939, p. 78.)

Plate 15.6 A trendsetting maternity pantsuit and yet another tea gown, 1942. (Redrawn from an illustration in Anonymous, "Cool Enough for Two," *vogue*, vol. 99, June 15, 1942, pp. 60, 61.)

the maternity market. The only exception to this is the T-shirt. This casual male garment was appropriated by women's high fashion around 1948. Maternity T-shirts appeared in the 1970s.

During the 1950s and early 1960s there was a preoccupation with weight gain during pregnancy that precluded advice on much else. Perhaps a reflection of a conservative era, pregnancy as a sickness was once again a prevailing attitude. This time it was expressed through stringent weight-gain requirements, sometimes attained by the physician-prescribed use of amphetamines (Shauffler 1963:40–F) or hospitalization.[2] Dr. Samuel Meaker's views complete the picture of prenatal care in the late 1950s and early 1960s. As a young doctor, Dr. Meaker wrote a book on prenatal care in 1927. In 1965, by this time professor emeritus, Dr. Meaker published a second book on the topic. Meaker writes that tennis, golf, and dancing are now acceptable, but bowling, horseback riding, skiing, and swimming are not. Train and plane travel are not injurious; however, automobile trips longer than one hundred miles are apt to be so fatiguing as to effect miscarriage. No pregnant woman should be behind the wheel of a car after the seventh month (Meaker 1965:66–67).

The 1970s brought a general relaxation by medical doctors of rules and restrictions during pregnancy. Travel was no longer considered threatening; hence, it was rarely mentioned. Exercise, rather than weight restriction, was perceived by editors as a topic of paramount importance to readers. There was a good deal of medical controversy over exactly what effect various types of exercise did have on pregnant women. However, very little of the professional controversy and data leaked into the popular press. Instead, how strenuous the suggested exercise could be was directly related to how pro-feminist the magazine was. Thus, conservative *American Home* told its pregnant readers to do between three and five rolls from side to side to tone the abdominal muscles (*American Home* 1972, Vol. 75:16F). More energy would probably be expended getting down to and back up from the carpet than in the exercise itself. Meanwhile, *Ms.* challenged its readers: "Who says athletes can't be pregnant? You can – and should – swim, run, jog, row, exercise, cycle, skate, and play tennis, squash, volleyball, soccer, softball, basketball, field hockey" (Kelley 1978:47). The article gives examples of athletes who have competed while pregnant and the opinions of several sports doctors that athletic women have an easier time from start to finish in pregnancy.

McCall's, meanwhile, walked briskly down the middle of the road wearing sensible shoes. A 1979 article suggested that each woman should do what feels comfortable, but that contact sports, competitive play with accompanying stress, and activities in which one can not maintain control, such as horseback riding and skin diving, should be avoided (*McCall's* 1979, Vol. 106:53).

These diverse views continue to have supporters to the present time. But which attitude any given pregnant woman may choose is hard to judge by observing her dress. There are many jogging suits and running shoes that have never been once around a track. The look, however, is one of health and complete inclusion in leisure activities, a look that was denied pregnant women a hundred years ago. The thought of participation then was not a matter for consideration. Therefore, there was no need for specialized leisure clothing. The basis for this judgment, made by physicians of the time, was not a vindictive one. Rather, it reflected their desire to protect women they thought to be sick from the rigors of casual social life.

Conclusions

A comparison of the phases evident in medical advice and practice from 1850 to the 1980s and the purposes of maternity clothing during that same time period show surprising congruity. From 1850 to 1870 prenatal care was practically nonexistent. So were maternity clothes. Between 1870 and 1930 medical science tried to protect the pregnant woman from inadequate diet and injurious activities. The result was a somewhat restricted lifestyle. Maternity dress during this time was promoted as healthful and germ-protecting. Clothing was viewed not as a "magical" but rather as a "scientific" shield from harm. Thus, science was accepted by people as the new magic, and promptly invested with the protective capabilities of the old magic. Pregnant women did not have the range of garments available to other women. Sportswear was a significant omission, reflecting conservative recommendations on exercise. All clothing was engineered to avoid constriction of any part of the body. From 1930 to 1970 prenatal advice repeated and refined ideas. Diet and allowable weight gain became progressively more limited. Concurrently, sports activities of all sorts became acceptable. In clothing, concealment of pregnancy by camouflaging any compromising outlines was increasingly important. Garments appropriate for most sporting events became available. Medicine and fashion tried to gain stricter control over appearances, while relaxing control over activities. The 1970s brought a cessation of this tension in both fields. Medical opinion on weight gain and diet became more moderate. The efficacy of letting nature take its course received official support for normal pregnancies. Maternity clothes approximated regular women's wear more closely than ever before (Plate 15.7). Thus, the situation by 1980 was that neither watchful medical attention nor maternity clothes were "needed" by the majority of pregnant women as they had been in the past, since their activities and clothing deviated little from their prepregnant condition. They were no longer sick, just experiencing a normal life process.

Women, however, will undoubtedly continue to take preventive prenatal trips to their obstetricians, and they will continue wearing maternity clothes. Both have become culturally ingrained psychological comforts and socially correct behavior for the middle-class women in

Plate 15.7 Maternity dressing in the 1970s: swinging clothes. (Redrawn from illustrations or photographs in Anonymous, "Big Mama Goes Couture," *McCalls*, vol. 99, November, 1971, p. 33; Anonymous, "Bellies are Beautiful," *Time* vol. 97, May 31, 1971, p. 58. Anonymous, "Happy Clothes for the 'Lady in Waiting,'" *Ebony*, vol. 30, June, 1975, pp. 120–F, p. 121.)

America today. Modern diagnostic techniques and advances in corrective in utero surgery make any other course of action seem incredibly oblivious to the very real science of the twentieth century. Yet, for most normal, uncomplicated pregnancies, prenatal visits are more a matter of propriety and custom than medicine; it has been so from the mid-nineteenth century, when women's reproductive processes were first included in the realm of professional care. From that time forward health-care advice for pregnancy has been burdened with many culturally accepted stereotypes and generalizations, a product of the limited fund of the scientific knowledge of the last century combined with a vast store of prejudices. The rapprochement of socially accepted activities for women and those allowed during pregnancy, and of the diversity of styles – including body-revealing ones – available to nonpregnant versus pregnant women has only recently been accomplished. One could not occur without the other, but differentiating cause from effect is a difficult task. In the final analysis, it was changing attitudes, greater equality between women and men in society, and the demystification of medical science as the exclusive realm of educated men that made pregnant women's voices no longer mute.

Notes

1. Research by Daniels (1965) and Wilson (1968) on pregnant woman's attitudes toward self and clothing strongly supported Hall's findings. They both reported that pregnant women would rather stay home than attend an event dressed unattractively or inappropriately.
2. A personal communication from Barbara Hawkins regarding advice during her first pregnancy in 1957: Mrs. Hawkins related that she did not gain any weight during the first three months of her pregnancy, and so could not gain more than twelve pounds for the remainder of the pregnancy. Her doctor, whom Hawkins felt was both progressive and knowledgeable, said he would hospitalize her if she gained more than two pounds in any month. Mrs. Hawkins is very petite and slender and had no complicating conditions at the time.

References

Anonymous, "For Mothers of Tomorrow," *Vogue*, Vol. 93, 15 June 1939, pp. 78–80.

———, "Cool Enough for Two," *Vogue*, Vol. 99, 15 June 1942, pp. 60–61.

———, "T-Shirts," *Life*, Vol. 24, 7 June 1948, p. 103.

———, "Short Shorts Become Permanent in U.S. Scene," *Life*, Vol. 41, 10 September 1956, p. 49.

———, "Pre-Baby Figure Trimmers," *American Home*, Vol. 75, January 1972, p. 16F.

———, "Fitness for Mothers-To-Be," *McCall's*, Vol. 106, July 1979, p. 53.

Ardener, S., ed., "Introduction," in *Perceiving Women*, London: J.M. Dent and Sons, Ltd., 1975, pp. vii–xxiii.

Bailey, R., "Fashions in Pregnancy: An Analysis of Selected Cultural Influences, 1850–1980," Ph.D. diss., Michigan State University, 1981.

Beecher, C.E., and H.B. Stowe, *The American Woman's Home*, New York: J.B. Ford and Co., 1869.

Daniels, A.C., "Certain Factors Influencing the Selection of Maternity Clothing," MS thesis, University of Tennessee, 1965.

France, B., "Are You Participating in the Baby Boom?," *American Home*, Vol. 28, August 1942, pp. 44–45.

Gerdes, M.M., "New Concepts and Procedures of Maternal Care," *American Journal of Public Health*, Vol. 29. September 1939, pp. 1029–33.

Hall, G.S., "Some Agents of the Early Sense of Self," *American Journal of Psychology*, Vol. 9, 1897–1898, pp. 351–95.

Keating, J.M., *Maternity, Infancy and Childhood*, 2d. ed., Philadelphia: J.B. Lippincott Company, 1891.

Kelley, J., "Who says Athletes Can't Be Pregnant?" *Ms.*, Vol. 7, July 1978, p. 47.

Mahoney, T., "Maternity Mart – The Story of Lane Bryant," *Reader's Digest*, Vol. 57, November 1950, pp. 99–101.

Meaker, S.R., *Mother and Unborn Child*, Baltimore: Williams and Wilkins Company, 1927.

———, *Preparing for Motherhood*, 2d. ed., Chicago: Yearbook Medical Publishers, 1965.

Mooney, B.S., "A Child is to be Born," *Hygeia*, Vol. 4, October 1926, pp. 581–582.

Napheys, G.H., *The Physical Life of Woman: Advice to the Maiden, Wife and Mother*, 6th ed., Philadelphia: George Maclean, 1872.

Neal, M., "My Experience in Babies, Sir!," *Godey's Magazine and Lady's Book*, January 1854, pp. 63–64.

Oliphant, H.N., *Maternity and the Care of the Babe*, Frankford, Indiana: H.N. Oliphant, 1909.

Owen, R.D., *Moral Physiology*, London: Holyoke and Co., 1859.

Parsons, T., *The Social System*, Glencoe: The Free Press, 1953.

Porter, A., "You'd Never Know," *Collier's*, Vol. 113, 29 January 1944, p. 17.

Rothman, D.J., and S.M. Rothman (eds.), *Birth Control and Morality in 19th Century America: Two Discussions*, New York: Arno Press and the New York Times, 1972.

Shauffler, G.C., "Will My Baby Cost Me My Figure," *Ladies Home Journal*, Vol. 80, May 1963, p. 40.

Skene, A.J.C., "The Status of Gynecology in 1876 and 1900," *Transactions of the American Gynecological Society*, Vol. 25, 1900, p. 476.

Stuart, B.T., "In Short," *Collier's*, Vol. 93, 24 February 1934, p. 20.

Sweeney, M.T., "Your 'Daily Dozen' During Pregnancy," *Hygeia*, Vol. 17, September 1939, pp. 795–98.

Van De Warker, E., *Woman's Unfitness for Higher Education*, New York: The Grafton Press, 1903.

Van Gennep, A., *Rites of Passage*, trans. Monika B. Vizedom and Gabrielle L. Caffee, Chicago: The University Press, 1960.

Wilson, S.M., "Attitudes Toward Maternity Wear," MS thesis, Colorado State University, 1968.

16

Dress and Modes of Address

Structural Forms for Policewomen

Malcolm Young

It is not every day that Metropolitan Police Orders appear to be pandering to the disparate erotic fantasies of devoted readers, but a recent issue dealt with the Order of Dress for ceremonial and public order events. Female commanders, it decreed, shall be attired as follows:

Mounted: As for dismounted but with pantaloons, riding boots, spurs, steel chain, black leather straps, mackintosh in wet weather . . .

Down, Dogberry, down Sir, I say!

— "Dogberry" column, *Police Magazine*

Police society is a fiercely masculine domain. Metaphors of warfare predominate. Always it is the "front line" where "real" police work is pursued, with high status attributed to operational activity in the "war against crime," or the "campaign" to beat the burglar or vandal.[1] Crime fighting is *the* status activity in a culture that is heavily indebted to binary images of right and wrong, order and disorder, and that contrasts directly with the "soft" world of "community affairs" activities. These "service" aspects of policing carry less symbolic import, although an institutional defensiveness means this can hardly ever be officially acknowledged to the outside world; indeed the reverse is the case. Protestations of a commitment to "care and service" matters are only so much camouflage, however, and any participant observation of the day-to-day nuances of policing reveals that regardless of declamations to the contrary, such areas of policing remain the province of "old women" or "troops with no bottle for the real work of dealing with angry men."[2] This is a society obsessed with the rigid classification of behavior, dress, deportment, and speech. An inculcated knowledge of the nuances of a correct cultural order and disorder in all things is imbued into the police neophyte, and within a very short space of time the probationer understands and lives a "habitus of practice" (Bourdieu 1977) as if it were natural. On joining "the family" in what is always firmly defined as "the job," these metaphors and symbols of the warrior life are taken on as basic ideological tools of the male "prestige structures" (Ortener and Whitehead 1981:13–21).

Women have always been marginalized in this institution, where gender hierarchy (Cucchiari 1981) sets "soft" against "hard" and attributes status to male constructs. As Ardener (1978:33) suggests, there are British parallels with the Islamic construct, which requires women in the public sphere to remain structurally invisible, veiled and hidden. Women are allowed into male police space, but reluctantly and always with conditions; for the female loose in the depths of male territory is provocative and offensive, producing something of a spiritual and conceptual problem for male prestige.

Asymmetry therefore predominates, with women always directed to those areas of work considered less important or even ignominious for men, assigned to areas concerned with the "welfare and care" of women and children – as an extension of their domestic role. Steered away from the "tougher" work, they are said to be too weak for "real police-work," and furthermore are believed to possess a natural animality and sensual helplessness which has to be guarded and guarded against.

One primary means of directing this marginalization of women has been to effect a total control of the body, for the police understand perfectly that by ordering the demeanor of the body physical, it is easier to define the body social and thus ensure conformity to the prescribed "natural" order of things. As a result, the carriage and clothing of the women reflect their peripheral situation in the culture, symbolizing their repressed sociosexual state. An all-encompassing code defines every nuance of dress, hairstyle, bodily ornament, and use of makeup. Since women started becoming members of the police force some seven decades ago, this code has carried intimations of how the men symbolize these intruders into their space. From the outset, women found that "the uniform was unspeakable . . . designed surely by men who had a spite against us. . . . When, at last, I stood before a mirror clad from head to feet in police provided clothing, I shuddered, and for the first time regretted my choice of career" (Wyles 1952:44).

The Early Days

The social upheavals caused by the First World War saw two major reports recommend the use of women in the police force and a few of the hundreds of police forces then operating in England and Wales appointed women to their establishments, although the vast majority resisted their inclusion for an additional two or three decades. In these early days, their grudging acceptance was the result of concern for the morality of women exposed to the rigors of metropolitan life during the war, and numbers of unpaid patrolling policewomen were taken on "as problems of order and decency in public places cried out for urgent solutions . . . [with the women police required] to deal with stray girls, begging children [and] amorous couples in public" (May 1979).

An armband was issued to these first policewomen to indicate their membership in a controlling organization as they patrolled the parks, railways stations, open spaces, and streets to assist "the great increase of women workers, many far away from their homes, often obliged to be out late in the evenings on account of their work or having no other possible time for fresh air, exercise, or amusement. These girls often run into danger and not infrequently come to grief just for the want of the friendly help and counsel of a member of their own sex" (May 1979:359). Yet even as they patrolled in pairs to sustain the physical and moral purity of these women, so their own fallibility was at risk, and the first women patrols were closely followed by two male constables, both to protect them and to ensure that they avoided the pitfalls of their own perceived sensual helplessness. This allegedly uncontrollable nature in women has consistently been used over the years to deny policewomen access to certain areas of the male domain.[3] For example, the early constitution of the police did not provide for female detectives, for, as a Scotland Yard spokesman explained, "women are particularly adapted for work which comes outside the scope of the ordinary detective, but unfortunately it is sometimes unsafe to trust a woman with an important investigation where young men are concerned. They are swayed by emotion. They can't help it: it is their nature, and they have been known to fall in love with the man they have been sent to watch" (May 1979:359). In effect, the few women who joined the police force in these first days had to follow the dictum that women stay out of the male public sphere, or venture in only if they could function as pseudo-males (Heilbrun 1979); the uniform of the women police symbolized this fact to a significant degree.

Photographs of Dorothy Peto, the first woman Superintendent in the Metropolitan Police (*Police Review* 9 July 1979; 28 November 1986), indicate the severity of this defeminization. Only the name beneath the photographs reveals that she is a woman. The hair is cropped behind the ears and Ms. Peto wears the male peaked cap, with collar, tie, and uniform tunic. In another photograph (*Police Review* 28 August 1981) four senior ranking policewomen of 1923 are shown. All have their hair cut short in back and on the sides to reveal their ears, and all wear the male uniform cap and long greatcoats, with knee-length leather riding boots. For the most part, however, the women wore a topee-style pith helmet, a belted tunic closed at the neck, with an ankle-length skirt hiding knee-length leather boots, all of which Lilian Wyles (1952) found so dispiriting (Plate 16.1).

Plate 16.1 The "unspeakable" uniform "designed surely by men who had a spite against us"... Wyles: 1952. (*Police Review*)

The Contained Woman

Mauss (1935) in his seminal essay on the psychosocial variations imposed on bodily activity in different societies, showed these are invariably determined by a preconceived understanding of what that society considers to be biologically correct. This "natural" state in police society requires women to be physically bigger than is normal in the rest of society. The setting of a minimum height restriction (although lower than that for the men) means a number of the women in the service are "large" ladies.[4] So that in the early 1980s when I recorded a conversation about the latest intake of probationer constables, it included typical references to the size and shape of the women: "Have you seen the latest batch of 'burglars' dogs'; most of them are built like brick shit houses! How do we pick them, with their upside-down Queen Anne table legs and faces like a bag of spanners!"[5]

Despite this alleged grossness, sexual dimorphism has been used to deny women access to areas of police work. Since the Sex Discrimination Act of 1975, their lack of inches and a perceived physical weakness has paradoxically been used as a male strategy to exclude women from many of the specialist roles, or has been used as an excuse to make calls for a reduction in the number of women recruits, and even to exclude the police altogether from the provisions of the Act. In some instances the women have fallen into this male trap, using their body size to define their social value to "the job," while denying the male opinion that women are always too big (butch and unfeminine) or too small (weak and in need of protection). Sergeant Janet Curtis is only one of a number of policewomen who have written to *Police Review* about her size. She told her predominantly male audience 'I have had experience of all the arduous duties quoted as being the province of male officers alone, and there is nothing unusual about me. I am but 5'6" tall and weigh 9 stone" (6 October 1972). At the 1978 Police Federation Annual Conference,[6] a policewoman told the audience she was the tallest and heaviest constable on her shift, and was rewarded by the patriarchal daily newspapers who all featured pictures of this "amazon" on street patrol. In August 1979, West Yorkshire police raised the minimum height for women recruits to 5'6" because they "now had to tackle the same jobs as the men," although at the same period the Police Federation was reported to "still be against an equal role for women" (*Daily Mirror* 3 August 1979).

Rarely do we see letters or articles from men defending their physical state. Always it is the women who are measured and weighed, even though there are some equally small, thin, or excessively fat male officers. As Coward (1984) indicates, however, men's bodies and their sexuality are taken for granted, whereas women's bodies are extensively defined, and sexual and social meanings are imposed upon them.

During the whole of my police service since the mid-1950s, I have heard little change in the repetitive remarks about the larger women. Unendingly the men comment on their ugliness, joke about their unfeminine form or marvel at the continual stream of "bulky maidens" who apply to join "the job." These consistently disparaging comments implicitly repeat the belief that any female entering police society will necessarily abandon the norms of femininity; yet will still be denied full acceptance into the male world.

Even when the tall policewoman is slim and petite she will be defined as too weak to be effective, while her perceived sensuality will almost certainly pose a threat to the integrity of the male order. By her very presence she risks becoming labelled as either an icy virgin if she resists male approaches, or becomes something akin to the "scarlet woman" if she shows any inclination to respond positively to those approaches. This "Catch 22" situation occurs simply because she is loose inside a male-oriented world. It is the equivalent of a woman having joined the Freemasons or having led the singing of bawdy songs in the Rugby Club bar after the game, both of which activities are dear to many male police hearts!

Terms used to describe the allegedly "lumpen creatures" who join the service are clearly inculcated. For more than thirty years, I have heard men complain that we seem to recruit women who are "built battleship-style" with "upside-down legs," or have "faces like a bag of chisels or a bag of hammers." These "butch burglars' dogs" with the "build of a store-horse" deny the stereotypical perfect woman, with the cover-girl image (Plate 16.2). Of course, this ideal woman is also unacceptable inside the institution, and indeed the presence of the slim, petite woman within the domain is equally resented, for the hostile reaction is to women in general. In effect, masculine police culture prefers women to stay outside, so that only when the female invades police society does the hostile imagery really begin to develop. To this end, the police tend to exaggerate a view of women as being naturally passive, obedient, quiet non-achievers, and to repress any social credibility for women's intrinsic mental abilities. This rejection and hostility to women (see Smith and Grey 1983) inside the domain means that cultural beliefs are convoluted and yet linked together to maintain a mode of thought that ascribes to women those characteristics of irrationality, emotional illogicality, and feminine instinct.

Even if she contradicts the norms of femininity, discarding a soft

Plate 16.2 The sensual "burglars dog" as lampooned by John Witt in *Police Review.*

image by taking on a hard, masculine form in which she achieves metaphoric invisibility by "drinking pints in the club like one of the boys," she can only be partially acceptable. She may be a "seven-footer with a face like a cathedral gargoyle" (all phrases recorded in field-notes), but she is still a woman and is therefore structurally marginal.

The Dressed Woman

There has been relatively little change to the basic uniform for women since the time that Wyles (1952) shuddered at its design. For the most part they have been designed by men, reflecting what men consider suitable. Usually there has been some form of tunic or box jacket with a hat parodying the military-style peaked cap. The jacket inevitably denies the bust, while the cap hides the hair, which has to be shorter than collar-length. If the hair is any longer, it must be pinned up or rolled to keep it well above the collar, and detailed written orders confirm this demand. Over the years many career women have adopted a totally masculine style, and their cropped hair, uniform, and build have earned them a partial right to maneuver in male social space.

In subtle ways, the various garments and fashions for women police parallel those described by Okely (1978:130–31) in the girls' boarding school, where the body is "subjugated and unsexed," and where the neutralizing effect of the uniform demanded the "denial of an identity which asserted the dangerous consciousness of sexuality necessary to oppose the notion of sexuality in the world outside."

In the closed environment of the police this neutralization is accomplished by a preference for the male hairstyle, short in back and on the sides; for the black flat-heeled, laced shoes; and for the female form to be concealed beneath the military-style uniform and submit to the constraints of a collar and tie. All these demands of style, like the thick black stockings that enhance the "upside-down legs" or the abhorrence of jewelery and makeup, are bodily controls that deny women a choice in the conception of self available to their peers elsewhere in society.

C.S.S. Kerswell-Gooch (1980), a sergeant from Cambridge, tackled what the *Police Review* 12 December 1980 described as "the vexed question of the impracticality of many women police uniforms." Her findings were that short tight skirts, handbags, capes, and soft unprotective "hostess" hats were handicaps women police could do without. Sergeant Kerswell-Gooch claimed that to do a police officer's job effectively, trousers were essential and should be regular issue, not just optional as in some forces. They should be wearable at all times, she declared, and not just at the dictate of some senior (male) officer, who would order skirts for some occasions and trousers for others. It was "too bad if some women don't look good in trousers," she decided, "fat policemen don't either."

She also mentioned the endless redesigning of the uniform and the resultant air-hostess-type gear. Again, this symbolizes the male view that uniform fashion must match the obsessive changes in fashion for women in the outside world, which rarely affects men in a similar manner. Such "fashion wear" was considered by a North-East policewoman to be "an absolute misery for wearing to work in a town center beat in January – pitifully inadequate to ward off the cold even with three pairs of tights, boots, and a concealed woollen jumper" (*Police Review* 12 December 1980).

Two years prior to this, a policewoman from Devon and Cornwall wrote to the *Police Review* (6 January 1978): "It came to me in a blinding flash . . . culottes! That's what we emancipated policewomen should be wearing in these modern times. They combine the smartness and femininity of a well-cut skirt with the practicality of slacks, in which, let's fact it, the majority of female forms look less than elegant." The magazine responded (24 March 1978) and Woman Constable Glover of Surrey became a cover girl in culottes. The illustration cannot be said to have depicted the anticipated femininity in the elegant "smartness of a well-cut skirt." Rather it reproduced a creature who perfectly restates the unspoken principles of police society, which demands that ideas of order are "placed beyond the grasp of consciousness, and hence cannot be touched by voluntary, deliberate transformations" (Bourdieu 1977:94). This culotted policewoman stands with her legs wide apart, showing that any possible feminine exposure is impossible in such a garment (Plate 16.3). In many ways they compare with the

Plate 16.3 "Culottes! That's what we emancipated policewomen should be wearing in these modern times . . ." (*Police Review*)

school shorts, which, Okely (1978:130) tells us, were garments that "concealed the existence of a split between the thighs. Two deep pleats in front and back made them like a skirt, but one which did not lift to reveal the thighs or buttocks. . . . The lower abdomen retained its mystery."

In addition to the control exercised by these long shorts, the legs of this culotted woman are neutralized in thick black lisle. Her shoes are laced and flat, her tunic is buttoned in regulation style and at her throat she has the male version of collar and tie with a large knot. She has "short back and sides" (hair that is short in the back and on the sides) or her hair is pinned up, revealing both ears. Unlike the men, however, she is denied a helmet, for she wears the white soft-topped, air-hostess hat fashionable at the time.[7]

The autobiography of the ex-Metropolitan Police Commissioner, Sir Robert Mark (1978) has only two short items on policewomen in its three hundred twenty pages. One relates to their perceived sexual license when he jokes about their breeding potential for recruiting, while the other relates to their uniform clothing (1978:90). Sir Robert, praised for dismantling the separate departments for women some three years before the Sex Discrimination Act, seems unable to write about women without making weak jokes about their biology. He recalls:

> The last change I made as Assistant Commissioner 'D' Branch related to women. This does not imply any need for alarm. I had always recognized that women were biologically necessary for the continuance of the force and were better able than men to persuade the public of our virtues as a service. In Leicester I had boldly ignored all the various Home Office exhortations and equipped them with court shoes, short skirts, air-hostess tunics and shoulder bags. The effect was electric, our recruitment rocketed. So, alas, did our matrimonial rate of wastage. My predecessor in the Met had asked Norman Hartnell to do something similar for the women and we had a special press showing of the result. It took time to bite, but gradually had an effect on recruitment (Mark 1978:90).

Sir Robert may have "boldly ignored Home Office exhortations" in his pursuit of short skirts and air-hostess type tunics, but seems to have ignored the practical mastery of those like the North-East policewoman quoted above, who deplored the impracticalities that resulted from male opinion.

This "Norman Hartnell" creation for the Metropolitan women was only one of many attempts to deal with the integrated women. In

December 1977, a *Police Review* cover previewed another "New Uniform for Met. Ladies" created by the design team of "Mansfield Originals." The hat is "by Mme. Simone Mirman, the Royal milliner" and we are told that "the women will be able to mix 'n match their garments to suit themselves, their duties and the weather conditions. The jacket is designed to be worn with skirt and trousers and outer garments include a double-breasted coat, a straight cut raincoat and a three quarter length coat. Officers can choose between long or short sleeved white coloured tailored shirts and a cravat replaces the tie" (*Police Review* 9 December 1977). This is palpable nonsense! Most police forces maintain strict orders dictating when trousers, skirts, and short- or long-sleeved shirts can or can not be worn, and I have worked with senior martinets who issue their own divisional orders to prevent any freedom of choice. In my last force, one divisional chief banned the use of the NATO sweater for male and female officers long after they had become "force-issue" uniform wear.

Another aspect of the regulation of the body that reflects the social experience of being a policewoman in a man's world is revealed by this same *Police Review* cover, where the new uniform is shown replicated on a set of marching clones. In an institution where principles of control always prevail to entwine the social, the cultural, and the biological, a preferred bodily carriage and an obsession with the discipline of posture is enhanced by the use of drill. From the time of its reception into the male police world the female body is made to regulate its deportment. Drill is mandatory at the initial Training Schools, with marching, saluting, parades, and inspection. Wyles (1952:20) enjoyed the drill immensely: "We went to Wellington Barracks where under the strict eye of our drill Sergeant, we were taught to march." Sixty years later, the *Police Magazine* cover (March 1978) shows the modern police equivalent of Wyles's drill Sergeant. This shaven-headed policeman, with his slashed cap-peak, row of medals, and swagger stick, mimics a military model of reality and leans forward to scrutinize a rigidly immobile female cadet. She has short hair, wears a collar and tie (no cravat for her yet), a tunic, and epaulets. This young girl, perhaps eighteen years old, clean-cut, and totally without make-up, presents an image and style which was almost the symbolic antithesis of the prevalent punk culture of the time.

Makeup was banned for years in many forces by written order. A touch of lipstick might have been acceptable, but even in the permissive 1960s when many bodily symbols of control were being diluted, a heavily made-up policewoman in my force was derogatively nicknamed "the painted lady," while another who wore a rather pervasive perfume and had visibly dyed hair was dismissed as "the peroxide hooer [whore]." In 1919, Wyles found that "all make-up had been strictly forbidden and hair had to be severely dressed, in fact, not an atom, not even a stray end showed itself from beneath the close-fitting helmet, which looked so much like an inverted soup plate upon the head" (1952:44).

The 1960 Northumberland Constabulary Force Order, Section 6, details the "Conditions of Service and Instructions for Police-women" (and links them with Cadets, Police Reservists, and Special Constables). Allocation with such other marginals further reinforces my point that policewomen stand defined as "outsiders" and remain ambiguous to categories of "real" policemen. The tiny establishment of fifteen women in their separate department was reminded by written directive that:

> The following instructions regarding dress apply:
>
> (a) black shoes and stockings must always be worn with uniform
> (b) cosmetics must be used in moderation
> (c) hair must be neatly arranged and must not fall below the top of the collar of the jacket nor show under the peak of the cap
> (d) jewellery will not be worn with uniform except a plain wrist watch, a metal identity wristlet, a plain gold ring or simple dress or engagement ring. If the two gold rings are worn they must be both on the same finger (Northumberland Constabulary Force Orders 1960: Sec. 6, Par. 6).

In 1980 the Orders of the amalgamated Northumbria Force were reappraised. (In 1969 the old Northumberland County force merged with two others; in 1974 several other borough, city, and county forces combined with them to form the "Northumbria Police.") Not a lot had changed in the subsequent twenty years. The new Orders set out the instruction relating to Policewomen's dress:

> (a) Cosmetics may be worn in moderation
> (b) Hair must be neatly arranged and must not fall below the top of the collar of the jacket nor show under the front of the hat
> (c) Jewellery will not be worn with uniform except a plain wristlet watch, wedding ring, engagement ring or simple dress ring. Earrings will not be worn (Northumbria Police Force Orders 1980, Sec. 2, Par. 27).

At my first Superintendents' Conference, after my transfer on promotion to West Mercia police (Hereford, Worcester, and Shropshire) in 1983, I listened with fascination as my colleagues spent an hour worrying over an order issued by the Chief Constable. This allowed officers to dispense with a tie and go open-necked in "shirt-sleeve order" in summer weather, but failed to define the number of buttons that should be left undone. The problem was that some officers had loosened more than one button, thus revealing chest hair and medallions; although there was no mention of unsuitable décolletage! This fear of an indiscipline in uniform matters is a constant concern, and in March 1987 the weekly Force Orders reminded officers that in relation to jewelry the Force Policy General Order 6, as reproduced below, remains unchanged:

> The wearing of jewellery by male and female officers whilst on duty will not be allowed, with the following exceptions:
>
> > Earrings will only be worn when specific permission has been granted by the Officer's Divisional or Departmental Commander. Officers may insert a small sleeper or stud during the immediate period after piercing to prevent natural healing (normally six weeks).
> >
> > Necklaces, neck chains and pendants may be worn if completely obscured by being worn underneath clothing.
> >
> > Wedding rings, eternity rings, engagement rings and signet rings may be worn, but the wearing of dress rings or a multiplicity of rings is not permitted.
>
> All officers must clearly understand that the wearing of jewellery whilst on duty in uniform for decorative purposes is totally unnecessary and contrary to the principles of a disciplined service (West Mercia Police Force Order, 14 March 1987).

Riot Gear

One of the most potent images of policing in Britain in the last decade has been of lines of officers in full riot gear, with shields, helmets, visors, flame-proof overalls, steel-capped boots, and long and short batons. Not unexpectedly, women have largely been denied any access to these male areas of operation, just as the sight of a woman police motorcyclist in full leathers is a rare occurrence. Most forces have simply ordered that women will be kept off "the front line" in such situations (Plate 16.4). As the police periodicals reported, "although the [three policewomen photographed] have received public order training, women officers in riot gear still have a novelty value for the press" (*Police Review* 27 February 1987).

Plate 16.4 "Not Yet One of the Boys" (*Police Review*)

P. W. Fiona Roberts's "novelty value" made headlines when she lined up in full riot gear with male colleagues at what *Police Magazine* (March 1986) described as "Fortress Wapping" (see also *Police Review* 3 April 1987; 1 May 1987). In the main, however, the men have denied women the right to move into such areas, arguing that they form a double indemnity because of their weakness and feminine susceptibility. That the men deplore the need to watch over the women indicates a true ambivalence in the ideology, for surely such massively butch creatures can look after themselves and need no protection. This ambiguity is recognized in the *Police Magazine* cartoons, where "Doreen," their regular cartoon "burglars' dog" (drawn by an ex-policeman "Jedd"), carries many signifiers of the difficulties caused by the presence of women inside the institution.

Hess and Mariner (1975) suggest that the use of such cartoons may well be the most effective vehicle for expressing opinion and beliefs, for they carry familiar symbols of cultural identity. Indeed, many cartoons in *Police Review* and *Police Magazine* over the years provide clear structural insights into the social beliefs of the police, which might otherwise go unspoken or unthought. As Cathy Morrison suggested in a review of *Police Review's* "Cartoon Coppers," "policewomen are either young, shapely sex-bombs or singularly unattractive spinsters" (*Police Review* 22 October 1982).

The "burglars' dog" tag certainly relates to "Doreen." She is perhaps eight feet tall, for she towers over men in her gargantuan height and bulk. In the March 1986 *Police Magazine*, following riot training for Metropolitan policewomen at the Hounslow Training Centre, "Doreen" is shown being introduced to visiting senior officers who fall back in amazement at "our Hounslow Boadicea." But it is how "Doreen" is dressed that reveals all! Blonde curls bush unacceptably out from beneath her riot helmet, and although she carries a shield and baton, there are no flame-proof overalls; rather, she remains in a skirt, and forsakes the protective boots for slip-on shoes. To complete the picture, a flounce of petticoat peeps from beneath her knee-length skirt. This petticoat has become her trademark, for it sneaks coyly into view in all her appearances.

This glimpse of underwear is a typical marker; ensnaring and deflecting the men, even though the massive "Doreen" is beyond the normal bounds of sexual desirability, for "petticoat police power may be attractive to the men in the street [but] is a distraction to the policeman on the beat, for while it is better for a woman to interview sexual assault victims, they fall from grace on such physical occasions as pub brawls, [and the men have to] spend more time looking after them than arresting criminals" (*Daily Express* 24 January 1978). Again the systems of belief are so insidiously impressed on and inculcated into the minds of the officers that the policewomen themselves often use the same visions of social disorder that "Doreen" clearly promulgates. On BBC TV's "Forty Minutes," a show entitled "A Policewoman's Lot" (aired on 10 November 1988) featured Sergeant Sheena Thomas giving an amazing description of how "yobs" set out to throw her from the balcony of a block of flats in the West Midlands. Her main concern, she reflected, had been that she was wearing orange knickers, which would have been revealed to all. In the twenty-first-anniversary commemorative issue of the West Mercian Force newspaper (October 1988), Inspector Janet Field recalled her days in 1971 as one of the first two women traffic patrol officers in the force: "The fact that we wore skirts caused problems – and a traffic hazard, as motorists were distracted by the sight of next week's washing as we carried out examinations underneath vehicles. The problems were solved, however, when we were allowed to design our own special uniforms with trousers and new style trilby hats, which attracted press headlines." It seems unlikely we will see the underwear of the men featured to such a degree, or hear of the changing fashions of their "mix 'n match" design initiatives!

Conclusions

Inevitably in such a macho society it seems the women will continue to be stereotypically portrayed as being weak, yet big and ugly. They will remain a danger simply because of their propensity to "fall from grace" and need masculine protection, yet at the same time they will be guilty of distracting the policemen by their Medusan charms. As a result of their presence in the wrong social space, a range of symbols of feminine weakness and sexual voraciousness seems destined to be repeated *ad infinitum* and become embodied in aspects of dress and deportment.

On the day I received the letter inviting me to contribute to the workshop at Oxford University where these papers were first presented, the minutes of the March 1988 meeting of the Joint Negotiating Consultative Committee (the police staff associations) arrived on my desk at Police Headquarters. Those present at the meeting included the Chief Constable, variously ranked male officers, and one woman police constable. One short item concerned the Uniform Subcommittee meeting of 3 February 1988, when two matters were discussed. The first concerned "headgear of female officers," where changes in fashion were once again in evidence – "it was agreed the bowler design was smarter but the hostess design was thought to be more comfortable and was reflective at night." The second item concerned truncheons for female officers: some officers apparently "questioned the effectiveness of the short truncheon. The Deputy Chief said he would enquire as to the level of training given in their use. Otherwise female officers could be issued with full size truncheons which fitted within the inside pocket of a utility coat." As might have been anticipated, the minutes produced one inevitable comment. A chief inspector in the office joked, "Short truncheons – dildos for the girls! . . . Don't need to enquire into the level of training they need there, do we chaps?" Many of these attitudes toward women reveal a deeply entrenched set of beliefs in an ideological difference between men and women, which are then dichotomized and set out as a "natural divison." However, women do not "naturally" disappear from police social space; rather, their absence is socially created and constantly reaffirmed until it then becomes the norm (Edholm, Harris, and Young 1977). At times, there is an almost religious zeal and fervour in the use of metaphors of "social chaos" posed in the symbols of female dress, deportment, and modes of address. These metaphors support a culture that still holds to the principles contained in a Biblical text that the sole woman Superintendent (out of the top seventy-one ranking officers) in the Northumbria Police in the early 1980s used as a frontispiece to her lecture notes on "policewomen's work":

> As in all congregations of God's people, women shall not address the meeting. They have no licence to speak but should keep their place as the law directs. If there is something they want to know, they can ask their own husbands at home. It is a shocking thing that a woman should address the congregation (1 Cor. 14:34–35).

Notes

1. The everyday use of terms such as "vandal" indicates the archaic strength of police language. The analysis of the use of everyday language (see Crick 1976) has been crucial to my explorations of police culture.
2. For further discussion on the masculine, warrior style of police culture, see

Reiner 1985, especially Chapter 3; Holdaway 1983; Smith and Grey 1983; and Young 1984; 1991.

3. In the late 1970s in a vain attempt to deny the equal role for women brought about by the Sex Discrimination Act, one "folk devil" raised in police circles was the problem men would face in having a female partner in a patrol car on nightshift. A heated correspondence in the *Police Review* spilled over into the daily papers, and headlines such as "Steamed Up Panda Cars" ran above stories that intimated that young policewomen would be unable to resist their own natural desires. The men were, of course, to remain blameless, for the fault remained in the sensual helplessness of the women. See *Police Review* 24 August 1979; 12 October 1979.
4. I am indebted to Sarah Ladbury for drawing my attention to Lakoff (1975), who identifies the pejorative nature of many unconscious uses of the term "ladies" or "girls." I had entitled an early seminar paper on policewomen "Ladies of the Blue Light" (Young 1979b).
5. In northeast England, where most of the field material was collected, the phrase "she's as ugly as a burglar's dog" was widely used by the men to refer to certain female colleagues. This may well relate to the bullterrier featured in Dickens's *Oliver Twist*, which belonged to the notorious burglar Bill Sykes. "Prig" – which means thief – is another archaic term used by Dickens's team of pickpockets, and is still the common parlance of policemen to define "real villains" in a small area of northeast England around Newcastle (see Young 1979a).
6. The Police Federation is the body that represents the lower ranks (Constable to Chief Inspector) in statutory negotiations.
7. There has never been any attempt to put the women into a replica of the somewhat phallic male helmet in the United Kingdom, although it has been taken up in some European forces.

References

Ardener, S. (ed.), *Defining Females: the Nature of Women in Society*, London: Croom Helm, 1978.

BBC TV "40 Minutes," *A Policewoman's Lot*, transmitted 10 November 1988.

Bourdieu, P., *Outline of a Theory of Practice*, Cambridge: Cambridge University Press, 1977.

Coward, R., *Female Desire*, St. Albans: Paladin, 1984.

Cucciari, S., "The Origins of Gender Hierarchy," in S.B. Ortner and H. Whitehead, eds., *Sexual Meanings: The Cultural Construction of Gender and Sexuality*, Cambridge: Cambridge University Press, 1981.

Crick, M., *Explorations in Language and Meaning*, London: Malaby, 1976.

Daily Express, "Petticoat Police Power," 24 January 1978.

Daily Mirror, "Increase in minimum height for policewoman," 3 August 1979.

Edholm, F., Harris, O., and K. Young, "Conceptualising Women," in *Critique in Anthropology*, Vol. 3, Nos. 9–10, 1977.

Heilbrun, C.G., *Reinventing Womanhood*, London: Gollancz, 1979.

Hess, A., and D. Mariner, "On the Sociology of Crime Cartoons," *International Journal of Criminology and Penology*, Vol. 3, No. 3, 1975.

Holdaway, S., *Inside the British Police*, Oxford: Basil Blackwell, 1983.

Kerswell-Gooch, C.S., "Policewomen's Uniform: The Unconsidered Handicap," *The Bramshill Journal*, Police Staff College and Police Review, 12 December 1980.

Lakoff, R., *Language and a Woman's Place*, New York: Harper Colophon Books, 1975.

Mark, Sir R., *In the Office of Constable – An Autobiography*, London: Collins, 1978.

Mauss, M., "Les Techniques du Corps," in *Journal de Psychologies Normale et Pathologique*, in E. Brewster (trans.), *Economy and Society*, Vol. 2, No. 1, February 1973, pp. 70–88.

May, D., "Women Police: The Early Years," *Police Review*, 9 March 1979, pp. 358–65.

Morrison, C., "Cartoon Coppers," *Police Review*, 22 October 1982.

Northumberland Constabulary, Force Orders, 1960.

Northumbria Police, Force Orders, 1980.

Okely, J., "Privileged, Schooled and Finished: Boarding Education for Girls," in S. Ardener (ed.), *Defining Females: The Nature of Women in Society*, London: Croom Helm, 1978.

Ortner, S.B., and H. Whitehead, *Sexual Meanings: The Cultural Construction of Gender and Sexuality*, Cambridge: Cambridge University Press, 1981.

Police Magazine, March 1978, March 1986.

Police Review, 1972–1987.

Polhemus, T., *Social Aspects of the Human Body*, Harmondsworth: Penguin, 1978.

Reiner, R., *The Politics of the Police*, Brighton: Wheatsheaf Books, 1985.

Smith, D.J., and J. Gray, *Police and People in London: Vol. 4, The Police in Action*, London: Policy Studies Institute, 1983.

West Mercia Police, Force Order, w/e 14 March 1987.

West Mercia Police, J.N.C.C. Minutes, 1 March 1988.

Wyles, L., *A Woman at Scotland Yard*, London: Faber, 1952.

Young, M., "Pigs 'n Prigs: A Mode of Thought, Experience and Action," *Working Papers No. 3 in Social Anthropology*, University of Durham, 1979a, pp. 67–167.

Young, M., "Ladies of the Blue Light: An Anthropology of Policewomen," seminar paper, 1979b.

Young, M., "Police Wives: A Reflection of Police Concepts of Order and Control," in S. Ardener and H. Callan (eds.), *The Incorporated Wife*, London: Croom Helm, 1984.

Young, M., *An Inside Job: Policing and Police Culture in Britain*, Oxford: Oxford University Press, 1991.

Notes on Contributors

Rebecca Bailey is an associate professor in the Art Department of Meredith College, Raleigh, North Carolina, where she teaches drawing and art education courses. Bailey also serves as a consultant to the Education Department of the North Carolina Museum of Art and conducts art workshops for children and adults. Conflicting advice given by different doctors during her own pregnancies piqued Bailey's interest in the origins of such prescriptive dictates.

Suzanne Baizerman teaches at the University of Minnesota, Department of Design, Housing, and Apparel, and is Director of the Goldstein Gallery. Her research focuses on the sociocultural context of hand-produced textiles. Fieldwork in Guatemala and the American Southwest has led to publications and papers on craft technology and the economic aspects of craft, particularly the effects of tourism. She is currently working on a book about Hispanic weavers of northern New Mexico, under contract with University of New Mexico Press.

Ruth Barnes is an art historian who has done field research on the textiles of Lembata, in eastern Indonesia. The results are published in her book *The Ikat Textiles of Lamalera: A Study of an Eastern Indonesian Weaving Tradition,* and in several articles. She also has worked with ethnographic collections at the Pitt Rivers Museum, Oxford. Currently she is preparing a catalogue of the Newberry collection of Indian block-printed textiles at the Ashmolean Museum, Oxford University.

Helen Callaway, a social anthropologist who did fieldwork in Nigeria, is Deputy Director of the Centre for Cross-Cultural Research on Women, Queen Elizabeth House, Oxford University. Her interest in the anthropology of dress evolved during her study of the symbolic structures of imperial domination, published as *Gender, Culture and Empire: European Women in Colonial Nigeria.* She continues research in the field of imperialism and gender for a biography of Flora Shaw, a joint project with Dorothy O. Helly. Coeditor of *Caught up in Conflict: Women's Responses to Political Strife,* she has published numerous papers relating to the anthropology of women.

Catherine A. Cerny is an assistant professor of Textiles, Fashion Merchandising, and Design at the University of Rhode Island. Her interest in the role of clothing traditions in the lives of American women has been expanded to include the wedding trousseau; specifically, its characterization during the nineteenth century and its use in postmodern society.

Louise Allison Cort is the assistant curator for ceramics at the Arthur M. Sackler Gallery and the Freer Gallery of Art, Smithsonian Institution, Washington, D.C. She has conducted extensive research on ceramics, textiles, and other craft forms in Japan, India, and Thailand, combining the methodological approaches of art history, archaeology, and ethnology.

Penny Dransart is affiliated with the Donald Baden-Powell Quaternary Research Centre, where she has completed a doctoral thesis for the faculty of Anthropology and Geography, Oxford University. She has done ethnographic and archaeological fieldwork in Chile, Peru, and Bolivia. Her publications include articles in *Images of Women in Peace and War, Hombre y Desierto: Una Perspectiva Cultural, Contributions to New World Archaeology* (Forthcoming), and *World Archaeology* (Forthcoming).

Joanne B. Eicher is a professor in the Department of Design, Housing, and Apparel at the University of Minnesota. Her current fieldwork focuses on the significance of dress and textiles among the Kalabari of Nigeria. She has authored *Nigerian Handcrafted Textiles and African Dress: A Select and Annotated Bibliography,* and coauthored *Dress, Adornment, and the Social Order and The Visible Self: Perspectives on Dress.* Other publications include articles in *African Arts* and chapters in books.

Tonye Victor Erekosima is a senior arts fellow and director of the Instructional Resources Center at the University of Port Harcourt, Nigeria. His research interests mainly focus on the innovative use of cloth by the Kalabari people of Nigeria as an effective medium of communication to solve problems of community integration, distinctive collective identity, and intragroup role demarcations. He believes similar situations confront larger Third World societies.

Danielle C. Geirnaert is a lecturer in Social Anthropology at the University of Leiden in the Netherlands. In the late 1970s, she spent several months in Central Java, where she developed an interest in Indonesian textiles. She later did field research among the Laboya, a community on the island of Sumba in eastern Indonesia. She is now finishing a monograph on the Laboya. She is a member of the Dutch-French cooperation research team C.A.S.A./E.R.A.S.M.E., based in Leiden and Paris.

O. P. Joshi has devoted his studies to the social anthropology of art. He is the author of *Sociology of Indian Art* and *Folklore Painters and Painted Folklore of India.* He chaired and organized the session on "Human Body Decoration" at the Eleventh International Congress of Anthropological and Ethnological Sciences, held in Canada in 1983. *Anthropology of Symbols*, a book edited by Joshi, is in press. He has recently joined the Jawahar Art Centre, a multi-arts center, where he is studying the anthropological and sociological context of the arts.

H. Leedom Lefferts, Jr. is a professor of Anthropology at Drew University, Madison, New Jersey. He has conducted ethnographic research in northeast Thailand since 1970. From 1989 through 1991 he lived in Southeast Asia, focusing on the study of T'ai textiles in preparation for a major exhibition and catalog on "The Textile Arts of the T'ai People."

Julia Leslie has been a member of the Center for Cross-Cultural Research on Women, Queen Elizabeth House, Oxford University, since 1984, and is currently a senior member. In 1987–88, she was a visiting lecturer and research associate in the History of Religions in the Women's Program at Harvard Divinity School, and is currently a lecturer in Hindu Studies at the School of Oriental and African Studies, University of London. Apart from a number of articles, her publications include *Perahera, The Perfect Wife: The Orthodox Hindu Woman according to the Stridharmapaddhati of Tryambakayajvan, Rules and Remedies in Classical Indian Law,* and *Roles and Rituals for Hindu Women.*

Susan Michelman is Assistant Professor, University of Massachusetts, Amherst. Her doctoral research focuses on dress in Kalabari (Nigeria) women's societies. Her publications include a coauthored article in *Adolescence* and an article in *Critical Linkages in Textiles and Clothing Subject Matter*, published by the International Textiles and Apparel Association.

Cherri M. Pancake was the founding curator of the ethnological textiles museum in Guatemala City. She has worked in publications design in the United States, Peru, and Guatemala. Pancake became curator of the Museo Ixchel in 1976 and established its reputation as the most comprehensive collection of Guatemalan textiles in the world. She also instituted an extensive program of field research involving ethnographers, linguists, cultural geographers, and ethnohistorians, as well as textile specialists. In 1981, she returned to the United States to become a professor in the College of Engineering at Auburn University (Alabama), where she continues to be active in textile studies, particularly the use of computers to analyze the communicative content of handwoven garments. She is associate editor of *Mesoamerica,* a journal devoted to historical and anthropological research on Central America and southern Mexico.

Mary Ellen Roach-Higgins is professor emeritus, University of Wisconsin-Madison. She has published a number of articles on the sociocultural aspects of dress and has coauthored three books: *Dress, Adornment, and the Social Order, The Visible Self: Perspectives on Dress*, and *New Perspectives on the History of Western Dress.*

Lidia Sciama has lectured on Italian literature at the Cambridgeshire College of Arts and Technology and has been a visiting lecturer in Social Anthropology and Comparative Literature at Mount Holyoke College. She is currently involved in anthropological research in Venice and on the island of Burano. She has published articles in *Women and Space, The Yearbook of Agricultural Cooperation for 1981–1982, The Incorporated Wife,* and *International Journal of Moral and Social Studies.*

Malcolm Young read anthropology on a Home Office Scholarship halfway through a thirty-year police career. After ten years in CID as a detective, he eventually reached the rank of Superintendent, and spent the final decade of his working career analyzing police culture. Retiring early, he is now a freelance writer, whose interests not unnaturally lie in the analysis of systems of power and control, the culture of institutions, and counter-cultural formations. His first book, *An Inside Job: An Anthropologist in the Police* is to be published by Oxford University Press. A further volume on an anthropology of a rural police force is in preparation, to be followed by review of the idea and use of surveillance as a means of social control. He also has a strong interest in feminist anthropology and in the rituals and symbolism of contemporary culture.

Index

Books that have been published in association with the Centre for Cross-Cultural Research on Women, Queen Elizabeth House, Oxford include:

NARROWING THE GENDER GAP
Edited by G. Somjee

GENDER, CULTURE, AND EMPIRE
By H. Callaway

IMAGES OF WOMEN IN PEACE AND WAR
Edited by S. Macdonald, P. Holden, and S. Ardener

ANTHROPOLOGY AND NURSING
Edited by P. Holden and J. Littlewood

ROLES AND RITUALS FOR HINDU WOMEN
Edited by J. Leslie

RULES AND REMEDIES IN CLASSICAL INDIAN LAW
By J. Leslie

VISIBILITY AND POWER
Edited by L. Dube, E. Leacock, and S. Ardener

WISE DAUGHTERS FROM FOREIGN LANDS
By E. Croll

ARAB WOMEN IN THE FIELD
Edited by S. Altorki and C. Fawzi El-Solh

GROWING UP IN A DIVIDED SOCIETY
Edited by S. Burman and P. Reynolds

THE PERFECT WIFE
By J. Leslie

WOMEN'S RELIGIOUS EXPERIENCE
Edited by P. Holden

FOOD INSECURITY AND THE SOCIAL DIVISION OF LABOUR IN TANZANIA
By D. Bryceson

CAUGHT UP IN CONFLICT
Edited by R. Ridd and H. Callaway

PERCEIVING WOMEN
Edited by S. Ardener

MARGERY PERHAM AND BRITISH RULE IN AFRICA
Edited by A. Smith and M. Bull

THE INCORPORATED WIFE
Edited by H. Callan and S. Ardener

FIT WORK FOR WOMEN
Edited by S. Burman